McNamara's Old Bronx

THE BRONX

(The Bronx County Historical Society Research Library)

McNamara's Old Bronx

by

JOHN McNAMARA

THE BRONX COUNTY HISTORICAL SOCIETY
The Bronx, New York
1989, 1996

Manufactured in the United States of America

THE BRONX COUNTY HISTORICAL SOCIETY
3309 Bainbridge Avenue, The Bronx, New York 10467

EDITORS
Dr. Gary D. Hermalyn
Prof. Lloyd Ultan

Dedication

This book is dedicated to A. Gerald Doyle, esteemed Editor of *The Bronx Press-Review* for 41 years, who gave permission to reproduce these articles.

My thanks to Myron Garfinkle, Publisher, and Eric R. Gerard, Managing Editor of *The Bronx Press-Review,* Ronald and Theodore Schliessman, Rose Politi, Robert R. Hall, Laura Tosi, Kathleen Pacher, Mary Ilario, Katherine Gleeson, Gary Hermalyn, Kathleen A. McAuley, Joe Connors, Lisa Seifert, Myrna Sloam, Sol Elbaum, Raymond Crapo, Lloyd Ultan and Arthur Seifert of The Bronx County Historical Society.

This publication was made possible by the generous support of Larry Barazzotto and The Commission Celebrating 350 Years of The Bronx.

FOREWORD

Almost everyone in The Bronx is — or should be — familiar with *History in Asphalt: The Origin of Bronx Street and Place Names* by John McNamara. Out of a lifetime of experience he has compiled an absorbing encyclopedia of the origin and significance of the name of every street in the borough. Now, in *McNamara's Old Bronx*, he has peopled many of those streets with an intriguing array of personalities, much like a still life photograph becomes a moving picture. For McNamara, no falling afoul of the temptation to write in broad, splashing strokes about grandiose events described in terms of towering individuals. He is in tune with much of the modern emphasis in historical research, which someone has described as "looking at history from the bottom up" — the individual, the local, the personal, the particular. He is aware of the law of historical diminishing returns: the greater the ground or area of interest covered, the more the author has to resort to generalities, and the more discursive his account becomes. And McNamara is as adept at handling a turn of phrase as he is a turn of events.

Everyone who reads *McNamara's Old Bronx* will feel indebted to its author. The Bronx County Historical Society is to be congratulated for making this publication possible.

WILLIAM A. TIECK
Official Historian, The Bronx

TABLE OF CONTENTS

Foreword vii

List of Illustrations xix

Introduction xxi

Section 1

MELROSE, MOTT HAVEN, NORTH NEW YORK,
OLD MORRISANIA, PORT MORRIS

Dome of U. S. Capitol Was Cast Century Ago
in a Bronx Foundry...3

The Mighty Gouverneur Morris Was Testy,
One-Legged Bronxite..4

Early Mott Haven Recalled: Horse Cars, Bath Houses,
Franz Sigel...5

Famous Piccirilli Studio Birthplace of Great Statues............................6

The Name of Jordan L. Mott Stamped on Iron, Worldwide 7

Scout Camp Reminds of Old Indian Name.......................................8

St. Mary's Park Revolution Site of "Refugee Huts"............................9

John Jacob Astor Bought Land of Morrises in 1840s 10

"Dutch Broadway" Busy Street in Boro for Nearly Century 11

Bronx Public Bath Was Held as World's Finest 12

Story of Boro Boy Gone Bad: Rise, Fall of Dutch Schultz 13

First Irishmen in the Bronx? Maybe Soldiers
for Dutch (1642) 14

First Jewish Temple Here Now Church for Baptists 15

Attorney's House was "Station" on "Underground Railroad" 16

Pulaski Park Named for a Pole...17

Ancient Police Blotter Cites Site of Gold-Laden British Frigate 18

Paderewski's Bronx Visit Enriched Piano Teacher 19

Bronx, Queens Claim So. Brother Island;
Only Seagulls Inhabit It..20

Section 2

HUNTS POINT, LONGWOOD, OAK POINT

Name of Hunts Point Avenue Goes Back in History to 1668 23

Dinner Given British Colonel in Mansion Proved His Last 24

The Leggett Family 25

Bank Note Firm's Engraver Was Master Counterfeiter........................26

West Bronx Had Indian Trail to Quinnahung Settlement 27

Old Oak Point Resort Area 28

Duck Island — Another "Lost" One — Lay Off the "Debatable Lands".......29

Country Seats Once Abounded in Bronx 30

Hunts Point Cows Monopolized The Spring at Leggett's Lane..............31

Cowboys in the Bronx? Certainly! At Springhurst Dairy in the 1880s.....32

Steamboat on East River Tipped Hookey-Players 33

"General Slocum Disaster" of '04 Recalled This Month.......................34

Seven Hispanic Names Listed in Bronx Directory 110 Years Ago 35

Drake, "Poet of Bronx" Asked Burial by Its River.............................36

Historic East River Isn't River At All..37

Late Bert Sack Recalled Days Before Gas, Sewers 39

First Theatre of Bronx Opened in '08 in "Neo-Grecian" Splendor 40

Titanic Sank (for Movie) In Bronx River, 1914–15 41

Section 3

CROTONA, MORRISANIA,
TREMONT, WOODSTOCK

Old German Bands Oom-pahed Their Way through Bronx Streets 45

Old Germania Park Noted Picnic Grounds.....................................47

Burial Area Became Site of PS 38 in Morrisania 48

Bronx Landmark, House-Shop Five Feet Wide,
    Had Legendary Career...49

The Old Woodstock Community Was Peopled by Germans 50

Third Ave. "Bend in Road" of 1860's Became 161st St. 51

Who Named Indian Lake? 52

"Home News" World Series Replays on Panel Recalled 53

Morrisania Hand-Rolled Cigars Were Phased-Out by Machinery 54

Columbia (or Columbus?) Entertained Old ('12) Italians.....................55

Bronx "Bombed" by Plane in 1918 Liberty Loan Drive.......................56

Capitol of Mandolin-Making Stood on "Dutch Broadway" 57

Black Settlements Started Here at Turn of Century...........................58

Old Vasa Hall Was Scene of St. Lucia's Observance 59

Lady Washington Co. Old Morrisania Pride 60

Second Gouverneur Morris Was Heir of Sire's Manor, Bluntness..........61

Tremont-Morrisania Index of '71 Listed 51 Saloons 62

Section 4

CLAREMONT, CONCOURSE,
HIGHBRIDGE, MACOMBS DAM

"Castle on the Concourse?" It's Special School No. 31 65

Continentals in Bitter Cold Attacked Highbridge Outpost 66

Claremont Park's "Black Swamp," Terror of Old,
Still Gives Trouble 67

Franz Sigel Park Formed Spot Where Washington
Once Watched British 68

Bronx Race Track Was First Opened in 1750 69

Old Fleetwood Hotel on Morris Ave. Was Favorite Spot
of President Grant...70

Balanced over River, Aerialist Made Cakes.....................................71

Nickname of "Dangerville" Once Applied to Highbridge 72

Grand Concourse Planning Work of Three Bronxites 73

Bronxite Recalls Building of Grand Concourse.................................74

Shakespeare Ave. Named for Bronx Formal Garden...........................75

Yankee Stadium's Golden Anniversary Stirs Memories........................76

Italian Bronxites Scarce in Area's 1870 Directories 77

Footraces on Bronx Streets Commonplace in 1920s–30s......................78

In Pre-1910 S. Bronx Ethnic Areas Were Many, Varied 79

Navigable River Flows Beneath Bronx from Croton Reservoir.............80

Section 5

MORRIS HEIGHTS, MT. HOPE,
UNIVERSITY HEIGHTS

Forts 5 and 6 Peaceful Posts in Revolutionary War 83

British "Fort No. 8" Artifacts Recovered by Bronx Historian 84

Ye Wickerscreek Trail Stemmed From Indian's "Weckquasgeek"............86

The Naming of Featherbed Lane: Four Varying Versions Offered 87

Street Names in the Bronx Come from Many Countries......................88

35 Hotels, Inns of Yore Served Travelers in Bronx 89

Old 24th Ward of Bronx Was "Western Reserve"...............................90

DSC "Horse Amulets" Once Warded off "Evil Eye" Here....................91

Old Pine Block Boro Roadways Were Easy on Hooves of Horses 92

Rivers of Bronx Were Courses For Impromptu Steamboat Races 93

Five Bridges Over Harlem River Were Constructed
  by A. P. Boller 94

Horsecars of Old Bronx Were Commuters' Specials of Time 95

High Bridge Built with Arches In 1840's, to Carry City Water.............96

Old Jerome Park Reservoir Gave Name to Boro Avenue 97

Section 6

BELMONT, BRONX PARK,
BRONXWOOD, WEST FARMS

First Bronx Phone Demonstrated In Wray's Hall
  107 Years Ago 101

The Bronx in Prehistory: "Rocking Stone" in Park...........................102

DeLancey's Pine, 122 Feet Tall, Long a Landmark...........................103

Monterey Ave. Named for Battle In Which Bronx
  Officer Fought 104

First Newspaper Published Here (1812) Put Out
  by Matthias Lopez...105

Carpenter of West Farms Devised Looms
  Which Popularized Carpets...106

Letter and Tomb Commemorate Fallen Officer of Civil War..............108

150 Inventions Work of Charles Tarbox...109

Busy Dr. Becker (Bronx 1903): Farmer, Banker, Realtor 110

Arthur Ave., in Belmont, Named for U.S. President 111

Bronx Zoo's Dr. Ditmars And His Snakes Recalled...........................112

Van Zandt Murals in Zoo Adorned Old Lion House..........................114

Southern Blvd. Planned In 1870s "Annexed District"...........................115

Rockefeller Zoo Gift O.K. to Mention Now 116

Chinese First Came to Bronx In 1890s and Kept to Selves 117

Old Roadhouse Yarn Wakes Half-Century Recollections 118

Section 7

FORDHAM, GUN HILL,
KINGSBRIDGE, NORWOOD

How Poe's Cottage Was Saved From Demolition in 1895 121

Nieuw Harlemites Grazed Cattle on Bronx Meadows........................122

Rose Hill Name Arises from Madison Square 123

Fordham Manor Church Set Up by 1684 Bequest 124

Villa Ave. Reminders of Jerome's Racetrack 125

Landowner N. P. Bailey Ruled Roost, Century Ago...........................126

Old Edison Studios Were Birthplace of Cartoon Films......................127

Actor Frank McGlynn, of the Bronx, Had Notable
    Lincoln Screen Career 128

"Ye Wading Place" in Time Came To Bear Present
    Name of Fordham 129

Kingsbridge Kids in '16 Found Washington's
    Cannonball Hoard 130

Jerome Park Race Track Gave Tone, Excitement to Old Bronx...........132

Lorillard Bros. Advertised Snuff And Segars 'way Back in 1787...........133

Stagecoaches Rumbled over Old Bronx Roads................................134

Valentine-Varian House Survived 1777 Warfare 135

Old Jesuit Cemetery at Fordham One of Dozen
    Small Ones in Boro...136

Section 8

FIELDSTON, KINGSBRIDGE HEIGHTS, RIVERDALE, SPUYTEN DUYVIL

Mounted Fire Chief Faced Perils of Irate Bulls as Well as Flames........139

Spuyten Duyvil Creek Rich in Ancient Lore 140

Bronx's Fort Independence Didn't Live Up to Name 142

"Henry Clay" Steamboat Disaster Of '52 Preceded "Slocum" Tragedy....143

Stature Added to Henry Hudson Statue by Sculptor Karl Bitter 145

Claflin Ave. in W. Bronx Named for Quaker Tycoon........................146

That Unlucky Friday the 13th When 8 Were Killed in Crash.............147

Kingsbridge to Lose Landmark, Ahneman & Younkheere Building 149

Valentine Family, Father Zeiser Both Figure in History of Bronx 150

Hudson Memorial Bridge Plan of '03 Just Didn't Get Across 151

Riverdale "Jumbo's Corner" So Called for Innkeeper........................152

Buffalo Once Roamed Home at Van Cortlandt Park, 1907 153

Mt. St. Vincent College Once Actor's Estate 154

One of Tallest Bronx Landmarks Isn't Visible from This Borough 155

Shad Fishing Started with Early Dutch 156

Riverdale's Arrowhead Inn Drew Cafe Society of 1930s....................157

Ploughman's Bush Really Exists — But There Wasn't Any Plough 158

Section 9

CASTLE HILL, CLASON POINT, PARKCHESTER, SOUNDVIEW, UNIONPORT, WESTCHESTER SQUARE

Indian Craft Used Pugsley Creek, Then Sloops,
  Now, the Tugboats...161

Park Versailles Naming Traced To Influence of Lewis Guerlain..........162

Dominick Lynch Name Once Locally Famous 163

Old Westchester Village Was Home For Some
  Colorful Sea Captains...164

First Boro Catholic Church Was on Bear Swamp Road 165

Unionport (Parsonage) Rd. Was Site of Black Workers' Church 166
Unionport Hotel...167
Zerega and Castle Hill Aves. Touch Twice at Their Ends 168
World War Changed Things For Odd Fellows Orphanage..................169
Castle Hill Point Has Designation—From Ancient Greece and Rome ...170
Open Trolley Ride Led to Finding Indian Village 171
Oldtime Milkman Trashes Police Booth 172
Kane's Park Resort Recalled By Oldtimer of Clason Point 173
Catholic Protectory Boys Didn't Run Away Sundays.........................174
Our Lady of Solace Catholic Church...175
No Working Farm Vehicles Left In Bronx, Crops Are Shrinking.........176
"Great Race Track Fire of 1910" Is Recalled in Detail by Woman........177

Section 10

CITY ISLAND, CO-OP CITY, COUNTRY CLUB,
FORT SCHUYLER, THROGGS NECK

Hot Horse Races Developed On Old E. Tremont Ave. 181
Old Stream Recalled by Weir Creek Park.......................................182
Ancient Locust Point "New Found Passage" 183
Devil Moved in Old Bronx On "Belt," Stepping Stones......................185
Anne Hutchinson Home Site Is Still Debated 186
Famed Cedar of Lebanon Toppled by 1944 Hurricane 187
The Time That a Shell, Fired To Warn Ship, Hit Fort Schuyler 188
No Tunnel Ever Connected Two East River Fort Sites.....................189
Ancient Eastchester Covenant Set Rules for Rattlesnake-Killing 190
Palmer Cove Bears Name Of 1740 Bay Lands Owner.......................191
Volunteer Fire Departments Still Keep Vigil in Waterfront Areas........192
Monorail Line to City Island Derailed on First Run 193
Historic Little High Island Sold To NBC for Transmitting Base..........194
Dynamite Johnny O'Brien Was Noted Pilot, '90s Filibuster.................195
Co-op City Was Once A Cucumber and Pickle Farm.......................196

From Cucumbers to Strawberries at Co-op Site 197

Freedomland..198

Section 11

BRONXDALE, MORRIS PARK, VAN NEST

Morris Park Race Course Drew Crowds, 1890–1904 201

Morris Park Track Was Site of World's First Airfield......................202

Bat-Like Glider Used by Youth To Soar Over Van Nest in 1908 203

Louis Chevrolet Raced Cars At Old Morris Park Track....................204

Bronx River Boundaries Caused 1884 Row for Bolton Family.............205

Tangle Woods Often Searched By Boys Hunting "Kidd's" Treasure......206

Gypsy Encampments Held by Bronx River Years Ago 207

Parade in Van Nest Bade Adieu To Old Volunteer Fire Fighters 208

Recalled Are Woodmansten, Pelham Heath Roadhouses....................209

Historians Seek Source of "Woodmansten" Name 210

How About That Bus Ride That Ended in '28 Arrest?......................211

Kings Road Trustee – MacAdam Built One in The Bronx, Too...........212

Gen. Collins Recollects Boyhood in Van Nest 214

Why is Our Borough Called THE Bronx 215

Section 12

BAYCHESTER, EASTCHESTER,
WAKEFIELD, WOODLAWN

1860 Restaurant Attracted Artists, Writers to Boro...........................219

Long-Gone McLean Brook Flowed in Family Estate 220

Wakefield's Black Settlement 221

Woodlawn Cemetery More Than a Burial Ground 222

Ill-Fated 1879 Explorer's Statue Adorns His Grave 223

"Sweet Adeline" Renamed To Honor Bronx Diva Patti.....................224

Nieuw Haarlem Patentee Gave Bussing Ave. Name..........................225

"Irish Fifth Avenue" Lost Lace Curtains in 1930s 226

Awning Makers Became Early Boro Movie Moguls 227

Bronxite Helped Carry Lincoln On Night He Was Assassinated 228

Wakefield and Joseph Conrad 229

Mystery of Buried Bones Solved by Capt. McKeown 230

Havemeyer Avenue Named for Bronx "Sugar Kings" 231

First Bronx Schoolhouse (1683) Served Children of "Ten Farms" 232

Scenes From The Old Bronx 233

Index 243

LIST OF ILLUSTRATIONS

Frontispiece: Map of The Bronx ii

Painting of the 1642 peace treaty in Jonas Bronck's home....................1

John Alf's Hardware Store, c. 1880s 2

View from Oak Point in 1889 21

Casanova Mansion in 1893...22

North Side of 169th Street and Franklin Avenue in 1900.....................43

Allen's Drug Store, Northwest Corner of 168th Street, c. 1870s 44

Volunteer Firemen Parade, Washington Avenue, c. 1900 63

High Bridge, around 1915...64

Lewis G. Morris Mansion in Morris Heights.....................................81

Bronx Borough Day Parade, June 14, 1924 82

The Conservatory in Bronx Park, 1905 99

Department of Highways—Webster and 180th Street, 1910 100

West Farms Square in 1940 100

Chateau Thierry Army Base Hospital
    and Columbia War Hospital, c. 1918 119

New York Harlem Railroad Timetable, c. 1848 120

View from the Hudson River in the 1880s 137

Spuyten Duyvil on October 1, 1928 138

Broadway at Mosholu Avenue in 1899...138

Phil Dietrich's Restaurant & Tavern in 1918 159

Bailor's Hotel in 1900 160

Fixing a flat in 1921 160

Aerial view of Freedomland in 1960..179

Automobile accident on April 1, 1918 180

Indian Trail in Silver Beach, c. 1920s 180

The Morris Park Racetrack and Grandstand in 1899 199

The Morris Park Racetrack Clubhouse in 1899................................200

Gun Hill Road and Edson Avenue vicinity in 1909..........................217

The End of Jerome Avenue, c. 1900 218

The Bronx Old Timers Parade, May 30, 1932.................................233

John Damm's Segar Store, c. 1900..234

Haffen Family, c. 1861. 235

Skating on Indian Pond in Crotona Park, c. 1900 235

Bailey Avenue, 1912 236
Diehl's Brewery on Westchester Avenue in 1954 236
Granite blocks at foot of Miles Avenue in 1919 237
Looking north to Hunter Island Bridge in 1931 237
Pauline and Betty McNamara in 1947 238
Author's Son, John in 1952 238
The Valentine-Varian House in 1985 239
Edgar Allan Poe Cottage in 1985..239
The Research Library Building of The Bronx County
    Historical Society in 1986 240
Early Leaders of Historical Society, Nov. 11, 1960..........................241

INTRODUCTION

From its initial publication in 1938, a weekly newspaper, *The Parkchester Press,* now called the *Bronx Press-Review,* reserved a corner of its editorial page for articles on Bronx history. Having always had an avid interest in the Bronx past, I read that column through a succession of writers. Several men, Joe Kerr, Charles Grabe, and Martin Gross, wrote the column, and their topics ranged over the entire Bronx, crossed centuries, and covered every facet of the past.

With the departure of Martin Gross, I was invited to take over the weekly column, and I did so in 1955 with the idea of publicizing the newly organized Bronx County Historical Society. My fear of "running dry" soon disappeared when I realized the vast lode of history running through The Bronx from Indian times to the present day.

The Bronx County Historical Society believed that these articles should be read together and so reproduced a number of them herein. To the question of how to organize and arrange the articles it was decided that grouping them by neighborhood would make the most sense. However, the precise boundaries, and even the proper names, of most Bronx neighborhoods is a matter of dispute.

For example, the New York City Planning Commission in its publications officially defines the South Bronx as that region from the Harlem River to the East River, below E. 180th Street. By pure coincidence this is the approximate bounds of the Morris Manorlands, known for three centuries as Morrisania.

Among Bronxites there is much difference of opinion about the South Bronx, for older inhabitants habitually refer to themselves as coming from a specific neighborhood such as Tremont, Hunts Point, Longwood or Melrose. To this older generation, anywhere below East 149th Street was considered the South Bronx but, even then, the people below East 149th Street thought of themselves as living in Mott Haven, Port Morris or North New York, and never referred to themselves as living in the South Bronx.

After World War II, officialdom took to including areas up to East 167th Street as "the South Bronx" but the residents of Melrose, Morrisania, Fleetwood and the Concourse stoutly held to their local names. It is a rare individual who would say, "I was born (or raised) in the South Bronx." He or she is more apt to name a certain section in the lower end of the borough.

This process of assimilating other names is not new. A century ago in the North Bronx, for example, there were three communities, side by side: Jacksonville, Wakefield and Washingtonville. In 1895, the last named village was annexed to Wakefield and today it is doubtful anyone remembers the old name. Shortly after 1900, Jacksonville was as well absorbed by Wakefield.

Therefore, the editors divided The Bronx into twelve large sections. Within each section would be found the historic Bronx neighborhoods. The frontispiece shows a map of The Bronx to help in locating the sites of the stories.

No matter what a neighborhood is called or how it is defined, this material is meant to inform, enlighten, and, perhaps, entertain. If it makes the reader want to know even more about The Bronx past, this book will have served its purpose.

JOHN MCNAMARA

Section 1

MELROSE, MOTT HAVEN, NORTH NEW YORK, OLD MORRISANIA, PORT MORRIS

Painting of the 1642 peace treaty in Jonas Bronck's home. By John Ward Dunsmore, c. 1908. (The Bronx County Historical Society Research Library)

John Alf's Hardware Store, near Westchester and Bergen Avenues, c. 1880s. The "Hub" was the principal shopping center of The Bronx by the turn of the century. (The Bronx County Historical Society Research Library)

2

Dome of U.S. Capitol Was Cast Century Ago In A Bronx Foundry

Few Bronxites know that the iron framework for the dome of the U.S. Capitol was cast in a Bronx foundry about a century ago. This writer did not know it either until a chance paragraph in *History of Bronx Borough* by Randall Comfort (1906) told part of the fascinating story.

When the Capitol dome order was secured, back in 1858, by a Manhattan foundry called Janes & Kirtland, it was so large an undertaking that the partners searched for a site that could contain the work. The firm finally located in the countryside of Westchester, next to a small brook and the Westchester Turnpike, and hard by a newly-laid railroad called "the Pocahontas Line." (Today's directions would be Brook and Westchester Avenues.)

A brick foundry was built there and, for three years, hundreds of workmen busied themselves on the 5,000 tons of ironwork to support the Capitol dome. Janes & Kirtland also did work for the U.S. Treasury building. The immense fountain for the city of Savannah, considered one of the finest examples of ironwork in America, originated in the Bronx foundry. The firm also supplied the iron railings for the Brooklyn Bridge, and also the numerous iron bridges for Central Park. Artisans cast wrought-iron deers, dogs, dragons and lions which found a ready market in China, South America and Cuba.

Mr. Janes lived in a mansion overlooking St. Ann's Avenue and for many years, his estate (now inside St. Mary's Park) was called Janes' Hill. The foundry buildings still stand, although most of them have been remodelled into warehouses, lofts and ice-plants; none of the present inhabitants of Brook Avenue know of their former use.

The Mighty Gouverneur Morris Was Testy, One-Legged Bronxite

Governor Peter Stuyvesant is remembered mostly for his terrible temper and his wooden pegleg, but the Bronx also had a testy, wooden-legged public figure in the person of Gouverneur Morris (1752–1816), who was noted for the high offices he held during the Revolution.

He was a member of the Continental Congress, a Senator, and General Washington's minister to France. However, he was never given any later diplomatic post, as he had a rough and caustic tongue. This was outweighed by his training in governmental affairs and his knowledge of French. Incidentally, he had been taught French by a Swiss clergyman named Jean-Pierre Tetard who lived in Kingsbridge (and a John Peter Tetard High School in the West Bronx has been named in his honor.)

In his wild and reckless youth, this heir to the Morrisania Manorlands would risk his neck by driving a team of horses without use of reins. Sitting in the coach, he would direct the racing thoroughbreds with shouts and the cracking of a whip, not caring a whit for the warnings of his friends. But one May day in Philadelphia, his team ran away with him, and one of his legs was crushed. For the rest of his life, Morris hobbled along on a wooden leg.

Once a religious friend called on him and assured him that all this was all for the best, as it was an act of Divine wisdom. He went on in this vein until Gouverneur Morris tartly replied: "My good sir, you argue the matter so handsomely, and point out so clearly the advantages of being without a leg that I am almost tempted to part with the other!"

Early Mott Haven Recalled:
Horse Cars, Bath Houses,
Franz Sigel

"Mott Haven, at the turn of the century, depended on one-horse streetcars for its transportation. The cars had straw on the floor and small coal stoves, and ran about every half-hour. The driver, sitting or standing on an outside platform, was without protection from rain or snow, and often suffered from frozen ears and feet."

So wrote Hester Smith, harking back to her girlhood in which she describes an early Mott Haven "where there were two newspapers *The Union* and *The People*. I remember General Franz Sigel. The General, who was a friend of my father's, wore a blue military coat and a cape lined with red flannel.

"When I first went to live in Mott Haven there was no gas or sanitary plumbing. There were only a few churches and no synagogue. When the Mt. Morris Theatre opened at E. 130th St. I remember seeing the play called *The Black Flag*. Other plays I saw were *The Two Orphans* and *Uncle Tom's Cabin*.

"There were floating bath houses at the foot of 138th St. Wednesdays and Thursdays were 'Ladies' Nights' and I always went when the weather permitted. I had a bad experience once with a goat who came alongside me as I left the baker's. It pulled the paper cover from the pan and ate the cake. I was so frightened that I ran home as fast as I could. At another time, a goat came into our garden and ate some of the clothes placed on the grass to bleach."

Hester Smith, were she to return to her Mott Haven today would not recognize it: No Mount Morris Theatre, nor bath houses on the Harlem River. No one-house street cars, and certainly no goats.

Famous Piccirilli Studio
Birthplace of Great Statues

How many Bronxites are aware that the world-famous marble statue of Abraham Lincoln, seated in the Lincoln Memorial, Washington D.C., was sculpted in the Bronx?

Today, E. 142nd St. between Willis and Brook Aves. can hardly be considered a rural spot recommended for its healthy air but, some 90 years ago, doctors advised a frail Italian woman to move to Old Morrisania for her health. Signora Piccirilli's six sons, who were stonemasons, then decided to establish their business uptown, and by 1892 their Piccirilli Studio had become a landmark.

The Carrara-born family of sculptors had already attracted nationwide fame with their extraordinary statues, bas-reliefs and busts. The oldest brother, Attilio Piccirilli, was the foremost artisan of the family, and he became a close friend of Enrico Caruso, Mayor Fiorello La Guardia, John D. Rockefeller, William Randolph Hearst and later, sculptor Daniel Chester French, one of the foremost sculptors of the post-Civil War years, who came to the workshop. French was commissioned to create a 17 foot statue of a seated Abraham Lincoln. He made clay models and had the Piccirilli family carve the 17 foot marble statue. Attilio carved the head and hands and the others did the rest, using 26 massive stone blocks, at their Bronx studio. It was shipped to Washington, D. C. assembled and then dedicated in May, 1922.

Newspaper accounts of the early 1900s tell of three U.S. Presidents—Woodrow Wilson, William Howard Taft and Theodore Roosevelt—who visited the Bronx studios where the family invariably invited them to a typical Italian meal. The Bronx Home News also noted schoolchildren were just as welcome to come in, with their teachers, and watch the brothers working on their granite, bronze, marble or limestone masterpieces.

Attilio's handiwork can be seen in the Maine Memorial monument at Columbus Circle, and in Mrs. La Guardia's tombstone in Woodlawn Cemetery. His other creations stand in many places throughout the world.

The Name of Jordan L. Mott Stamped on Iron, Worldwide

A sturdy brick building stands alongside the Harlem River near E. 136th St. and passing boatmen and sightseers might notice, on its wall, the faded spelling of Mott Iron Works. The name is a symbol of a vanished era when Jordan L. Mott ran a prosperous industrial complex, owned 100 acres west of Third Ave., and put Mott Haven on the Bronx maps. Mr. Mott was of a mechanical turn of mind and, at age 15, had invented a machine for weaving tape. More than 50 patents were granted him, and his most important and remunerative invention was the cook stove for burning anthracite coal.

Most of the foundry buildings have been torn down since the Iron Works ceased operation in 1906, while Mott Ave. was renamed the Concourse, and the Mott Haven Canal has been filled in. The name survives in the Mott Haven Reformed Church on E. 145th St., and on the subway station at E. 149th St., but the most lasting reminder of all are the manhole covers on our Bronx streets, and the wrought-iron bridges in Central Park.

Trellises and ornamentation that were cast in the Bronx foundry are encountered worldwide, from Turkey to Japan and throughout South America, for Mott's name was invariably stamped on a rim or pedestal. On a visit to San Jose, California, this writer was taken on a tour of a "House of Mystery" — an architectural oddity of peculiarly built rooms and stairs. The tour was intriguing enough, but it was the wrought-iron statue on the lawn that drew this Bronxite's attention: it was stamped J.L. Mott.

Scout Camp Reminds Of Old Indian Name

The Indians who lived west of the Bronx River were ruled by the Sachems of the main tribe located in what is today Dobbs Ferry. Therefore, to these chieftains, the lower end of The Bronx represented the southern limit of their tribal lands and this they called Wanachquiwiauke, the End Place.

This End Place aptly described the rounded peninsula where it met the waters of the East and Harlem Rivers. In time, this difficult Indian name was reduced by the white men to Wanachqua and Wanaqua.

Jonas Bronck's homesite was on this same peninsula but he discarded the "heathen" name and gave it the Biblical one of Emmaus. Later, the Morris family built their first mansion there, west of the Mill Brook, and the land became known as Morrisania. Around 1860, it became known as Old Morrisania to distinguish it from the village, around E. 165th St., of the same name.

However, a landowner named B. G. Arnold revived the original name by calling his Oak Point estate Ranaque and this was so noted on the maps of 1868. This estate has since disappeared under the railroad yards at Oak Point Ave. and, with it, the name.

Today the ancient name survives but, oddly enough, not in The Bronx. Thanks to the Bronx Boy Scouts of America, their encampment on Ten Mile River is called Camp Ranaqua, as a reminder of their Indian past.

St. Mary's Park Revolution Site of "Refugee Huts"

On a British war map, showing what is now the lower Bronx, are a series of squares marked "Refugee huts." These huts (barracks) represented the temporary quarters of a constantly changing number of displaced persons who were victims of the Revolutionary War.

A considerable area of Westchester County was known as the Neutral Ground, as neither those active in the American cause nor the people loyal to the Crown controlled it. Raids and counter-raids made the County an ever-shifting battleground and, as farms were burned and cattle driven off, many Loyalists fled to the shelter of New York City. The City was hardpressed to accommodate this influx, so temporary camps were set up outside the city, but inside the British zone. Such a camp was laid out near the Mill Brook of Old Morrisania, and its location was at our present-day St. Ann's Ave. and E. 149th St.

The proximity to the brook ensured a supply of fresh water, and the hills of what is now St. Mary's Park provided shelter from the wind. Nearby woods were the source of firewood, and logs for the building of fences and more huts.

At first the barracks sheltered whole families but eventually the women and children moved into New York City, and military units took their place. Composed of men from upper New York and Connecticut, they were known as the Associated Loyalists, but the Americans called them the Refugee Corps. These Refugees raided into rebel territory, killed patriots and destroyed what they could and, in reprisal, the Americans penetrated into the British zone and attacked the Refugee huts.

This Corps finally was disbanded by Sir Henry Clinton, the British commander, because he disapproved of their excesses which were in the nature of personal vendettas against former neighbors. There were no traces of this military camp at war's end, and only squares on a faded military map tell us that once St. Mary's Park figured in our Revolutionary War.

John Jacob Astor Bought Land of Morrises in 1840s

A reader inquired about Astor Ave., and the acquisition of Bronx land by that wealthy family. The tract, alongside Pelham Parkway, was the third or fourth parcel that was bought.

The first purchase of property in our Borough was initiated by John Jacob Astor when the Morris family began selling some of their manorlands along the Harlem River in the 1840's. Mott Haven had already been sold to Jordan L. Mott and the Astors looked over the countryside directly north of it. The years following the Civil War had given New York City terrific impetus and its expansion included the Annexed District which was the Bronx west of the Bronx River. Small factories were being established and clusters of working class homes were in the making.

Astor envisioned industrial docks, factories and tenements for the workers when he purchased the tract on the Harlem River from E. 149th St. to approximately E. 156th St., extending inland to present-day Franz Sigel Park. In keeping with the family tradition of remembering their German origin, the main thoroughfare was named Waldorf Place.

Subsequent maps of the district show little or no progress. No settlement sprung up. No piers were depicted, and the only establishment this writer has ever heard about was a small amusement park and picnic grounds in the 1890's called Vineyard Beach. Believe it or not, today's congested, polluted stretch of the Harlem River at that point was an inviting beach with clear water suitable for bathing. Ashore were a dance pavilion, and a beer garden patronized by the Irish of Mott Haven and the Germans of Melrose.

In 1899, right after the entire Bronx became part of New York City, Waldorf Pl. was renamed Ferncliff Pl. and most likely heralded the fact that the Astor family no longer was the property owner. The area lay idle for many years until, in 1935, the Bronx County jail was built upon the site.

Today, Ferncliff Pl. and Waldorf Pl. are found only in old atlases.

"Dutch Broadway" Busy Street in Boro for Nearly Century

The intersection of E. 149th Street and Courtlandt Avenue today is a heavily trafficked crossing and has been a busy corner for almost a century. Its hilltop location has always given it importance, and no doubt in Indian times served as a lookout. This was Weckguasgeek Indian territory, just beyond the northern limits of Jonas Bronck's farm whose bounds ended at E. 148th Street.

In 1697 the Morris family was granted the entire South Bronx by the English crown, and the manorlands remained in the possession of Morris descendants for almost two centuries. Gouverneur Morris, in the 1850's, began to dispose of the family holdings, and small villages were laid out. The incorporated village of Melrose was subdivided and sold to families from lower New York City, and the surveyor was an Andrew Findlay of Scotch descent. Melrose South ran from E. 148th to E. 156th Streets, and Melrose North went on to E. 163rd Street.

Courtlandt Avenue was the main thoroughfare, holding its churches, theatres, social halls and stores. The Uptown News of November 1885 advertised apartments on Courtlandt Avenue were renting at $10 a month. The avenue had the highest elevation in the section, and — due to its heavily German population — was called "Dutch Broadway." The Haffen family, wealthy brewers, lived on Courtlandt Avenue, and one of the sons was the first Borough President.

E. 149th St. was originally a tree-lined lane called Benson St. after a local landowner named Benjamin Benson. E. 149th St. and Courtlandt Avenue flourished as a business junction and, through the years, boasted of many fine cafes and restaurants. Adam Hoffmann, who eventually operated eight different summer parks, hotels and saloons, opened his first tavern on the northwest corner of that crossing.

After World War I, the German population dwindled and a strong Italian influence became apparent. After World War II, Puerto Rican and Negro residents moved into the old-law tenements that were left, but still today the intersection is largely a business hub.

Bronx Public Bath was Held as World's Finest

With bathrooms so taken for granted and bathtubs such an accepted part of every household, it is difficult to imagine the time when many Bronxites had to go to a Public Bath. Oldtimers will recall the formal opening in May 1909 of the Public Baths on the southeastern corner of Elton Avenue and E. 156th St., a Roman-styled building with heavy ornamental stone cornice and copper roof, and an arcade of artistically carved ornamentation. There were separate entrances for men and women opening onto a spacious loggia that had a mosaic floor, massive stone arches, bronze tablets and even a bronze ceiling.

At the opening of this classic building, architect Michael Garvin modestly accepted the congratulations of Bronx Borough President Louis Haffen, Superintendent Reville and other dignitaries of the Board of Aldermen. The inspecting party toured the main and upper floors that contained 130 separate bathrooms, consisting of 2 compartments each: the outer compartment being the dressing room, and the inner, the bath proper. Besides showers, a number of porcelain tubs had been installed for people who preferred them, and each room was provided with a drinking fountain of iced water.

Competent judges who were familiar with public baths in America and Europe expressed their opinion that the Bronx installation was the finest and most complete public baths of its size in the world. Alas, modernization brought about its decline as every home built thereafter had bathtubs installed, and today the passerby on Elton Avenue sees nothing but an excavation where once the famed Public Baths stood.

Story of Boro Boy Gone Bad: Rise, Fall of Dutch Schultz

In the annals of the Bronx underworld there is hardly anyone better remembered than Dutch Schultz who got his start to the top, during the Prohibition Years (1919–1933).

Prior to that uneasy era, he had been a smalltime burglar and package thief named Arthur Flegenheimer, and having served a short term in prison, came back to the Hub where his pals in the Bergen Gang dubbed him Dutch Schultz. There had been a real Dutch Schultz, said to have been a brawler in the Frog Hollow Gang of the early 1900's, and Flegenheimer adopted his name and also his rough-house tactics.

At first he was just a bartender in a Bronx speakeasy (illegal saloon) but soon went into business for himself, acquiring delivery trucks, tough drivers and a certain ability to transport beer from the illicit New Jersey breweries. By 1931 Schultz had some 20 garages and storage sheds scattered around the Bronx, and a criminal workforce that delivered thousands of kegs of beer to small buyers.

One "drop" was a storage shed located near the Mott Haven railroad yards, and featured an elevator that took empty beer trucks underground, and brought them up again fully loaded. The location had the curious nickname of the Tins but this writer has never been able to pinpoint the exact location, nor unravel the origin of the nickname. Nearby was an office building at E. 149th St. off Morris Ave., and there Schultz established his executive office which was more like a command post, with bulletproof doors and steel-lined walls.

The Beer Baron had a few prosperous years in the Bronx, controlling the lucrative bootleg business while carrying on murderous warfare against rival gangsters, but a trip to Newark N.J. in 1935 witnessed his downfall. There he was gunned down by hired killers, and that ended the violent life of a Bronx boy gone bad.

First Irishmen in the Bronx?
Maybe Soldiers for Dutch (1642)

Around St. Patrick's Day each year, some readers inquire who were the first Irishmen to set foot in the Bronx. It is this writer's conviction that 1642 would be the date of this event, and that the men were soldiers in the pay of the Dutch West India Company.

The region around the thriving colony of Nieuw Amsterdam was, that year, the scene of Indian attacks on outlying farms, and settlers were massacred and their belongings destroyed. Governor Kieft ordered an Ensign Hendrick Van Dyck to proceed against the Weckguasgeek Indians who roamed the Bronx mainland between the Harlem and Bronx Rivers, and so an expedition was formed. With 80 men and a trusted guide, Van Dyck reached Bronck's land and at dusk found himself (according to old accounts) by a stream which was called Armenparel by the Indians. This was the Mill Brook of later times. Van Dyck's plan to surprise the Indians failed, for the red men had prudently retreated from such a large force: but it was this show of strength that caused the Indians to sue for peace, and sign a treaty in Jonas Bronck's house. That Armenparel was a stream on Bronck's land would be an indication it was the Mill Brook beyond a doubt.

A rollcall of the 80 men is still on record in the New York State historical section, and some of the names on this roster are quite curious: Nicholas Murfey, John Swilivan, Mathew Maguere, Jeremiah Sheredewyn. Are these not Murphy, Sullivan, McGuire and Sheridan? In addition there were men in another company named Kalleghein, Makneel, Hennisce, Makmihon and Obryan which surely was the result of a Dutch adjutant's trouble in spelling Callahan, McNeil, Hennessy, McMahon and O'Brien!

These Irishmen in the pay of the Dutch West India Company were most likely runaway servants from New England. In those days it was the practice to work seven years for a master to pay off the cost of transportation to America, but many indentured men tired of the work and regretted their bargain, so that the only solution was to begin a new life in Nieuw Amsterdam.

First Jewish Temple Here Now Church for Baptists

It may come as a surprise to some Bronxites of the Jewish faith that the first Temple in our borough is still standing, in good condition, on E. 169th St., East of Third Ave. However, it no longer is a synagogue but has become a Baptist church that serves the present population. Temple Adath Israel, organized by German Jews in 1889, is believed to have been the first Jewish organization in the Bronx.

Temple Hand-in-Hand might dispute this claim, for five years earlier Wilhelm Daub helped organize this house of worship on E. 145th St. between Willis and Brook Aves. *The American Jewish Yearbook, 1907–08,* gives the date of organization as 1895 in its *Communal Register,* but a biography of Mr. Daub credits him with being the president "of the first Jewish Synagogue in the Bronx."

William Daub (as he preferred to be called) came from Germany, trained in the clothing business, in 1866, and eventually moved to North New York (E. 145th St.) with his Austrian-born wife and five children. There the family became active in social events of Mott Haven, Melrose and Morrisania.

Very few Jewish families were then living in the Bronx and nothing was done for religious training. Mr. Daub spent his free Sundays looking for Jewish families and within a few months of the year 1883 he had gathered 35 boys and girls, and started their religious training. They first met in Kirchoff's Hall at Westchester and Third Avenues, later in a Turn Verein Hall on Courtlandt Ave. and E. 150th St., finally to their own Temple on E. 145th St.

In 1901 Mr. Daub retired from the clothing business and became superintendent at Lebanon Hospital, then located at Westchester and Cauldwell Aves. He was an honored man in the community, and a civic leader. He was a member of Beethoven Lodge, F. and A.M., of Palestine Lodge, the North Side Board of Trade and the Melrose Turn Verein, but he always regarded the Temple Hand-in-Hand as his especial accomplishment.

Attorney's House was "Station" On "Underground Railroad"

In the years preceding the Civil War, Villa Place was a tree-lined lane in the village of Mott Haven. The name referred to the attractive villa of Charles Van Doren, legal counsel to Jordan L. Mott, who had founded the settlement and given it his name.

Those were the agonizing years when the question of slavery was tearing the quiet fabric of rural America, and the village of Mott Haven was feeling its effects. It was the time of the Underground Railroad which was neither underground nor a railroad, but a secret system of aiding escaping slaves. The law had decreed southern slave owners could come north above the Mason-Dixon Line and recapture blacks, so even the northern cities of Philadelphia and New York were no longer havens.

Travelling by night and hiding by day, escaping slaves went from "station" to "station" aided, fed and clothed by people who were passionately opposed to slavery. One of these Abolitionists was lawyer Van Doren whose villa was a "station" of the Underground Railroad. This house stood alongside the road to Boston — now E. 145th St. and Third Ave. — and members of the nearby Dutch Reformed Church helped hundreds of unfortunate Blacks on their way up to Boston or Canada.

That a reputable lawyer and equally respectable church members would circumvent a heartless law proved to be yet another step that led to the Civil War, and the emancipation of the black population.

The Mott Haven Dutch Reformed church still stands, but now is situated some 50 yards from its original place on Third Ave. There is no trace of Charles Van Doren's villa, and not even a tablet or plaque marks the site of the long-vanished "station."

Pulaski Park Named for a Pole

With the Papal visit here things Polish are in the limelight. The Polish influence in our Borough has been limited mostly to two small communities — one in Melrose, and the other in Wakefield — and there is not a street or avenue honoring anyone of Polish origin.

We almost had a Kosciusko Ave., near Jerome Ave. and Gun Hill Rd., but there is an old story that when the city planners learned how much trouble Brooklynites had, trying to spell their Kosciusko St., they decided Kossuth Ave. would be easier to spell. (Incidentally, Kossuth was a Hungarian).

There is, however, a small park, overshadowed by the Major Deegan Expressway at Willis Ave. in the South Bronx, that is named after Count Casimir Pulaski of Poland who served as a general in our Revolutionary War.

The land had been private property from the time it was part of Jonas Bronck's farm until it was acquired for public use at the time the Major Deegan Expressway was being planned. Rows of old law tenement houses were razed along E. 133rd St., and this wholesale demolition resulted in an open space, suitable for a park.

Pulaski Park was named in 1930, but years of persistent questioning by this writer have never turned up anyone who attended the opening ceremonies almost 50 years ago.

Ancient Police Blotter Cites Site Of Gold-Laden British Frigate

Would you expect to find a bit of Revolutionary War history in an old police blotter? This unlikelihood can be read in the day-to-day reports of the Alexander Ave. stationhouse of a hundred years ago, when its outposts included Port Morris and adjacent North and South Brother islands. The Port Morris beat was clearly described as commencing at Locust Ave. and terminating at the Hussar, and thereby hangs a tale.

The Revolutionary War was in full swing when a British frigate, Hussar, was enroute to Rhode Island, via the East River. Legend has it that, besides carrying American prisoners, the Hussar was transporting the pay of the British army — a fortune in gold and silver coins. The ship was wrecked on the reefs of Hell Gate and the swift current carried it to the shores of what is now Port Morris, where it sank.

Many attempts were undertaken in subsequent years to locate the sunken treasure, and from time to time pieces of copper, ship's timber and an English coin or two were recovered, but the treasure — if there really was any — has never been brought to the surface.

Extensive landfill in the 1850s may have buried the Hussar, and the area around E. 133rd St. was always regarded as the possible site of the ship. The name, Hussar, was transferred to that locality, even to the extent of being officially recorded in the police journals of the early Bronx.

Paderewski's Bronx Visit Enriched Piano Teacher

The Polish population in the Bronx has never been a large one, and only two colonies were ever cohesive enough to warrant their own parochial schools, churches and social halls in lower Wakefield, and in Melrose.

The Melrose Polish-Americans lived along Courtlandt, Melrose and Elton Aves., attended St. Adalbert's church on E. 156th St., and enjoyed their festive evenings in the Polish Hall on Courtlandt Ave. and E. 154th St.

When this writer was young he heard a bit of neighborhood folklore from a Mr. Tully (born Tuliszewski) concerning a perhaps unofficial visit by the Prime Minister of Poland, Ignace Jan Paderewski, to the Melrose church. The year would be approximately 1920, and as no one else ever substantiated the story, this writer always considered it just a pleasant joke. Until recently. Then, an article appearing in a foreign language newspaper repeated the selfsame story, ascribing it to "a suburb of New York" but not naming the Bronx in particular.

Mr. Tully's tale: Hoping for a few hours' relaxation from his round of receptions, the Prime Minister left St. Adalbert's church and sauntered along Elton Ave. Paderewski was far better known as a concert pianist, famed as an interpreter of Chopin, Rubinstein and Liszt, so it was with a critical ear that he heard someone playing a Nocturne by Chopin. A sign next to the open groundfloor window read "Ellen Smith, Piano teacher. $1 an hour."

Paderewski, on impulse, went into the house and knocked on the door, the story goes.

The young lady recognized him immediately and was astounded when he asked permission to come in and sit at her piano. Almost speechless, she listened as the maestro played the same Nocturne and gave her a few pointers. He then told her to play the song again, which she did, with Paderewski gently coaching her through the difficult passages. Satisfied, he left.

From that time onward, related Mr. Tully/Tuliszewski, the sign on Elton Ave. read "Ellen Smith (pupil of Paderewski) Piano lessons— $5 an hour."

Bronx, Queens Claim So. Brother Island; Only Seagulls Inhabit It

South Brother Island is a small isle of some four neglected acres, lying off the South Bronx shoreline. Thousands of ferry passengers pass it daily on their way to North Brother Island or Riker's Island, but it is doubtful if a dozen people set foot on it any given month. It contains no pier, no road, nor suitable landing, and is rimmed with uninviting boulders.

Recently this writer and a fellow-historian, Ronald Schliessman, paddled a canoe to South Brother Island, not knowing if we were landing on Bronx territory or not, for, according to some maps, it is considered part of Queens County. Other charts plainly include South Brother Island in Bronx territorial waters. This view is held by the Bronx County Engineers' Office, where officials assured us the island was definitely part of this Borough — but this is not the viewpoint of the Municipal Reference Library.

Its history is as scanty as its aspect: originally Indian territory, it was claimed for the Dutch West India Company by Adrian Block who dubbed it and neighboring North Brother Island De Gesellen (The Brethren.) Colonial maps show it as the smaller of The Two Brothers. In the mid-nineteenth century North Brother Island and Riker's Island were acquired by New York City and considerably enlarged, but little South Brother remained unchanged.

Colonel Jacob Ruppert bought it in 1894 and erected a summer home there, which he occupied until 1907. The house burned down in 1909, and the Colonel's estate sold the island to John Gerosa in 1944. Gerosa, in turn, sold it to the Manhattan Sand Company in 1958 and this company, to date, has not used the island for anything.

In the interest of The Bronx County Historical Society, a landing was made and the canoe drawn up on the beach. Paradoxically surrounded by the crowded Boroughs of Queens, Manhattan and The Bronx, little South Brother Island was entirely deserted — and really belongs to the seagulls!!

Section 2

HUNTS POINT, LONGWOOD, OAK POINT

View from Oak Point in 1889. The steamboat in the center was traveling to Long Island Sound. The hospital and power plant of North Brother Island are in the background. (The Bronx Old Timers Collection, The Bronx County Historical Society Research Library)

Casanova Mansion in 1893. This property was located in Hunts Point facing the East River. The mansion was called Castello de Casanova after the owner, Innocencio Casanova y Fagundo, a Cuban importer. The structure was formerly the Whitlock Mansion, and originally the Leggett Mansion. (The Bronx County Historical Society Research Library)

Name of Hunts Point Avenue Goes Back in History to 1668

Hunts Point no longer is the beautiful peninsula of the previous centuries, but its street names faithfully retain memories of the Colonial families and the later squires that lived there.

Hunts Point Ave. remains the main artery, and that name goes back to 1668! Gabriel Leggett's name is just as ancient, and a nearby avenue carries on his memory. Gabriel Leggett II was the progenitor of the Fox and Tiffany families and every Bronxite knows those names.

For years The Grange, ancestral home of the Hunts, was a haven to Joseph Rodman Drake, and so we have a Drake Park and a Drake St. (In deference to this Poet of the Bronx, adjoining avenues were named for Halleck, Whittier, Bryant and Longfellow.)

Around Civil War times Hunts Point held the mansions of the Vyse family, Edward G. Faille, Paul Spofford, Innocencio Casanova and Benjamin Whitlock and all these prosperous squires are remembered to this day on street signs.

Few neighborhoods in the Bronx have so many historical connotations as Hunts Point.

Dinner Given British Colonel in Mansion Proved His Last

There must have been monumental Thanksgiving dinners served in the Bronx during the past three centuries, but only one has ever been accorded a place in our history. Officially it was not a Thanksgiving dinner, although it took place two hundred years ago this month, during our American Revolution, but instead was a farewell dinner given by a British colonel named Fowler.

James Graham, Attorney-General of the Provinces, had been given a grant of land by his son-in-law, Lewis Morris, in the 1740's and on it, Graham had built a fine mansion. It was located on Oak Point in the vicinity of today's Leggett Ave., and commanded a broad view of the East River. The Attorney-General died just before the Revolution, and his widow sold the property to the Leggett family who were living in the mansion when the British army occupied what is now the South Bronx. The Leggetts were then dispossessed to make room for the British officers.

Colonel Fowler received orders to vacate the Morrisania area, so he arranged a farewell dinner to which he invited Loyalist neighbors and fellow officers. The convivial party had just sat down at the tables when orderlies discovered the mansion was on fire. Colonel Fowler immediately gave orders that all the tables, chairs and dishes be moved to the lawn, where the diners continued to enjoy their dinner. To the clinking of wine glasses and toasts to His Majesty, George III, the Leggett mansion burned to the ground without any attempts being made to save it from destruction! And to this day the cause of the fire has never been ascertained. The event proved definitely to be a farewell dinner for Colonel Fowler for, that same night, he led a marauding expedition to Eastchester and was mortally wounded.

The Leggett Family

An ancient cemetery belonging to the Hunt and Leggett families still can be visited on Hunts Point, but the burial grounds of their slaves has long been obliterated by the manufacturing and marketing complex that makes up the Point today.

In 1891, some nine Leggett graves were opened and the remains removed and transferred to St. Peter's churchyard at Westchester Square. The crude headstones were left behind, and a Mr. Spofford used them to build a rookery on his grounds nearby.

An eyewitness account by a 19th century Leggett emphasized the height of the men "We were surprised by the stature of the men, for although the bodies had crumbled, the space they occupied was well defined, and measured almost seven feet. I had often heard my mother say the Leggetts were very tall, my grandfather 'high as the door.'

"In one grave, copper nails on the coffin lid spelled out 'Wm Leggett — Aged 71 Years' and of him I had heard many tales. The 1730 records of the Boroughtown of Westchester listed him as an Alderman. One family record noted that on February 13th, 1740 Captain Wm. Leggett went over to Long Island with a slay (sleigh) as the Sound was frozen, and brought over 30 bushels of corn.

"He was gone from home on long sea voyages, and on one such venture he returned to the family and covered the entire dinner table with Spanish dollars."

Bank Note Firm's Engraver Was Master Counterfeiter

Anyone interested in money (and who isn't?) may find an absorbing hour or two reading William Griffith's *The Story of the American Bank Note Company.*

People who travel abroad, particularly in South America, often remark on the colorful attractiveness of the bank notes they see, not realizing that the paper currency originated right here in the Bronx. The American Bank Note Company had been on Hunts Point for decades, rolling off the currency of a half-hundred nations [but since 1984 has moved to New Jersey].

The least publicized man in that closely guarded trade was a master-engraver named Joseph Ford. He was referred to as "the honest counterfeiter" and his specialty was a bizarre one: that of testing the security of the bank notes by attempting to counterfeit them. Mr. Ford spent his working hours in a secluded workshop attempting to duplicate the various currencies that were being run off on the presses. Provided with all the necessary chemicals and photographic equipment, Ford's failures were cause for satisfaction; but when he succeeded in counterfeiting the bank notes, it led to subtle changes in design, or tinting or grade of paper to foil any other ambitious counterfeiter.

His son, William Ford, became known as the world's foremost portrait engraver, and was widely acclaimed for his fine work — a fame his father never aspired to, as his specialized lifework demanded the utmost secrecy.

West Bronx Had Indian Trail To Quinnahung Settlement

An Indian path ran alongside Bronx Park and, reaching West Farms Road, followed the Bronx River downstream. At today's Westchester Ave., it turned towards Southern Blvd. and out to the tip of Hunts Point.

There, the Native Americans had a large settlement for there was plenty of game and abundant fishing, and it was called Quinnahung — or as close to that pronunciation as the Dutch and English could manage. In the aboriginal tongue, it meant the Planting Neck, and the incoming Europeans and their African slaves farmed the land and raised corn, tobacco and much the same crops that the Weckguasgeek had harvested.

Before the region became industrialized in the late 1800s, amateur archeologists could scour the shoreline of the East and Bronx Rivers, turning up arrowheads, flint knives, stonetipped spears, axe heads and flat scrapers for skinning animals. Clay pottery, along with layers of clamshells, indicated centuries of Indian occupation before the coming of the Hunt family. The Hunt cemetery that is still in existence is said to overlay a far more ancient Indian burial ground, but civilized conduct (and Parks Department regulations) would not allow any exploratory digs to be carried out.

Old Oak Point Resort Area

A far corner of the Bronx is Oak Point, lying alongside the East River below Hunt's Point. Hardly anyone goes there these days, it being an industrial zone of small factories, warehouses, vacant lots and railroad yards. There is little reminder of its bucolic past.

The pre-Revolutionary name of the area was Jeafferd's Neck, but became better known as Leggett's Point once that prominent family took possession of many holdings on the peninsula. For a brief time, in the mid-1800's, charts of the Sound steamers noted Arnold's Point, when B.G. Arnold was the landowner, whose mansion was used as a checkpoint.

At the end of the 19th century, Oak Point became a popular pleasure resort, and flourished until 1905 or 1906. The Oak Point Road (no longer in existence) was the shortest route to the picnic groves, baseball fields and amusement center.

Duck Island—Another "Lost" One Lay Off the "Debatable Lands"

Another lost island that has disappeared under the relentless reclamation of land is the East Bronx islet once known as Long Rock, or Duck Island.

Some 300 years back, the region between present-day Bruckner Blvd., Hunts Point and the East River was a swampy track threaded by some winding creeks. The Morris family claimed their bounds extended to the eastern-most creek, which they called Bound Brook. "Not so," said the Hunt family, "this is not your Bound Brook but our Wigwam Brook which is inside our grant. The true boundary is farther west at Sackwrahung Creek." "It is not Sackwrahung Creek," retorted the Morris family, "we call it Bungay Brook and it is well inside our Manorlands of Morrisania!" Thus this region became known as the "Debatable Lands," and many a decade passed in dispute.

It was only in 1740 that the land between both creeks was adjudged part of Morrisania, and it was sold to James Graham, Attorney-General of the Province. It passed through several hands, including the Leggett family, and in the 18th century, Leggett's Creek was noted on maps, displacing the earlier names of Wigwam Brook and Bound Brook.

At the mouth of this creek, a small island was situated offshore and was used as a landmark. On an 1850 survey, it was marked "Long Rock" when Benjamin Whitlock bought the estate from the Leggett family. Next, Innocencio Casanova, a Cuban, purchased the property after the Civil War and the little island was included in the sale. Senor Casanova's mansion became a secret cache for Cuban arms to be used in a revolution, and local lore tells of mysterious ships that ventured up the creek on moonless nights, with Spanish-speaking sailors cautiously sounding the channel. No doubt the little island served as a smugglers' haven when low tides prevented the ships from reaching the Casanova mansion itself.

Around the turn of the century, lads from Hunts Point and Springhurst used to swim out to Duck Island—a local name for the same island—but after 1910, landfill operations began in earnest, and in a short time both creek and island were engulfed. Tiffany St. was extended, and it now overlays the lost island at East Bay Ave., a prosaic intersection some 50 yards inland.

Country Seats Once Abounded in Bronx

Today we Bronxites know Hunts Point as an industrialized peninsula, with barren stretches of scrub and fen, so that it is hard to realize it was once a wooded, pleasant abode of farmers and land owners.

On 1858 map one finds the Hunts Point Road a meandering path that made a wide loop south of the Joseph Rodman Drake cemetery, whereas the 1958 visitor will see that the road has been straightened out to pass on the north.

Most of the land owners maintained business houses on lower Manhattan and commuted daily by private sloop, or by coach. A few merchant princes had carriage connections with the steamers that docked at Morrisania, but one squire (E. G. Faile) preferred to remain in his carriage and continue on into Harlem. There, he had a fresh team of horses waiting to carry him on his way. In the late afternoon he reversed the procedure. These horses, by the way, were imported from Argentina and each one cost the squire $1,000 in transportation alone!

The gentlemen of those days gave descriptive names to their country seats and, oddly enough, only one of these names survived the passage of a century and is in use today. On the other hand, the names of almost all the landed gentry are preserved as avenues and streets: Ranaque at the end of Oak Point was owned by B. G. Arnold; Castello de Casanova by Senor Innocencio Casanova; Blythe by Francis J. Barretto; Elmwood by Paul N. Spofford; Springhurst by George S. Fox; Greenbank by C. D. Dickey; Sunny Slope by P. A. Hoe; Woodside by E. G. Faile, who has already been mentioned.

Then there was Ambleside, owned by J. B. Simpson; Brightside by Colonel Hoe (who invented the rotary printing press); Foxhurst which belonged to H. D. Tiffany, and Rocklands owned by T. A. Vyse.

Finally there was Minford Place, the country seat of Thomas Minford, and Longwood Park—owned by S. B. White—and the only estate in that vicinity that became a street name.

Hunts Point Cows Monopolized The Spring at Leggett's Lane

James Reuel Smith, on his bicycle tours of the early Bronx, before 1900, was no stranger to Hunts Point—his photographs show springs on Faile Street, Whitlock Avenue and Leggett's Lane.

The last-named provided a good picture of the rural aspect of Hunts Point as we read: "A few feet north of Leggett's Lane a rough country road branches off to the east of Southern Boulevard and crosses the New York, New Haven & Hartford Railroad. Some 200 feet west of the railroad there is a spring. The property was formerly owned by Judge Dennison White and is bounded by a low stone wall which once retained water for an ice pound that was fed by this spring. There is a small grove of cedar and cherry trees near the spring, and over the wall of the ice pound glimpses are caught of ships passing on the East River, behind Oak Point, a half mile distant.

"The neighborhood of the spring is now given over to a herd of cows. They monopolize the spring, and make it difficult to work with a camera. They are very good-natured beasts, but they nose around and peer into the lens and rub up against the photographer in pushing past to get their drink, as if human beings were trespassers on their private domain.

"October, 1897. On the west side of the Southern Boulevard about 500 feet north of Intervale Avenue, a spring rises just on the inner side of the sidewalk. The water is very cold but has a slightly salty taste."

And this observation: "A few feet north of the west platform of the Hunts Point railroad station is what a casual passenger takes for a kennel, perhaps wondering that such a location should be selected for a dog house. This is the box of one of the best-kept springs in the city. The stationmaster cleans it out often, limes it, and always has several pieces of iron coupling in it to add to what he believes are its natural virtues. The water comes through rocks at the bottom and is about eight inches deep. It has never been known either to freeze or go dry. The water is said to have been analyzed by the Board of Health and found to rank with the purest in the city. Anyone drinking from it, however, would pronounce it pecularily tasteless if not actually flat. It has no frogs. The overflow, collected an eighth of a mile north, forms a good-sized pond on Mr. Ives' place, from which two crops of ice are cut in winter."

Cowboys in the Bronx? Certainly! At Springhurst Dairy in the 1880s

Some 75 years ago there were many small dairy farms operating in the rural countryside now called The Bronx. A half dozen were to be found in the Hunt's Point section, and the largest was that of Hugh Duffy, who operated the Springhurst Dairy.

Some 33 cows grazed on leased property of the Faile family, and this herd supplied milk for housewives as far off as the South Bronx and Yorkville. The price? 8c a quart! The milk wagons were driven by Duffy's sons; and, in winter, they switched to horsedrawn sleds. Springhurst was located east of Southern Boulevard, extended to Hunts Point and encompassed about 40 acres. Eight of these acres were set aside as cornfields, to supply cattle fodder. Sons Jack, Ed and Joe Duffy were youthful cowherders but they lightened their tasks by rounding up the cows by horseback.

One of the vivid boyhood memories was the weekly balloon ascent by a Dr. Thomas. Across the flat fields (now covered by factories on Tiffany Street) they could watch the balloon being inflated down at Port Morris, and then the thrilling skyride of the daredevil doctor. One time the argonaut landed in their farmlands, and Farmer Duffy loaded the basket and deflated balloon in his haywagon and hauled Dr. Thomas back to his launching spot.

When the Faile Estate was subdivided, the Springhurst Dairy did not go out of business. Hugh Duffy leased an adjoining tract — the Spofford Estate — and continued operations into the 20th century. By that time, health regulations, labor laws, zoning restrictions and licenses hedged and hemmed in the small dairymen and, one by one, they went out of business — and so did Hugh Duffy.

A prized possession of son Ed Duffy, now living on Country Club Road, is a quart milk bottle, marked Duffy's Springhurst Dairy — certainly a collector's item!

Steamboat on East River Tipped Hookey-Players

Ed Duffy, once of Springhurst (Hunt's Point) but now of Country Club, thinks back to the large steamships that plied between New York City and the New England ports, and he remembers watching them as they steamed by majestically on their way to Long Island Sound.

"Some of these boats were sidewheelers and carried freight as well as passengers. They came up the East River in the evenings—large and beautiful white steamers with Colonial names such as the 'Priscilla,' 'Commonwealth,' 'Puritan' and 'Providence.'"

One boat that ran to New Haven was the "Richard Peck" and, because it passed Baretto Point and Hunt's Point at 3 p.m., any boy playing hookey knew it was time to go home. There also were a couple of ferry boats that went from Port Morris at E. 134th St. over to North Beach, which was a large amusement park in those days. Today it is part of La Guardia Airport. Another ferryboat system operated from Clason Point to College Point, Queens, but the Bronx-Whitestone bridge ended the era of the ferryboat.

If you lived along the Hudson River side of the Bronx, there were the Day Liners enroute to Poughkeepsie and Albany. These boats were a different type than the Sound steamers, with fewer staterooms and more deckspace. The Albany Night boats made the trip from 6 p.m. to 6 a.m. One steamship line played its searchlight on both shorelines. People on the hillsides would wave their hats and kerchiefs as the boat passed, and it was a grand sight. The fare was more reasonable than the train, but it took much longer.

This, of course, didn't matter to most people, as it was such a pleasant trip.

And thanks for pleasant memories, Mr. Duffy!!

"General Slocum Disaster" of '04 Recalled This Month

This year and month commemorates the 75th anniversary of the General Slocum ship disaster wherein over a thousand people died in what was described as "the worst ten minutes in New York history."

On St. Mark's Day—June 15th, 1904—this excursion boat came up the East River from lower Manhattan, carrying over 1,200 excited and happy people, bound for Long Island Sound on a Lutheran church outing. As it was a weekday, very few men were aboard. Approaching Hell Gate, a fire broke out and forced hundreds of women and children to jump into the water, where they drowned in the swift currents. The captain elected to run through Hell Gate and rammed his vessel on the southwestern shore of North Brother Island where hundreds more perished in the flames.

This tragedy had several Bronx aspects in that many of the parishoners were from this borough—the ship caught fire in Bronx waters and was beached on a Bronx island. Port Morris firemen were summoned to the scene, and it was the Alexander Ave. police station that dispatched men to aid in the rescue, prevent looting and transport bodies back to the precinct house. An oldtime resident of Willis Ave. once told this writer that she remembered the rows of victims laid out on the narrow lawn that, at the time, surrounded the police station.

Furthermore, the victims who were still alive from their harrowing experience, were brought over to Lebanon Hospital which was then situated on Westchester Ave., on a rocky plateau overlooking Cauldwell Ave. The head nurse there happened to be the fiancee of the luckless Captain Van Schaick, but that was just an unfortunate coincidence.

Memorial services are held every year in the Lutheran Cemetery of Middle Village, Queens, and although many years have passed, there are still a few survivors of that disaster—two of them being Bronx residents.

Seven Hispanic Names Listed In Bronx Directory 110 Years Ago

With the Bronx telephone book fairly containing many Spanish names, it is interesting to check back some 110 years and look through a directory of those times to find surnames of Hispanic origin.

Only seven names were found, with the Cordes family (changed from Cortez) leading the short list. Frederick Cordes was a Washington Ave. grocer and a son, Henry, was a clerk. A Christopher Cordes of Elton Ave. was registered as a laborer.

A piano manufacturer with the aristocratic name of DeNobriga lived off Elton Ave. and a Jose Santos of Courtlandt Ave. was a stevedore. Ernest Vasquez was listed as a cook, with his residence given as Robbins Ave. and Lexington St., now Jackson Ave. and E. 147th St.

Best known was a wealthy importer named Casanova whose impressive home Castello de Casanova stood on Hunts Point in the 1860s. He was known to shelter Cuban political exiles, and strong rumor had it that guns and ammunition to fight the Spanish authorities in Cuba were cached in his mansion. The building, incidentally, was partially built of stone, imported from France, and the local people referred to it as the Castle.

The colorful and controversial merchant returned to his homeland where he died in Havana in May, 1890. His last will and testament, written in Spanish, was probated in New York City and was signed Innocencio Casanova y Fagundo. Casanova St. on Hunts Point is named in his honor.

Drake, "Poet of Bronx" Asked Burial by its River

Mention of Joseph Rodman Drake, "Poet of the Bronx|," reminds this writer of a littleknown facet of his short career.

The Drake family had been prominent in Westchester during Revolutionary times, but after the war, removed to lower New York City where Joseph was born. Early in life he discovered the bucolic fields of Hunts Point and spent many happy times roaming the meadows and rowing a boat past the swamps of the Bronx River. He lived in "The Grange" with some of the Hunt family, and knew the other pioneer families named Richardson and Leggett. Many times he made the long overland trip up from Little Old New York to the far reaches of the Point — but water travel (around 1810) was much more feasible, so young Drake occasionally journeyed by rowboat up the East River to the mouth of the Bronx River. There he visited his favorite haunts and wrote poetry that endures to this day.

Needless to say, water travel required a knowledge of tides and currents, and more than a passing acquaintanceship with the reefs and rocks of Hell Gate. The general impression of an 18th century poet is of a pale and wistful youth, but if Drake rowed up the East River to the Bronx he must have had a set of muscles to do it.

However, he did die of consumption at the age of 25, but not wishing to be buried in the Drake family vault in Eastchester, he begged to be laid to rest beside his beloved Bronx River. So it is that the tiny Drake cemetery off Hunts Point Avenue contains a bit of Early Americana that is a legacy to future generations.

Historic East River Isn't River At All

The East River, of course, is not a river, it is a salt water estuary, or tidal strait, connecting Upper New York Bay with Long Island Sound, and is subject to tidal fluctuations which its varying depth and narrowness accentuate.

It separates western Long Island (Brooklyn and Queens) from Manhattan Island and The Bronx. From the Upper Bay, between the Battery and Governors Island, to Long Island Sound at Throgs Neck, the river is 16 miles long. About eight and one-half miles north of the Battery, it is joined by another estuary, the Harlem River, and turns east toward the Sound.

Near the meeting of the Harlem and the East Rivers, and wedged between The Bronx, Manhattan and Long Island are Randall's Island, and Ward's Island. In the wider eastern arm of the river, between the Bronx and the northern shore of Queens, Riker's Island and North Brother and South Brother Islands lie near the entrance of Bowery Bay.

Facts — relevant and otherwise: Just north of the New York Connecting Railroad Bridge across Hell Gate the river is 168 feet deep at mean low water. Politically, Welfare, Ward's and Randall's Islands belong to Manhattan; Riker's and North Brother Islands are part of The Bronx; and South Brother Island is in Queens.

Abraham Rycken (or Riker) obtained a patent for his island — 87 acres of unwanted land — in 1664. In 1884, New York City annexed it from Newtown, Queens, and promptly began to increase its size. The dumping of old metal, refuse, cinders, and dirt from subway excavations no doubt made it one of the least desirable pieces of real estate in the Bronx. For 30 years, subterranean fires burnt in the rubbish, and hordes of rats monopolized the site.

In 1935 the model penitentiary, which replaced the Welfare Island prison, was built. Twenty-six fireproof brick buildings, at a cost of nine million dollars, make it one of the most modern penal institutions in the country.

The prisoners have remade the island into a garden spot. A 50-acre farm is steadily enlarged every year, and most of the artificial land has been landscaped.

North Brother Island was the thirteen acre site of Riverside Hospital for communicable diseases. In 1904, the burning excursion steamer, General Slocum, carrying thousands of children from the Lower East Side was beached on this island.

South Brother Island was owned by the estate of Colonel Jacob Ruppert, of brewery and ball team fame. It is seven acres of unimproved brush.

Late Bert Sack Recalled Days Before Gas, Sewers

The Bronx lost one of its most active oldtimers a few years ago when Bert Sack died. He busied himself in all kinds of civic work and was responsible for the maintenance of the West Farms Civil War cemetery, and the restoration of the military statue that stood in the Bronx River. One of his last letters will intrigue present day Bronxites with its description of Hunts Point of 80 years ago:

"I was born on Fox St. in 1896 when the area was still virgin green and countrified. My family was on Fox St. before gas and sewers were put in, and yes they had an outhouse.

"My three uncles liked fishing and often took their creel and went, either by foot or horse and carriage, to Hunts Point for a day of angling. They brought home flounders, flukes and crabs and I can still remember how sweet they tasted. My aunts took me to Hunts Point by a little stagecoach from the corner of Southern Blvd. and Hunts Point Rd. for a wonderful day of picnicking and bathing. The water was clear as crystal, for no sewers were built yet to befoul the river.

"I remember when the area around Randall Ave. was filled with fruit orchards, and there were several dairy farms. The Duffy brothers used to round up the cows, cowboy-style, on the Springhurst Dairy meadows.

"Hunts Point then became a commercial area, and Consolidated Gas built a huge gas tank and plant there, but that was short-lived.

"Yes, I grew up in the Bronx and lived to see it burn down, but it looks like it's on its way up again."

First Theatre of Bronx Opened In '08 in "Neo-Grecian" Splendor

After 1900, the population of the Bronx grew to such proportions that theatre operators in Manhattan began to see possibilities in and around E. 149th St., which was "the Hub of the Borough."

The first to take advantage of the Hub as a theatrical center was Percy Williams, who acquired a site at E. 150th St. and Melrose Ave., on which he built the Bronx Theatre. It opened in a blaze of glory in 1908, calling attention to its resemblance to the Paris Opera House and its luxurious appointments "harking back to the Neo-Grecian days."

Another showman, H. C. Miner, already had a famous burlesque institution on the Bowery, billed as the home of the "Get-the-Hook" amateur nights. He, too, invaded the Bronx to erect a theatre on 3rd Ave. at E. 155th St. (now the Victory Theatre). Miner kept to his successful program of vaudeville and amateur nights, adding such novelties as "country store" raffles, and even wrestling matches. A 1910 ad reads: "A Night in Minstrelsy introducing the Three Leightons. Others on the bill are O. Duncan, ventroloquist; Peters and Rogers comedy skaters; and Will Rogers, a real cowboy in a lariat-throwing exhibition."

Later on, Miner moved to the Bronx Theater on Melrose Ave., and Miner's became a Bronx byword for bigtime actors. Who remembers Sliding Billy Watson, Jimmy Savo and the outsized chorus girls known as The Beef Trust? There were also travelling theatrical companies — one led by Cecil Spooner — who presented mysteries, dramas and comedies at Miner's through the years.

The Bronx landmark eventually became a movie theatre, and finally went out of existence altogether leaving nothing behind except dim but pleasant memories.

Titanic Sank (for Movie) In Bronx River, 1914–15

The Bronx River has served in many capacities over the centuries — as an Indian canoe-route, a boundary water, a busy steamboat course to the river port of West Farms, a source of waterpower to grind snuff and flour, the scene of Revolutionary warfare and also the watery grave of the illfated Titanic. In reality, the sinking of the Titanic, pride of the British merchant marine, occured in 1912 when it collided with an iceberg, but a Bronx film studio re-enacted the disaster in the waters off Hunts Point.

Murray Haas, a Hunts Pointer from way back, remembers the filming of this epic in 1914 or 1915. The Union Railway carbarns were located at Randall Ave., next to the Bronx River, and these buildings served as work-shops, dressing-rooms and studios of the film company. Carpenters built a realistic hull of the transatlantic liner, complete to portholes and lifeboats, which was then anchored in the river. Extras were hired, provided they knew how to swim, and the final touch was a replica of an iceberg — a jagged combination of wood and canvas, painted a dazzling white, that was towed past the Titanic.

Actual filming was done at night under flares and arc-lights, and Hunts Pointers on shore watched the extras diving and jumping overboard, the repeated scenes of life-boats being lowered, and the sinking of the big ship. This last was accomplished by having the Titanic collapse in horizontal sections until the funnels were at waterlevel. The scenes were shot over and over again, until the wet actors and actresses shook with cold despite the mild weather.

Mr. Haas recalls the actress who took the part of Lady Duff-Gordon and the actor who portrayed Nathan Strauss the millionaire who, with his wife, went down with the ship. What impressed him were the cameramen in rowboats, grinding their comparatively primitive cameras, while their assistants pulled on the oars.

The filming of the Titanic was the biggest event on Hunts Point in many a year, and oldtimers took to pinpointing anything else with the expression "Before the Titanic" or "After the Titanic."

Section 3

CROTONA, MORRISANIA,
TREMONT, WOODSTOCK

North Side of 169th Street and Franklin Avenue in 1900. Franklin Avenue was considered a better street than Washington Avenue as it was up the hill and away from the railroad. William Jennings Bryan campaigned against William McKinley in 1900. (The Bronx Old Timers Collection, The Bronx County Historical Society Research Library)

Allen's Drug Store, Northwest Corner of 168th Street and Franklin Avenue, c. 1870s. Charles J. Allen's Pharmacy reflected the Germanic influence of Morrisania; one of the signs reads, "Deutsche Apotheke." (The Bronx County Historical Society Research Library)

Old German Bands Oom-pahed Their Way Through Bronx Streets

Some 80 years ago Harper's Weekly had this to say of street musicians: "The German bands are becoming a feature here, and there and be no doubt in the minds of our citizens that if we are to be compelled to listen to music whether we will or no, at almost every hour of the day, the brass band is a great improvement on the Italian hand organ."

In the Bronx, German bands are well remembered by oldtime residents. These street musicians usually numbered from two to five, and were found in neighborhoods that were more or less German in composition. Apartment house dwellers, in the days before radio, knew them well, for these men — dressed in ordinary clothes but with semi-military caps — trudged the thoroughfares in all seasons. Occasionally they essayed "O Sole Mio" or "My Wild Irish Rose" to woo additional listeners, but they specialized in music that originated in their Fatherland.

Their route might have seemed erratic to a casual observer, but there was a definite pattern to their itineraries, and also in their choice of music. It was the unvarying custom of these bandsmen to give a nostalgic concert of music hall airs, dating back to the Germany of the 1890s, and this was played in front of pork stores and bakeries frequented be German housewives. Sentimental *Hausfrauen* invariably dropped a coin in their basket in exchange for a fleeting memory of their girlhood in some provincial town, and sometimes they would ask the musicians to play a favorite waltz.

In front of gymnasiums (called *Turnhalle*) the German bands would render drinking songs doubtlessly reminding the men of their student days. The groups of athletes who might be lounging outside the gymnasium entrance loved to join in the songs, and enrich the musicians' wage.

Pausing outside saloons, the band would always play stirring martial airs that recalled days in the German army, and there would sometimes be a sad cornet solo that harked back to *die Heimat*. It was a rare saloon-keeper who did not invite the thirsty musicians in for a drink, and in those days of free lunch counters, the bands then would time themselves to reach a favored saloon at the lunch-hour.

Another stop was at the loading platforms of the Bronx breweries then concentrated in Morrisania and Melrose. There the German bands serenaded the wagon-drivers, loaders, coopers, bottlers, and blacksmiths with a medley of airs, after which they trooped inside to sample the brewer's beer.

These musicians exist now only in fond memories of Bronx oldtimers, for after World War I the German band had become a rarity, and then was gone forever.

Old Germania Park Noted Picnic Grounds

Many years ago, when there was plenty of elbow room in the Bronx, picnic ground and amusement parks were fairly plentiful.

One of the best-known was situated east of Willis and Bergen Aves., from 147th St. to 149th St. although in those days, none of the streets or avenues mentioned were in existence. The other side of the park was bordered by the Mill Brook from which Brook Ave. gets its name. It was a sylvan spot with shady trees and picnic tables, and this glade formed a green retreat for the citizens of Melrose and Mott Haven.

One large building contained a ballroom, dining room, a saloon and private rooms for card parties. On the grounds was an outdoor bowling alley, and also one of the largest shooting galleries in the entire State. This center was known as Karl's Germania Park, or simply Karl's Park, and was a favorite spot for the German rifle societies who enjoyed venison dinners or clambakes.

Later, ownership passed to a Jacob Cohen who changed the name to the 23rd Ward Park. An interesting event was the wedding of Miss Cohen in 1882. Her father had a special dance pavillion constructed on the lawn trimmed with red, white and blue bunting and illuminated with calcium lights. The trees were hung with Japanese lanterns which gave the park a fairyland appearance at dusk. The wedding was celebrated in the grand ballroom, which was decorated with flowers and palms that had been especially raised in hothouses. Such lavishness was the talk of Old Morrisania. Mr. Cohen was best remembered, however, for his public spirit, for annually he gave the use of the park for a three-day picnic—the proceeds going to charity.

The park again changed hands, and it became known as Loeffler's Park . . . but its days were numbered. Soon 148th St. was laid out and cut through, and most of the main building, with its picturesque turrets, was demolished. The park could not exist with the city street cutting it in half, so around the turn of the century, the property was sold for building lots and the pleasant retreat became just a memory. Even Retreat Ave. lost its name, and henceforth was known as Bergen Ave., so nothing at all is left but the name of Brook Ave.

Burial Area Became Site Of PS 38 in Morrisania

The Bensonia Cemetery was eliminated by St. Ann's Ave. almost 100 years ago. Once it had been a picturesque spot, densely shaded by elms, poplars and evergreens—and there were eight footpaths in it named after eight apostles, with the main carriage path being called Zion Ave. Records show the land had previously been the property of Robert Elton in 1853 who sold it to the Town of Morrisania.

It should have been added that, when St. Ann's Ave. was cut through, a small portion of the burial grounds did remain, west of the avenue, but no further interments were allowed. The bounds of this surviving portion were Rae and Carr Sts., St. Ann's Ave. and the Mill Brook. Later, a country lane, German Pl., was laid out next to the brook.

The little graveyard became sadly neglected, and oldtimers recall there were still some forgotten gravestones to be seen as late as the 1920's. During World War I, German Pl., had its name changed to Hegney Pl., to honor Arthur V. Hegney who was killed in action during that conflict. Officially, he was the first Bronxite to become a war casualty.

What was left of the Bensonia Cemetery was, by now, a rubblestrewn lot, a seasonal ballfield and a year-round weed-choked area. The Town of Morrisania, having been absorbed by The Bronx, ceded the property to the borough's Board of Education with the result that PS 38 was built upon the abandoned graveyard.

Bronx Landmark, House-Shop Five Feet Wide, Had Legendary Career

Around Christmas, 25 years ago, a Bronx landmark disappeared, leaving not a trace behind. Oldtimers will recall the narrow house on the northwest corner of Melrose Ave. and E. 161st St. which was the smallest house in our borough. It measured 20 feet in length, and five feet in width — but despite its tiny size it had a colorful history that dated back to 1891, when Melrose Ave. was cut through.

It was then that the owner of the property learned that almost all of his lot would be taken over by the City with the exception of a strip of land, 58 feet deep and six feet wide. Melrose Ave. was cut through, paved and curbed but still the owner stoutly refused to sell his remaining strip. Instead he erected a picket fence and built a house which became the focus of local legend, jokes and tales.

For a number of years it was a tailorshop, and then a dog and cat hospital that gained wide publicity as a progressive pet sanitarium. Dr. Lebish handled skunks, monkeys, trained white mice and guinea pigs, and newspaper articles told of his patients which included a collie with artificial legs, a cat with a glass eye and a police dog with gold-capped teeth.

Eventually the veterinarian moved to larger quarters and the midget house became in turn a lunch counter, a photography shop, seafood stand, a license bureau and then for the last five years of its existance, a tightly-shuttered relic of an earlier era.

In 1959 a service station next to the house bought the hold-out strip and within a very short time wreckers appeared — and the little house disappeared from the Melrose scene.

The Old Woodstock Community was Peopled by Germans

The Woodstock branch of the Public Library system is about the only reminder of the village of Woodstock that flourished from the 1860's onward. Its limits were approximately E. 160th St. north to Boston Road, Cauldwell to Jackson Avenues. On centuries-old maps belonging to the Morris family, the hilly land was marked "Shingle Plain" and the tract was sold by Gouverneur Morris in 1858. It was surveyed by Andrew Findlay, of Scotch descent, and he is credited with naming the wooded area Woodstock. Sir Walter Scott's novels enjoyed wide popularity in those days, and many of his titles and scenes were given to localities in Canada, Australia and America. One of his novels was *Woodstock.*

Largely deserted until after the Civil War, Woodstock became populated by German immigrants who brought with them their Turn Vereins (athletic clubs), Singing Societies and social clubs and, of course, the saloons. Two of the most famous clubs were the Tallapoosa Club on Tinton Avenue and E. 161st St., and the Schnorer Club at Eagle Avenue and E. 163rd St. The firstnamed club was notable for its wine cellars and its political outings, while the latter club was a civic and social hub for many years, and was composed of Bronx businessmen. At first, the membership was of German stock, but later on, all nationalities were admitted.

While the poorer German element centered in nearby Melrose, professional people — doctors, architects, lawyers and businessmen — lived on the higher grounds of Cauldwell, Jackson and Trinity avenues. In the 1890's the mansions and roomy frame houses began to disappear as the district built up, and apartment houses lined E. 163rd St. to Prospect Avenue. Woodstock remained heavily Teutonic well into the 1920's, but then the ethnic composition changed to Puerto Rican and Black. Lutheran churches became Baptist or Spanish-speaking Catholic houses of worship, and the synagogues followed the same trend.

Forest Houses, a housing project, vastly changed the appearance of the neighborhood, and today a trace of Old Woodstock would be hard to find.

Third Ave. "Bend in Road" Of 1860's Became 161st St.

A bend in the Post Road past the village of Melrose was once enhanced by a typical country inn by the name of Hammer's Hotel. In the 1860's and 1870's, Edward Hammer owned this sprawling frame building with its shady backyard and attached stables.

His lodgers and some residents of Melrose would sit in comfortable rocking chairs on the sheltered front porch, and from this vantage point they watched the leisurely traffic of drivers, carriages, horsemen and pedestrians. This constant flow came down from Fordham, or up newly-opened St. Ann's Ave. which joined the Post Road at that turn.

Later, the thoroughfare was renamed Third Ave., and the bend became E. 161st St.

Hammer's Hotel survived into the 20th century until it was replaced by a court house in 1906. This was a handsome structure in Classic Revival style, and on its south facade, a leaf-crowned, seated statue of Justice was raised to the level of the Third Ave. El. A joke was circulated that not an El passenger could look Justice in the eye as the train went past.

Some 70 years of smoke, soot and grime did not give a patina of charm to the courthouse, and the El rumbling past, spoiled its classical lines. Now that Third Ave. is once again a broad street emerging from under the shadow of the elevated railroad line, let's hope the old courthouse gets a long overdue cleaning, and regains a beauty so long hidden.

Justice no longer stares at the El passengers, but out onto a wide, roughly-triangular area "where St. Ann's meets Third."

Who Named Indian Lake?

Usually names are conferred upon streets and landmarks by local politicians with, now and then, an assist from neighborhood historians. Not so in the case of Indian Lake in Crotona Park, according to Frank Wuttge, Jr. who quotes the late Frank Monahan, Asst. Borough Park Director. According to that gentleman, the neighborhood boys actually gave the name to Indian Lake. To those boys, the formation of rocks at the southern end of the lake was the site of a Great Council. In their minds' eye they saw tepees in the background, Indian braves sitting on the ledge of rock, and Ranaqua, their chief, smoking the pipe of peace with the Europeans who came to buy the land.

The overflow from Indian Lake made its way down present-day Wilkins Avenue, turning into Intervale Avenue, to widen out into a duck pond. A century ago, this pond was on Captain Samuel Kelly's farm — and today's Kelly St. is a legacy of that small body of water.

The brook meandered down to the East River, entering it at E. 149th St. To the Indians, this was the Sacrahung, but the English knew it as Bungay (or Bound) Brook. The waterway was the boundary between the lands of the Leggetts and Hunts on one side, and the Morris family on the other, and was the cause of many disputes. This brook still flows today, but inside a huge sewer that runs under Intervale Avenue.

Indian Lake remains, better known as Crotona Lake today, with its shoreline more constricted and of concrete, but little boys still climb the ledges, and dream of Indians.

"Home News" World Series Replays on Panel Recalled

Walter Hicinbothem, who has lived almost all his 72 years in the Bronx, was spurred by the recent World Series to send in his memories of how the baseball classic once was publicized.

"The old *Bronx Home News* was my favorite newspaper, and its offices on E. 149th St. was a favorite place for me, especially when it came to World Series time," he writes. "In those days, all games were played in the daytime and many rabid Bronx fans would not go to work that week, but congregated opposite the newspaper office to 'watch' the game.

"Many times the crowd, jammed between Courtlandt and Third Avenues just off the Hub, was so dense that traffic was unable to proceed. Autos and horsecarts could be sidetracked onto E. 148th St. or E. 150th St. but the trolleycar conductors had no choice but to inch their way thru the tightly-packed crowd. There were good-natured protests from the spectators, and the conductor clanged his bell for passage, with one eye cocked at the scoreboard. Policemen did their best to divert the east-west traffic, but they themselves were just as interested in the game and soon they, too, became spectators.

"*The Bronx Home News* staff received their play-by-play messages by telephone (no radio or television in those days!) and then would show the action on a huge wooden panel on the outside of the building. A baseball diamond, complete with scoreboard, was painted on this panel and, as the game progressed, a newspaperman would lean out the window and motivate the play with a long pole, and also change the numerals under 'balls' and 'strikes.'

"By present day standards this was pretty primitive, but it was a marvel of communications, to us. I was a Giant fan in those days."

Morrisania Hand-Rolled Cigars Were Phased-Out by Machinery

A Morrisania directory of a hundred years ago contains a list of cigar factories, and the addresses of men and women who rolled cigars at home. Third Ave., in the stretch from E. 162nd St. to E. 169th St., had many such factories, with Jacob Stahl's firm the largest, employing over 50 German immigrants. A photograph, dated 1889, shows his shop, with a large sign reading "Segars."

In those days, ships brought up bales of tobacco from Cuba and these produced the most expensive cigars, known simply as Havanas. Virginia leaf was transported by railroad, and unloaded in the freightyards at E. 164th St. and Brook Ave. Even closer was Connecticut tobacco. An uncle of this writer was a cigarmaker as a boy of 9 or 10, as there were no labor laws in effect, and he remembered the teamsters coming down Boston Road with bales of Connecticut tobacco piled high on their farm wagons. They would stay overnight in a hotel where the Third Ave. courthouse now stands, and start homeward the next day.

Around the turn of the century, a machine was invented that turned out cigars from the tobacco leaf to the finished product, with a further improvement that slipped on the cigarband, and boxed it — and that spelled the doom of cigarmaking by hand. Moss Hart, the Broadway producer, lived in Morrisania and in his autobiography, *Act One,* mentioned that both his father and grandfather lost their livelihood when this mechanization took place. When the factories closed, they bought raw tobacco, made cigars in their kitchen and peddled them from door to door, but it was a lost cause. The craft of making "segars" by hand died out in the Bronx.

Columbia (or Columbus?) Entertained Old ('12) Italians

Reader John Nargi and this writer have been carrying on a friendly argument about an oldtime theater that once was situated in the Frog Hollow section of Melrose, and was called either the Columbia theater (according to Mr. Nargi) or the Columbus Theater (on the say-so of this writer). But our differences are academic since the entire block of E. 151st St. from Morris to Park Aves. has been razed to make way for a low-income housing project.

This theater was a focal point for entertainment from 1905 to 1912 — a time when Italian troupes toured the eastern United States, giving farces, skits and sometimes melodrama for their immigrant compatriots. What is definitely known is that puppet shows were presented, and that is ascertained by a grandson, Nicholas Falco, whose grandfather Guiseppe Fusco was once the manager of the theater. These puppet shows, carried out in the traditional Neapolitan and Sicilian manner, were sandwiched in between the silent movies of those days. To those who did not understand the language, it was enough to watch the action, some of which embodied age-old stories about saints, Crusaders and Saracens.

Bronxites will recall the visit of Pope John Paul II to our Borough, where he addressed a crowd from a temporary stage off Morris Ave. The crowd stood in a cleared site on which the Columbus (or Columbia) Theater once stood, flanked by narrow old law tenements and some small factories. Italian-Americans such as Fiorello La Guardia and Mother Cabrini, some 70 years back, were well-acquainted with that particular street — but now the surrounding Little Italy has all but died out.

Bronx "Bombed" by Plane
In 1918 Liberty Loan Drive

Even though the Bronx was 3000 miles from the European battlefields of World War I, it was once "bombed" by a fleet of airplanes in October, 1918. The bombardment was part of a Liberty Loan drive, spurred by the *Bronx Home News,* in which 50 weighted copies of the newspaper were thrown down on various Bronx intersections.

Eight aeroplanes took off from Mineola, escorting the ninth, which was the bomber. Straight up over Willis Ave. flew this plane, the aviator keeping so low he could plainly be seen by the crowds that lined the sidewalk. The escort planes continued North, but the lone pilot went into a sidespin as he rounded the steeple of the Immaculate Conception R.C. Church at Melrose Ave. and E. 150th St.

Motormen and conductors left their trolleycars, as did the passengers, to watch the evolutions, and engineers on the Third Avenue El stopped their trains at the Hub, to watch. Two dozen "bombs" were dropped. The aviator then headed for Tremont Ave. to unload more "bombs," and finally sped off for the aviation grounds on Long Island.

Albert Goldman (later to become Postmaster) was chairman of the Liberty Loan drive publicity committee, and he expressed his satisfaction with the demonstration. Of the 50 "bombs" dropped, only 39 were retrieved from rooftops and on sidewalks (where several spirited scuffles were reported) and the 39 Bronxites appeared at the *Bronx Home News* office on E. 148th St., off Third Avenue, to take part in the final drawing for two $50 Bonds. A small boy drew out the two winning numbers, and a Robert Smith and an Albert Wittig were the lucky winners.

At the same time, another stunt to whip up the sale of Liberty Bonds was underway at Westchester and Third Ave., where a "mystery chest" from France was to be opened. Only when $15,000 in Liberty Bonds were sold would the mysterious trunk be unlocked. It was bound with wire, locked with steel and guarded by Naval Scouts.

On hand was "the Great Dunninger" to demonstrate his mind-reading abilities, and he listed what he thought was in the chest: a German hand grenade, some shells, a French gas bomb, an American flag and a mushroom hand grenade. More than $17,500, was raised by the spirited crowd, and the chest was opened to disclose exactly what "the Great Dunninger" had felt was there.

Capitol of Mandolin-Making Stood on "Dutch Broadway"

In the Melrose section of the Bronx, on what was once nicknamed Dutch Broadway, stands a two-storied frame building that somehow has survived the passage of almost a century, four ethnic changes and a variety of interior modifications.

Courtlandt Ave., long a stronghold of a German population, was not a likely spot for an Italian family to set up business back around 1918. But Angelo Mannello was not depending on the citizens of Melrose particularly for his livelihood, nor even on his countrymen who lived on nearby Park and Morris Avenues: he was already an established and famous craftsman of custom-made mandolins, and E. 150th St. was the site of his third (and last) factory to which his customers came from all over the world. Many of his instruments won prizes in the trade fairs in America and Europe, and some ended up in museums as priceless and rare examples of handcarved musical instruments.

Born near Naples, Mannello migrated to the States in 1885, aged 22, with a skill that brought him fame and modest fortune. Eventually he had a small staff of artisans, including his sons, who manufactured guitars, banjos and mandolins. Cramped quarters induced him to move to Eagle Ave. in the Bronx where his factory employed almost 70 men and women. The staff attended to standard instruments, but Angelo devoted himself to showpieces that took many weeks to complete.

Mandolin bands were popular in the early 1900s but somehow after World War I, they waned in the public fancy and Mannello & Sons had to cut down production. A fire then destroyed the factory and the family moved to Courtlandt Ave. and into much smaller quarters. Mannello continued to fashion custom-made mandolins with their elaborately intricate inlay work, up to his death in 1922. After that, the business faded and the final blow was the Depression that closed down Mannello & Sons.

Today, no one knows, or cares, about the old nondescript house on Courtlandt Ave. that was once a magnet for world-famous musicians.

Black Settlements Started Here at Turn of Century

Three separate black settlements began forming at the turn of the century, and these can be regarded as the first communities of their kind here. Their inception was brought about largely by the building of the railroads into the Bronx, for most of the male workers were trainmen, laborers, and Pullman porters.

In the 1890's, the black settlement of Mott Haven was located on the Ridge — the beginning of the Grand Concourse, which was then just an unpaved road called Mott Ave. The women were laundresses and maids in the Mott Ave. mansions, and the menfolk were railroad workers or, in some cases, dockworkers on the nearby Harlem River.

A smaller settlement was situated at E. 161st St. and Morris Ave in Melrose and was comprised of a better-paid workforce employed on the New York Central Railroad. These men were Pullman porters, trained cooks and stewards, and their families lived in a row of tidy brick homes. The children attended PS 3, off Courtlandt Ave. A localism for the colony was Georgetown from the fact that the inventor of the Pullman car was a George Pullman.

There seemed to be little or no contact with the next black community at E. 165th St. and Brook Ave. in Morrisania, and this was probably due to economic reasons. The men were employed as laborers and trainhands on the nearby Port Morris & Spuyten Duyvil Railroad, with some others working in a local iceplant. Some women worked as domestics, and the children attended public school on Eagle Ave. The 30 or 40 families were concentrated in a few apartment houses and a row of frame houses. Although separated by a mile and a difference in income, both groups attended the same Baptist church on E. 160th St and Melrose Ave.

Old Vasa Hall Was Scene Of St. Lucia's Observance

Alf Johanneson was a Washingtonian most of his life but never forgot the Bronx, where he grew up. One of his fondest memories was the Scandinavian feast day of St. Lucia that is celebrated on December 13, and how it was observed in the South Bronx.

Back a half-century ago, there were Swedes, Danes and Norwegians living in the Mott Haven section, and they never failed to assemble in Vasa Hall on St. Lucia's Day. Vasa Hall (sometimes called Vasa Temple) was an imposing brick social center on E. 149th St. just West of the Grand Concourse and was not limited to the Nordic element, but could be rented for Greek and Italian wedding parties, German beer festivals and Irish dances.

But every December 13th evening the hall took on a sedate, religious air as sober groups in their Sunday best took seats and waited expectantly for the stage curtain to rise. Prayers in Swedish and English were recited, Old Country psalms were sung, and then there was a short sermon by a minister.

The musicians struck up the opening chords of "Santa Lucia" and the curtain was raised to reveal a row of young girls in virginal white gowns carrying bouquets of flowers. On their heads they wore crowns of lighted candles and these tapers provided the only light in the darkened hall. The soft glow of the candles, the pure contraltos of the young girls raised in song, and the graceful sweep of their gowns as they filed into the aisles, was an unforgettable experience, and it never failed to thrill the audience.

Mr. Johanneson, now deceased, often wondered if St. Lucia's Day was still celebrated in the old-fashioned way, but this writer invariably let December 13th slip by and so was never able to find out for him.

Lady Washington Co.
Old Morrisania Pride

The Village of Morrisania must have had pleasant times, almost a hundred years ago, for I quote from yellowed pages, with present day placenames in parentheses: "There was an ideal grove and picnic ground (Crotona Park) extending to Fulton Avenue. Here the annual village celebrations took place for many years. On these festive days, all business was suspended and the fire department, military and principal societies paraded up Fordham Ave. (3rd Ave.) with music, flags waving, and women and children marching along.

"Lady Washington Engine Co. No. 1 was located on Fulton Ave., south of the picnic grounds near Sixth St. (E. 168th St.) and Michael Bergen was the Chief. The wives of the members and the other women of the village furnished the meeting room upstairs with Brussels carpet covering, upholstered chairs, desks and gilded mirrors. Ornately framed was a citation from the City of Yonkers presented in grateful appreciation of a run the Volunteers made, to assist that city when it was threatened with complete destruction by fire. The Lady Washington engine was painted a glossy white, the wheels a magenta brown with shiny brass hubs. The trimmings were also of highly polished brass and surmounting all was a beautiful gamecock. To all of our members this engine was a thing of beauty and a joy forever . . . the pride of our village."

When the district was annexed to the City of New York, the Volunteer Company was disbanded and the furniture was sold at auction to the people of Morrisania. The engine — a hand drawn pumper wagon, built in 1851 by James Smith — was called "The White Ghost." Anyone interested in vanished facets of the Old Bronx can see "The White Ghost" for it stands now in the New-York Historical Society's museum on Central Park West.

Second Gouverneur Morris Was Heir of Sire's Manor, Bluntness

The second Gouverneur Morris (1813–1888) inherited the bluntness of his father, and one story concerning it has come down from his day to ours.

Jordan L. Mott had purchased some 200 acres of lower Morrisania and laid it out into building lots. He sent one of his employees to Gouverneur Morris and asked if he objected to the new section being called Mott Haven. Morris replied gruffly: "I don't care what he calls it; while he is about it, he might as well change the name of the Harlem River, and call it the Jordan!"

Morris went on to sell portions of the Manorlands which became Melrose, Morrisania, Woodstock and other early Bronx settlements.

He was quite proud of his Indian blood, for his mother, Ann Randolph Morris, claimed descent from Pocahontas. St. Ann's Church was built in her honor, and this in turn gave its name to the avenue.

When the Port Morris & Spuyten Duyvil Railroad Company was organized by Gouverneur Morris it was called the Pocahontas Line. It did his blood pressure no good to learn the irreverent townspeople referred to it as "the Old Pokey" . . . a far cry from the majestic Indian name Gouverneur Morris had in mind. To make matters worse, the German settlers of Melrose and Morrisania called it "Pokey Hannes" — a mixture of German and English, meaning "Slow Johnny!"

Tremont-Morrisania Index Of '71 Listed 51 Saloons

A thin 138-paged Directory of Morrisania and Tremont, published in 1871, can provide hours of fascination with its wealth of history, strange street names and diverting advertisements. Names found in the alphabetical lists of almost a century ago may still be encountered in the Bronx telephone book of today, but of the businesses listed in that faroff year, not one remains.

Basket Makers (2) and Blacksmiths (20) and Brewers (14) Button Makers (2) Coachmen (14) Hides & Tallow Renderers (4) Lager Beer Saloons (51) Oyster Saloons (1) Saddle & Harness Makers (16) and Dealers in Firewood (5) have vanished entirely. Alexander Bathgate listed his calling as Farmer, and his land as being opposite Clinton Ave.

One-man businesses were very numerous, with the trade being carried on in the front rooms of private houses: John Van Horn manufactured base balls, D. L. Van Schaick was a spinner. Strange to us was the custom of specifying widows (wid), Negroes (col'd) and the forthright listing of washerwomen, peddlers and laborers.

The addresses were given in approximate terms, such as near 2nd house from and corner of. Today's postmen and taxi drivers would most certainly be stumped trying to find Grove Hill, Cromwell's Creek, Jayne's Hill, Wilton Hill, or Uncas, Denman and Schuyler Sts.

Although the names were about evenly divided between English, Irish and German derivation, only one advertisement was in the latter language but liberally laced with English:

Buchelberger's Wein — Handlung and Lagerbier Saloon, Third Ave., cor. Elton St., Melrose, N. Y.

Section 4

CLAREMONT, CONCOURSE, HIGHBRIDGE, MACOMBS DAM

Volunteer Firemen Parade, Washington Avenue, c. 1900. Before the Grand Concourse was built, Washington Avenue was the favored thoroughfare for patriotic parades and other public functions. The hand-drawn horse cart resembles that belonging to the Lady Washington Hose Company of Morrisania. (The Bronx Old Timers Collection, The Bronx County Historical Society Research Library)

High Bridge, Washington Heights, New York City.

High Bridge, around 1915. Looking east over the Harlem River at 175th Street. This postcard was a popular item with tourists and Bronxites alike. The bridge, opened in 1848, was a favorite strolling area for generations. It stands 116 feet above the river and is 1,460 feet long. Around 1928, the granite arches were replaced by a steel arch to facilitate river traffic. (The Bronx County Historical Society Research Library)

"Castle on the Concourse?"
It's Special School No. 31

Standing at 144th St., Special Primary School 31 has a well-deserved nickname of "the Castle on the Concourse." Its massive doors on Walton Ave., its stained glass windows and gargoyles, iron columns and Gothic architecture make this school unique. And recently its 100th anniversary was celebrated.

Mott Haven in the 1890s had farms and scattered small houses, and the dirt road in front of the school was called Mott Ave. A few substantial mansions fronted on it, with spacious lawns and gardens lending color to the properties. Franz Sigel, a retired Civil War general, lived "on the Ridge" as the locale was called, and in time his name was given to a nearby park.

P.S. 31 has the official name of the William Lloyd Garrison School and it honors an editor (1805–1877) who wrote of the evils of slavery in his newspaper *The Liberator*. By coincidence, an early Black settlement was located immediately south of the school. The menfolk were stevedores, foundrymen and railroad workers, and their wives were cooks and laundresses in the wealthier households.

"The Castle on the Concourse" began with outdoor plumbing, gas light and some pupils arriving on horseback, but it has been periodically modernized. Aside from not having elevators, the school is on a par with much later schools — and instead of being a strictly neighborhood school, has become a special primary school drawing pupils from all parts of the Bronx. It is the only school that has this program, and it has an enviable scholastic record.

Continentals in Bitter Cold Attacked Highbridge Outpost

The winter of 1778–1789 was so cold that New York harbor froze over, as did the Hudson River and Long Island Sound. Military records of the Revolutionary War tell of British cavalry galloping on the ice from Staten Island to lower Manhattan, and dispatches from the American side cite the arrival of 300 mounted men and a regiment of infantry in the village of Westchester (now Westchester Square) having crossed over from Long Island on the frozen Sound.

Despite the Arctic temperatures, the war went on and on one freezing night in January, 1779, a number of Connecticut volunteers marched over the icy roads to reach a British outpost in what is now Highbridge.

Three English sentries were killed in the sudden attack, and the garrison retreated inside the house and barricaded themselves on the upper floor. The Americans managed to get inside and set fire to the lower rooms, forcing the defenders to jump from the windows to escape the flames. The entire detachment was taken prisoner.

The precise location of this house has been a matter of conjecture, but it is a fair assumption the Connecticut men, led by captains Lockwood and Keeler torched the British outpost in the vicinity of Ogden Ave. and W. 170th St.

Claremont Park's "Black Swamp," Terror of Old, Still Gives Trouble

Claremont Park is situated on high ground and where it slopes to the west there was once a dismal quagmire known to our forefathers as the Black Swamp. Tales handed down to us from earlier times, indicate even the Indians gave it a wide berth, and it is a matter of note that no Indian trail was ever mapped in that vicinity.

Old records of Revolutionary times tell of cattle that wandered into the mire and disappeared, and farmers of the neighborhood suffered frequent loss of livestock to the Black Swamp. Not all the people believed their pigs and calves fell victim to the bottomless mud and suspicions was turned toward the slaves who used to go into the woods with dogs and guns. A 1691 Court Order was passed "that no Negro or Malatto bond slave be permitted to have with them any gun, dog or staffe when out of their masters plantations."

During the 1800s there were several attempts to fill in the Black Swamp, but the work was sporadic and ended in failure. Shortly after the Civil War, contractors brought in tons of rock, rubble and dirt, only to find their day's labor gone by next morning. The Black Swamp semed to be actually bottomless but more modern methods and machinery at the turn of the century finally filled in the morass.

Evidence of the vanished swamp is still visible in the buildings now standing in Claremont Heights: patched-up settlement cracks, out-of-level and out-of-plumb window sills and frames, with here and there a tilted stoop. These are signs that the feared Black Swamp has not entirely been conquered!

Franz Sigel Park Formed Spot Where Washington Once Watched British

Most of the parks in The Bronx were acquired from private ownership in 1888 by the Parks Department, but Franz Sigel Park was purchased from the Morris family in 1885.

The hilly tract, running from E. 151st St. to E. 160th St. along the grand Concourse (then known as Mott Ave.) had been the "Cedar Grove" estate of Gerard Walton Morris and his wife, Mary, although some maps listed their 17.5 acre property as "The Cedars." The newly acquired park was called "Cedar Park."

Once its high rocky ridge had figured briefly in Revolutionary War history when General Washington and Comte de Rochambeau and their staffs watched British troops bivouacking alongside the Harlem River. Andrew Corsa, one of the Westchester Guides, was a 19-year-old youth at Washington's side, and many years later he told of his experience at that summit.

"The enemy saw our men and horses and commenced firing at us, so that shots came perilously close. I dived for shelter behind the rocks, but the generals and their officers stood their ground, with spyglasses trained on the British. I felt a little shamed and returned to the General's side. No one was hit, and we then spurred our steeds and left for King's Bridge."

In 1902, a Civil War general who had lived on Mott Ave. died. He was Franz Sigel and, at the behest of the residents of Melrose and Mott Haven, Cedar Park had its name changed to honor the man and keep his memory green.

Bronx Race Track Was First Opened in 1750

The first reference in local history to a racetrack tells of a course laid out in the Mill Brook valley in 1750.

General Staats Morris was a noted horseman, and he imported and bred racehorses on his estates which consisted of the Morrisania manorlands west of the Mill Brook (approximately from Brook Avenue west to the Harlem River, and from 133rd St. to 167th St.). South of the ridge on which Claremont Park is situated was a comparatively level stretch, and on this grassy expanse the Morris family maintained a track which was much patronized by the landed gentry.

It remained in the family for more than a century. In 1870 Dater Brothers leased the property, lengthened it to a one-mile track, and it became known as Fleetwood Park. It was devoted to the distinctively American sport of trotting.

Robert Bonner, founder and proprietor of the "New York Ledger," had his stables not far from the track. In a book on notable New Yorkers published 60 years ago, he was listed as a turfman, and owner of the world's fleetest horses. He was noted for his flamboyant character, and an excerpt—dated 1866—has this to say about him: "People regarded Robert Bonner as having carried genuine advertising and its humbug style to an extravagant pitch."

After some ten years of operation, Fleetwood Race Track failed, and property and buildings reverted to the Morris estate. Next, the Gentlemen's Driving Association leased it until it finally closed down in 1898. The growing Borough had hemmed it in.

Today, the old trotting grounds are nothing but a nebulous memory, but three names survive its passing: Morris Ave., on which the Fleetwood theatre is located, and a short dead-end street called Bonner Pl.

Old Fleetwood Hotel on Morris Ave. Was Favorite Spot of President Grant

One hundred years ago on July 23rd, 1885, General Ulysses Grant died. He had been President of the United States and his funeral was an impressive one. Civil War generals Phil Sherman and William Sheridan were pallbearers, and it is no coincidence that three adjoining Bronx avenues now carry the names of those Union generals. Incidentally, two Confederate generals also were pallbearers.

The avenues are in an area known to generations of Bronxites as Fleetwood and the name harked back to Fleetwood racetrack—a trotting course that attracted socialites and horsemen. President Grant often attended races there. He was friendly with Robert Bonner, founder and publisher of the *New York Ledger* and a noted turfman, whose home was nearby. A lithograph shows Bonner and Grant in a carriage en route to the Fleetwood Hotel.

This well known tavern stood at E. 164th St. and Morris Ave. but has long since been razed. In its heyday the Fleetwood Hotel catered to a wealthy clientele, and the presence of Grant gave it added prestige, so much so, that the hotel was often referred to as Grant's Hotel even though he had no financial interest in it.

There are Grant, Sheridan and Sherman Aves., but the name Fleetwood did not survive.

Balanced Over River, Aerialist Made Cakes

During the summers of 1859 and 1860, a wiry blond Frenchman named Jean Gravelet crossed above the raging rapids of the Niagara River on a slender rope cable. His repeated performances, 200 feet in the air, made his professional name, Blondin, a household word in all America and huge crowds gathered whenever he made a crossing. In later years, other aerial daredevils duplicated the feat, for there are records of a Signor Farini in 1860, a Signor Balleni in 1873 and then a Maria Spelterini in 1876.

Around that time, in the Bronx, a tightrope artist by the name of Leslie announced that he would cross over the Harlem River from Washington Heights to Highbridgeville. In those days, Highbridgeville was a small village and on its Harlem River shoreline were piers at which excursion boats docked. Ashore were amusement centers and picnic spots, and the best known was Kyle's Park, which was situated just north of High Bridge itself, where the Major Deegan Highway is now laid out.

The tightrope was stretched from the Manhattan slope, passed over Kyle's Park, and was anchored firmly in the steep slope alongside High Bridge. Doubtlessly, the resort owner paid Leslie well, for the announcement attracted thousands of people to the park. Excursion boats and trains brought huge crowds, and families even rented rowboats and anchored out on the river to see the aerialist cross over.

Leslie (according to oldtimers) left the Manhattan side, carrying a small stove on his back. Balancing at the halfway point over the river, he set the stove down, lighted a fire, mixed batter and cooked pancakes! These he threw down to the people in the rowboats below him, while he waited for the stove to cool off. Then he deftly packed his portable kitchen, replaced it on his back and crossed swiftly over Kyle's Park.

There the story ends. No one is sure in what year the event took place, or if Leslie made any more crossings. Even today, the story is half-legendary and will remain so until the day someone discovers a photograph of Leslie cooking his pancakes high above the Harlem River.

Nickname of "Dangerville" Once Applied to Highbridge

In the 1800s, no doubt influenced by the French Revolution, earlier Bronxites followed the trend of embellishing their settlements' names with the French "ville." As a result, maps in the Civil War times show at least nine small communities beginning with Adamsville, progressing through Centerville, Connersville, Deckerville, Highbridgeville, Jacksonville, Mottville, Schuylerville and Warnerville, to end with Washingtonville.

As years went by, all these villages were absorbed into larger communities, and lost both their boundaries and identities. One settlement, however, once was facetiously dubbed Dangerville, and even newspapers of the 1880's used the nickname in referring to the area we now call Highbridge.

There are two different versions of how Dangerville got its name. The first is that it was considered dangerous to venture among the Irish who made up the bulk of the population.

The second tale is that a wealthy landowner, whose property included a sloping lawn facing the Harlem River, had the inspiration of naming his estate Garden Villa. To that end he ordered wrought-iron letters, each 4 ft. high, to be erected on the lawn. Upon uncrating them, it was discovered the letters spelled G-A-R-D-E-N V-I-L-L-E, so the squire refused to erect them until the error was rectified. During the night some pranksters climbed the hillside and set up the letters to read D-A-N-G-E-R-V-I-L-L-E.

Next morning, passengers on the railroad and on the riverboats were vastly amused, as were the residents of Highbridgeville. . . . and the nickname stuck for years afterward.

Grand Concourse Planning Work of Three Bronxites

The Concourse is a continuous chain of hills, and its development into a thoroughfare was the result of three men of vision: Louis Risse who was the planner and engineer; Louis Haffen, the first Borough President, who foresaw its importance; and Louis Heintz, Street Commissioner and champion of the venture, who fought long and hard for its acceptance by a reluctant Board of Estimate.

Louis Risse, a native of Alsace Lorraine, was an ardent hunter and, in the 1890s, shot pheasant in what were the hills of Tremont. The hills were known variously as Mount Eden, Union Hill, Mount Hope and Mount Sharon, and the few farmers there used them principally as woodlots.

Ordinarily, hunters keep their preserves unpublicized, but Risse, on his treks, envisioned a broad boulevard as wide as those he had walked upon in European cities. He mulled it over in his spare time, and then set to work.

His sketches of such a curving, treelined boulevard, with separate roads for carriages and equestrians, were appealing to Borough President Haffen, who became an enthusiastic supporter. The original plan called for the Concourse to run from E. 161st St. to Mosholu Parkway but, later on, the stretch from E. 138th St. up to E. 161st St., known then as Mott Ave., was added.

Today, in Joyce Kilmer Park opposite the County Courthouse, there is a statue of Louis Heintz. At Mosholu Parkway, there is located Risse Street, but no reminder of Louis Haffen appears anywhere near the Concourse. He is remembered, however, by a park off Eastchester Road, thanks to this writer's efforts.

Bronxite Recalls Building of Grand Concourse

At 91 years of age, Mr. Erich Marks is one of the very few Bronxites who saw the construction of the Grand Concourse across meadows, farms, hills and rock ledges. This broad swath extended north from E. 161st St. to Mosholu Pkwy. and, later on, the lower stretch to E. 138th St. was added.

The thoroughfare was intended as a Continental-styled boulevard for horses and carriages, and in the 1894 sketches drawn by the chief planner, Louis Risse, there is not an automobile to be seen. Equestrians and horsedrawn vehicles only, were depicted.

According to Mr. Marks, the sideroads were reserved for the few motor cars. A narrow belt of trees shielded them from the horsemen, for it was a widely accepted belief that the animals would bolt at the sight of a "horseless carriage." These sideroads were unpaved, so it was the motorist who had to contend with dusty roads whereas the carriages monopolized the paved center lanes.

Sundays were the days that the early Bronxites exercised their trotting teams, and tried to see how fast they could gallop the length of the Concourse. Mounted policemen discouraged this practice whenever they caught an offender, and began the deterrent of "writing out a ticket."

Then, automobiles increased to a point that the motorists demanded and got access to all lanes of the Concourse. After 1918, the horse population dramatically declined, and by the 1920s a Bronxite taking his family out for a Sunday spin in a surrey with the fringe on top was a rarity.

Shakespeare Ave. Named for Bronx Formal Garden

The watchman on the construction site of the Yankee Stadium was a storehouse of Highbridgeville history. After fetching a can of beer for him — a custom known as "rushing the growler" — this writer would be rewarded with folklore from that colorful West Bronx community.

One such tale concerned the naming of Shakespeare Avenue. The watchman — whose name has been long forgotten — was born in Highbridgeville shortly after the Civil War, and, being raised in that predominately Irish settlement, had a brogue as genuine as any son of the Emerald Isle itself. He started working as a stable boy and groom in the Marcher estate, and he recalled the fine view of the Harlem River, the extensive lawns and gardens, the carriage horses and valuable spaniels, and the Marcher mansion.

The eastern slope of the estate was a steep rocky set of cliffs, accounting for its name of Rockycliff while the western end was noted for its Shakespearean Garden. This was a formal garden containing many of the flowers mentioned in Shakespeare's plays, and embellished by marble busts of the Bard himself, and some of his creations, such as Puck, Romeo and Juliet, Hamlet, Shylock and Portia. Other statues were placed in arbors and along the footpaths. Rebecca Marcher, averred the old watchman, pursued the theme by naming her horses and dogs Macbeth, Pyramus and Thisbe, and Falstaff.

When the estate finally succumbed to an expanding city, the street that was surveyed and cut through the property was named Marcher Avenue. In 1912, however, its name was changed to Shakespeare Avenue, recalling the widow's beloved garden.

Yankee Stadium's Golden Anniversary Stirs Memories

The year 1973 marked the fiftieth anniversary of the opening of Yankee Stadium. Considering the wide variety of sports events, religious convocations and political rallies that were held there in the course of a half-century, there must be thousands of Bronxites who can recall a thrilling touchdown, an unbelievable home run, an unexpected knockout or a spectacular procession in the Stadium.

This writer has two vivid memories of Yankee Stadium, but both recollections concern its outside. The first knowledge he had of the Stadium was in its construction period (1922) when a watchman would periodically send him to a River Avenue speakeasy for a can of beer. The watchman, an elderly native of Highbridgeville, was of Irish stock and could pray in Gaelic — a minor accomplishment he passed on to this writer.

The second memory was Holding Babe Ruth's Coat! This momentous occasion occurred after a game, and the players' exit was lined with baseball fans, eager to see their heroes. Babe Ruth hurried out to the curb where a small roadster was parked, in readiness. It was a brisk Fall day and the Babe was wearing a raccoon coat, then so popular in the '20's, but when he attempted to get into the sportscar, he was too bulky to fit in. He straightway shrugged out of the coat, and looked around.

"Here, kid, hold this a minute," he said to this writer who was standing in awe and hero-worship. The Babe then seated himself in the car, and reached for his coat with a nonchalant "Thanks, kiddo" and drove off.

Needless to say, this writer was speechless with pride, and burst in on his family, shouting: "I held Babe Ruth's coat! I held Babe Ruth's coat!" and, next day, in school was the envy of his classmates.

In later years, this story was told to the writer's children. The son looked perplexed: "What's a raccoon coat?" he inquired. And the daughter (who hadn't been paying attention) asked: "Babe Ruth? Who is she?"

Italian Bronxites Scarce In Area's 1870 Directories

"I know Italians began to move into the Bronx in large numbers from 1895 to 1910," writes Fino John Pagliuca, "But were there any here, a hundred years ago?"

In 1850, the population of lower Westchester (now The Bronx) was 6,928 and that same year records were kept of the inhabitants for the first time. Not one Italian name was noted.

In 1870, directories of Highbridgeville, Tremont, Morrisania, Melrose and Mott Haven turned up very few names of Italian origin. In endless lists of German, Irish and English surnames, a few possibly harked back to Italy.

Anton Bultra, cigarmaker, lived on Washington Ave. John Carrissa was a peddler on Jackson Ave. J. Delgado was listed as a resident of Eagle Ave., but his trade was not mentioned. On present day E. 159th St., Angelo and Louis Delnoce were merchants, and J.B. Sanguinetti was a tailor on Courtlandt Ave. This last gentleman advertised that he had formerly been employed by the Manhattan establishment of Croney, Lent & Co. at 753 Broadway—and was now in business for himself.

Antoine Santalini of Mott Haven was registered as a laborer, and Joseph Petri was a baker in Tremont. This meager roll call was rounded out by a peddler, James Vanduza, whose name could possibly be Van Duzer, and be of Dutch descent.

Italian barbers and shoemakers, seamstresses, musicians, artisans, shopkeepers and restaurant owners would not appear on the scene for another 30 years. So it follows that pizza pies were in the far, far future for our Bronxites of 1870.

Footraces on Bronx Streets Commonplace in 1920s–30s

In these days of mini-marathons, semi-marathons and other variations of the 26-mile classic, it might surprise today's runners to learn that foot races through Bronx streets and along the Grand Concourse were weekly events in the 1920s and 1930s.

Jogging was commonplace in the West Bronx, for athletes from the Mohawk A.C. and the Pastime A.C., both located at E. 161st St. and Walton Ave., limbered up along Jerome Ave. and the Grand Concourse without a worry about automobile traffic.

Macombs Dam Park, a quarter-mile oval alongside the Yankee Stadium, was a favorite track for local and European aces, but that area has since been redesigned into a baseball field. Finnish runners who practiced there were Willie Ritola and Paavo Nurmi; and the 1912 Olympics triple-gold-medal winner, Hannes Kohlemainen, often worked out there despite the wintry weather.

The abovementioned athletic clubs offered the Finnish runners use of their facilities, and whenever the Throggs Neck Finns knew their heroes were there, they would congregate in the clubhouses or on the running field to speak to them. Prohibition was the law of the land but, somehow, vodka mysteriously became available and the result was a very convivial evening.

Neither clubhouse exists today as they were razed to make way for the Bronx County Building.

In Pre-1910 S. Bronx Ethnic Areas Were Many, Varied

Generations ago, most cities of America were patchquilts of closely knit ethnic neighborhoods—and New York was no exception. It followed that the Bronx, too, had distinct areas where foreigners congregated, particularly in the lower portion of the borough. Before 1910, the majority of Bronxites lived below E. 170th St., and places like Fordham, Throggs Neck, Wakefield and Riverdale were considered the country. It was the South Bronx, in the horse and buggy days, that could be considered a microcosm of various nationalities.

Italians dwelt along lower Morris Ave. Jews were concentrated around Brown Pl. and Brook Ave. The Irish filled Willis and Alexander Aves. Melrose and Morrisania were heavily German. There were Swiss in both these neighborhoods, and a small Scandinavian colony clustered around Mott Haven.

Poles and Lithuanians were scattered throughout Melrose from Elton Ave. to Courtlandt Ave., chiefly along E. 155th St. There was no Negro concentration, but a few Black families lived here and there on upper Brook Ave., and around Park Ave. and E. 161st St.

After World War I, the population shifted dramatically northward, and fell into less definable patterns. Oldtime designations such as Dutch Broadway, Irish Fifth Ave. and Little Italy fell into disuse, if not disfavor—and now those 19th century names have become obsolete and almost forgotten.

Navigable River Flows Beneath Bronx from Croton Reservoir

Although it appears on no map, there is a navigable river flowing down through The Bronx from the Yonkers city line, to Highbridge. This river, of pure fresh water, originates in Croton Lake, 33 miles away, and, underfoot and unseen, courses through subterranean pipes. The shoulder-deep stream has never ceased to flow since a June day in 1842, when the Croton Aqueduct was formally opened.

On that day, crowds had gathered at Highbridgeville where it was possible to actually see the water arrive, for there the aqueduct came to a temporary halt. The High Bridge had not yet been built, and temporary water mains were to carry the water high over the Harlem River to Manhattan's reservoirs. At this Highbridgeville valve station the stream would emerge after its leagues of sunless passage under the countryside of Westchester.

The reader might then ask: "A navigable river?" which leads to the retelling of the eerie voyage of a boat named The Croton Maid. Four men actually navigated this underground river in a wooden boat from Croton Reservoir to Highbridgeville, and careful regulation of the flow of water at the dam assured them of sufficient head room and reasonable safety. The release of the water was a controlling factor in the speed of the small boat, and this was later ascertained to be at a stroller's pace.

At dawn of June 22, the four men cast off, provided with oars, fending poles, torches and some provisions, and the little Croton Maid floated into the black tunnel and disappeared. Hours passed. The crowds at Highbridgeville waited through the long day. Night fell, while somewhere under the hills and dales of Westchester, four men poled along on their subterranean voyage. Midnight came and went. People slept on the grassy slopes, or sat and gossiped, wagering bets or praying for the men.

Around 3 o'clock in the morning there was a distinct rumble of approaching water, and the spectators hastily gathered around the terminal. As the water flowed into sight and gradually deepened, the crowd set up a cheer. Then someone glimpsed a flicker of torches reflected on the water, faint hallos were heard and soon the four heroes poled their craft out of the tunnel. Thus, the Croton Maid docked at the port of Highbridgeville, a very strange harbor indeed—some 120 feet above the Harlem River!

Section 5

MORRIS HEIGHTS, MT. HOPE, UNIVERSITY HEIGHTS

Lewis G. Morris Mansion in Morris Heights. Mount Fordham mapped in 1868 was the property of Lewis G. Morris and passed to his grandson, Charles Popham. (The Bronx Old Timers Collection, The Bronx County Historical Society Research Library)

BRONX BOROUGH DAY PARADE
JUNE 14, 1924.

Bronx Borough Day Parade, June 14, 1924. The Grand Concourse and Burnside Avenue from the top of the Elks building. The horse drawn house float was from the Real Estate Association of The Bronx. (The Bronx County Historical Society Research Library)

Forts 5 and 6 Peaceful Posts in Revolutionary War

Fordham Heights had Forts Five, Six, Seven and Eight guarding the countryside during the Revolutionary War.

Fort Number Five was a square earthwork surrounded by the customary wall of felled trees with sharpened branches facing the enemy. According to military maps of those times, it was perched on the uphill curve of Kingsbridge Road at about today's W. 195th St. It was built by Provincials, a term used by the British to denote Americans loyal to the Crown and, at times, the fort was commanded by Colonel DeLancey, a wealthy West Farms landowner, who had kept his allegiance to King George III.

Fort Number Five had no heavy cannon, nor did it figure in any action. DeLancey's orderly book mentions that two privates of the King's American Regiment were courtmartialed for quitting this post, and one wonders if it were from boredom. The little fort was destroyed and abandoned by the British in 1779.

Reginald Pelham Bolton, Edward Hall and W. L. Calver did important excavation work on the site in 1910, before apartment buildings were built there, and their finds were donated to the New-York Historical Society.

Fort number Six was a similar earthwork, manned by 25 Hessian privates, a sergeant and one drummer — according to Von Krafft's (translated) war journal. Later on the garrison was enlarged to 30 privates, two sergeants and a drummer of the Prince of Wales regiment, and Bayard's Orange Rangers — both units comprised of Americans who sided with the British. The men never participated in any action, but did sentry duty along Kingsbridge Rd. Fort Number Six was located on Sedgwick Ave. south of Kingsbridge Rd., on the grounds of the Veterans Hospital.

British "Fort No. 8" Artifacts Recovered by Bronx Historian

Revolutionary maps of the Bronx clearly define the location of eight forts, all of them located on the Fordham-Kingsbridge-Spuyten Duyvil heights, overlooking the Harlem River.

Of them all, Fort Number Eight was unique in that it remained in the hands of the British from the time it was constructed in the winter of 1776–1777, to the day it was demolished in October, 1782. All the other forts were attacked, besieged, captured, freed and stormed again and again, with Hessians, British, Americans, Scotch Highlanders, Irish Volunteers and Tories being the successive occupants of the stone, earthwork and timbered strongholds. Not Fort Number Eight: it flew the British colors throughout the entire war, until English army engineers blew it up on the day the departing redcoats hauled down their flag and left.

The hilltop, overlooking the Harlem River, soon lost its martial look, as trees and shrubs grew over the crumbled fort. The Archer family who had owned the land since the mid-1700s did not improve their property nor build upon it, but in 1857, Gustav Schwab and another wealthy man named Mali purchased the hillside at $1000 an acre, and there erected their mansions. The Schwab family, in particular, turned up many cannonballs, musket balls, coins and buttons, and, conscious of the historic setting they lived in, had an engraved marker placed on the property, not far from their house on the hill.

Today we know the spot as the site of N.Y.U., [now Bronx Community College] and what remained of Fort Number Eight lay underground. In 1959, work was begun on a new building near the Hall of Fame, and in January, 1960, Dr. Theodore Kazimiroff was given permission to dig in and around the excavations. In spite of the bulldozers and steamshovels encroaching upon him from all sides, the official Bronx Historian unearthed rum bottles, Hessian buttons, clay pipes, cannonballs and pikes, shovels and British regimental buttons. A most interesting find was a fireplace, the grill of which consisted of a bent iron hoop from a cask, on which . . . believe it or not . . . sat a rusted iron kettle.

One can imagine the British soldiers having a last mug of tea before the order came to assemble and march off, leaving the fireplace to be buried under an avalanche of dirt, as the Army sapper blew up the fort. The charcoal from the burning timbers was mute evidence of the thoroughness of their job! So, in the year 1960, Fort Number Eight was assaulted for the last time . . . a once-in-a-lifetime experience for even such a seasoned historian as Dr. Kazimiroff. Today a modern building stands on the site of the Revolutionary fort, but its historical reminders have been rescued, to beguile our coming generations.

Ye Wickerscreek Trail Stemmed From Indians' "Weckquasgeek"

Indian days continue to fascinate Bronxites of today, and a frequent question put to this writer concerns the trails that eventually became our modern streets.

The Bronx, west of the Bronx River, was Weckquasgeek tribal lands, and well-defined trails were in existence when the first Europeans came to this region. From ancient Dutch chronicles and subsequent English records we learn the main settlement and residence of the Grand Sachem was in present day Dobbs Ferry, and that a well-trodden path paralleled the Hudson River, to terminate at the lower end of the Bronx.

The English settlers simplified the Native American name and their references to Ye Wickerscreek Trail is frequently encountered. In time, the trail was widened to accommodate cars and carriages, finally to evolve into paved highways that we know today.

This trail followed the Hudson River down to Spuyten Duyvil, climbed up to Fordham Heights via Kingsbridge Road, then turned south on Aqueduct Ave. to approximately W. 172nd St.

From there, the trail angled down to Walton Ave., past present day Franz Sigel Park and onto the Grand Concourse (past Hostos College). Then it led over to Lincoln Ave. and E. 132nd St. where a sizeable Indian village was once situated. Early Dutch and English settlers knew it as Ranaqua (with various other spellings) which, in the Indian tongue, meant "The End Place" that it was. No trace of Ranaqua remains, save the name, as it has been buried under the railroad yards for over a century.

The Naming of Featherbed Lane: Four Varying Versions Offered

"How-did-Featherbed Lane-get-its-name?" is a favorite game of Bronx amateur historians, and all the versions of its origin have a measure of credibility to them. So, with no attempt to influence the reader, the three most accepted stories are offered.

During the Revolutionary War, patriotic inhabitants who lived alongside the steep road once laid their feather beds onto the frozen roadway so that the American cavalry could pass without being betrayed by the hoofbeats of their steeds. Military maps of this time do not show any lane—but sometime around the Civil War a road was shown, bearing the name of Belmont Street.

Two stories stem from this later period: farmers, driving down the steep rocky road, would upholster the wagonseat with old featherbed mattresses to ease the jolting journey. A variant of this is that the name really applied to the swamp at the bottom of the hill (now Jerome Ave.) for the marshy, boggy surface was as soft as a feather bed.

This writer believes in none of these stories, but feels the name originated unofficially in the 1840s when rough gangs of men worked on the Croton Aqueduct. As drinking was forbidden to the laborers, illegal "saloons" were set up on wagons and hidden in the nearby woods. Gambling, too, was frowned upon but sheds were set up on payday as temporary gambling halls. Special Aqueduct Police had to patrol the work area because of the animosity between the Irish workers who came from rival Counties in their native land. In short, there was a frontier atmosphere to the countryside, and the name Featherbed Lane might well perpetuate the temporary red-light district.

Once the workmen departed along with their attendant evils, the name remained in local folklore. In 1889, the name appeared in parentheses on a map, and a latterday real estate broker, having no idea of its origin and liking the homey sound of it, had the name officially adopted.

It is also likely that none of these stories is the true one, but until Featherbed Lane is explained with official records, the Bronxite has four stories from which to choose.

Street Names in the Bronx Come from Many Countries

When traveling in the Old World, one of the facets of European cities that Americans notice is their street names: in Italy, they are almost 100 percent Italian. In Germany, practically every street has a German name, and this practice holds true in all the other countries. The only exceptions to this rule are the names of internationally known people such as Dr. Schweitzer, President Kennedy, Albert Einstein, Christopher Columbus and a few more.

In the New World we have an ethnic mix that is reflected in our street names, and the Bronx is a good example, due to the many immigrants who have enriched our history.

Regrettably few Indian names have survived the centuries and we have only Mosholu and Katonah. Came the Dutch, so we have Verveelen Pl., Van Cortlandt Park and Steenwick, to name just a few. The English arrived soon after, giving us Livingston Ave., Pell Pl. and Bailey Ave. Scottish names, such as Bathgate, Findlay and Givan were mapped, as well as the Welsh names of Morris, Powell and Tinton. Kelly, McGraw and Brady are avenues with Irish names. Latkin Sq., Antin Pl. and Fischer Pl. are some streets that reflect our Jewish population, and the heavy German migrations of the 1850s resulted in Havemeyer Ave. and Bruckner Blvd., not to omit Franz Sigel Park.

Casanova and Manida Sts. and Roberto Clemente Park bring to mind the Hispanics, while the Italians can point to Crimi Road, Santo Donato Place and Donizetti Place. Ericson Place is a Scandinavian contribution to the Bronx map, with Korony Sq. and Kossuth Ave. adding a Hungarian touch.

The Poles are not left out, for there is Pulaski Park—and Scharansky Plaza and Kazimiroff Blvd. smack of Russia. Purdy, Tetard and Ferris (originally Ferriers) are reminders of the early French settlers in what is today the Bronx, and if any nationalities were left out, please forgive this writer!

35 Hotels, Inns of Yore Served Travelers in Bronx

Although the Bronx is larger than many American cities, it is uniquely lacking in hotels. A glance at a classified directory bears this out: Five hotels and eight motels, whereas the oldtime directories carried an impressive list of inns, taverns, hostelries or hotels.

True, many of them were small, two-storied wooden houses, but the weary traveller finding himself in any of the small villages above Manhattan had no trouble finding a room for himself and a stable for his horse. These public houses numbered approximately 35.

The Hotel Clausen was in Mott Haven, and the Winona Hotel was once located on Courtlandt Ave. St. Mary's Park Hotel stood on the corner of Willis Ave. and N. 148th St. On Brook Ave. were Seebeck's Hotel and the North Side Hotel.

Third Avenue was served by the Hammer Hotel, McLaughlin's Hotel, the Mount Morris Hotel and an inn known as the Stone Jug. Jerome Ave. had its Beaconsfield Inn, Judge Smith's Inn, the Jerome Park Hotel and the Grand View Hotel. Highbridgeville, overlooking the Harlem River, had no fewer than five: Patrick Clancy's Hotel, Conrad's Hotel, Karl's Hotel and Kyle's Park and the Woodbine Hotel. Continuing North, there was the Sage House at Spuyten Duyvil and the Riverdale Inn at W. 254th St.

The Fleetwood Hotel catered to the carriage set. The Hotel Gorbets on Gun Hill Rd. was popular with cyclists and Bronx River boatsmen. To the west, Van Cortlandt Park Hotel did a thriving business at Woodlawn Cemetery. Foley's Hotel was below Bronx Park, while Kipp's Parkway Hotel was above it, at Southern Blvd. and Fordham Road. Then there was the Adriatic Hotel with seven acres of land, near Crotona Park, and Bailor's Hotel, in Unionport. Odell's Tavern on the Boston Rd., near Dyre Ave., dated back to the 1830's and its business was taken over by Breinlinger, and then Dickert. Westchester Village had the Osseo Hotel, St. Boniface's Inn, the Westchester Hotel and, a bit below, on the Westchester Turnpike, the Swan Inn.

The Eureka House fronted on Eastchester Bay and on the opposite shore was the Colonial Inn, near the City Island bridge. On the island itself was the Monte Carlo Hotel at its southern tip, and the Macedonian Hotel on the eastern shoreline.

Old 24th Ward of Bronx Was "Western Reserve"

Last week's reference to the title "Territory of the Bronx (River)" was just one of the names applied to our Borough in earlier times. Politically, it was the 23rd and 24th Wards — as applied to all the land west of the Bronx River — the other 22 Wards being located in Manhattan. When the land east of the Bronx River, including City Island, was detached from Westchester County and added to the 24th Ward, the two countryfied wide expanses were lyrically referred to as "the Wards of Magnificent Distances."

"The Western Reserve" was yet another name of a sector of the 24th Ward as it was land reserved for the development of Upper Morrisania, which subsequently was renamed Tremont. "The Western Reserve" is now known as the area of Mount Hope.

Around the turn of the century, two names were in vogue for the new county, north of Manhattan: the more popular title was "The Great North Side" and this common usage resulted in one of our early newspapers being named *The North Side News* which had its offices and presses on E. 149th St. and Bergen Ave. "The Annexed District" was the second name, but its usage seemed to be confined to legal matters and real estate dealings.

In 1898 when Brooklyn, Richmond, Manhattan, Queens and The Bronx were incorporated into one city, there were various names suggested other than New York City. One public-minded citizen advanced his idea of combining the first two letters of Brooklyn, Richmond, Manhattan and Queens with the last letters of The Bronx. The result would have been Brimaquonx, but happily for all of us, the name was never seriously considered or adopted!

DSC "Horse Amulets" Once Warded Off "Evil Eye" Here

There are thousands of Bronxites who can remember the days when almost every conveyance in our Borough was horse drawn. These vehicles—fire truck, ambulance, police van, mailcoach, delivery cart and vegetable wagon—all moved at horse pace, and nothing was more commonplace and pervasive than the clop-clop of hooves.

Three nationalities seemed to dominate the wagon trade: native-born Americans were predominantly cab drivers and deliverymen; Irishmen drove the horsecars and garbage wagons; the Italians went in for ice wagons as well as fruit and vegetable wagons.

The Department of Street Cleaning (now our Sanitation Department, but then known as the D.S.C.) at first employed Irishmen who were familiar with horses, but as these men had no language barrier, they rose to more responsible positions within the Civil Service system. Their places were taken by Italian immigrants who soon brought to their work a certain Mediterranean flavor, already in vogue with their compatriots who drove the ice wagons and vegetable carts. This touch was the horse amulets that were so much in evidence in southern Italy and Sicily before World War I.

These ornaments or charms were dogs' heads, crescents, horns and bulls' heads in brass or silver, and were the property of the D.S.C. drivers. The Irish foremen might have disapproved of the heathen doodads on the harnesses, but there was much tolerance and no issue was made of it. The cart driver, at the end of his day's work, would turn in his equipment but took the amulets home with him.

A favorite place for such insignia was the horse's forehead, and the object most commonly hung between the ears was a pair of small, branching horns. Their object was to ward off the "Evil Eye" or "Contra la Jettatura" and hardly a horse in the early Bronx was without this safeguard. By the mid-1920's most wagons had been superseded by trucks, and the horses were sold. The magic amulets were no longer seen, and a little part of the Old World disappeared from the Bronx scene.

Old Pine Block Boro Roadways Were Easy on Hooves of Horses

Some Bronx thoroughfares are among the most beautiful in the world, and some have an ugliness hard to match anywhere. Visitors might say that in some neighborhoods the streets are monotonously the same, but if you were born and raised on, say, E. 152nd Street you know it isn't anything like E. 151st Street or E. 153rd Street. Each street in our Borough has a slightly different history from its neighbors, but they are alike in that the Borough President paves them all.

In Dutch colonial times, a 1642 Burgomaster proclaimed that "the streets were terrible, and becoming more and more unfit for human use" and he urged the public "for their own accommodation and the public good, ornament and welfare of the city, to pave the said streets with round (cobble) stone."

Some people did. Some didn't. So, paving was everybody's business and nobody's business. Even under British Colonial administration, wooden paving and a variety of badly laid stone paving was in use, and this hodgepodge system continued on in early American times. At one period, the Chief Engineer of the Fire Department was in charge of streets, and later the actual paving became the responsibility of the Croton Aqueduct Department. This chaos was largely rectified after 1898 when the office of Borough President was established for each Borough.

Not all citizens of the newly annexed Bronx (then called the North Side) were pleased at having their streets paved, to conform with Manhattan's system: they preferred pine block paving which was easier on horse's hooves, and were more quiet when carriage wheels rolled over them. Bitter political fights resulted, but eventually stone paving won out.

Although every effort was made to standardize Bronx paving, there are still holdovers from the old days: in Port Morris there are to be found granite Russ Blocks—two to three feet square—which were named after their inventor, Horace P. Russ. Oblong granite paving stones can be seen in Mott Haven's alleys, harking back to the Belgian Block method—so called because it was first used in Brussels, although made of trap rock cut from the Palisades. But, along with the horses and carriages they served, the stretches of pine slab paving has disappeared. The durable wooden streets of the early Bronx are now covered by a layer of asphalt.

Rivers of Bronx Were Courses For Impromptu Steamboat Races

Steamboat racing was once a well-publicized sport in the 19th century with the Mississippi River the most famous watercourse. The streams of our borough — the East, Harlem and Hudson Rivers — also were the scenes of rivalry, and at times, these contests resulted in marine disasters. The most common cause of the tragedies were overloading the furnaces so that the steam boilers burst. Steamship officials denied their vessels raced, stating the captains merely kept to a tight schedule, but the public was skeptical.

Prospect Ave., where it led down to the East River, was a vantage point from which Bronxites could view the thrilling sight of two steamboats racing each other, and another lookout point was Morris Heights in the West Bronx.

In a letter to the *Daily Graphic* in 1874, a reader complained that "The Sylvan Dell and the Shady Side went up the East River at a speed which convinced everyone who saw them that they were racing. Crowds of people at Oak Point were eagerly watching, and speculating on the chances of an explosion.

"Now it is said that the boats are merely hurrying to make their landings and not out to beat the competition, but last night the Shady Side was leaking steam in half a dozen places in her steampipes and attachments — sufficient evidence she had heavy pressure on her boiler. How long will this sort of thing be permitted to go on?"

The writer went on to cite the damage to small craft at their moorings, and to the docks along the waterfront when the gigantic waves rolled in.

Five Bridges Over Harlem River Were Constructed by A. P. Boller

Mention of A. P. Boller, whose Hudson Memorial Bridge was never built, may have given readers the impression he was a failure, but that was certainly not the case.

Sharon Reier's excellent book *The Bridges of New York* cites the five spans over the Harlem River leading into the Bronx that were designed and built by this man who was described as "intuitively artistic." His relaxation was painting landscapes, and his sense of harmony is seen to this day in the steel and iron of his bridges.

His initial work was the Park Ave. railroad bridge, financed evenly by the City and the New York Central Railroad and, his reputation established, Boller started his own consulting firm and built bridges for streetcar, horse and carriage, and pedestrian traffic.

Boller's structural artistry came out in the Broadway Bridge (1895) with its gazebos at both ends, and the iron ornamentation. When it had to be replaced in 1905 it was floated downstream to become the University Heights Bridge, at West Fordham Road. That same year, Boller won the acclaim of the American Society of Engineers when his Macombs Dam Bridge, a blend of Tudor and Gothic styles, was finished.

The E. 149th St. Bridge (1905) and the second Madison Ave. Bridge (1910) were the other Harlem River crossings to Boller's credit, although, according to Sharon Reier, these two were merely functional.

Daily, Bronxites by the thousands cross all these bridges without giving a thought to Alfred Pancoast Boller, but at least his name is on a Bronx street sign.

Horsecars of Old Bronx Were Commuters' Specials of Time

Today we tend to think of a horsecar as a bit of Early American comedy, but in 1886 there was nothing remotely ridiculous about horsecars. There were more than 500 horse railways in cities and towns then, powered by 100,000 animals. Purists referred to them as "animal railways" for both mules and horses were used in the mass transportation of those days.

The Bronx (or rather, the Annexed Districts above the Harlem River) had its horse railways too, and the best known and most ambitious one was the system running along Third Ave. Back in the 1880s this main artery was known as the Boston Road, from E. 134th St. to E. 163rd St., and from E. 163rd St. up to Fordham Road, it was called Fordham Ave. In time, the horse railway developed branch lines to West Farms and Hunts Point.

These lines, slow and small by our standards, nevertheless affected the patterns of city growth for they allowed a workman to comute six or eight miles to a small home in a countrified section, instead of being tied to a tenement close to his job.

High Bridge Built with Arches in 1840's, to Carry City Water

Most Bronxites have seen the single steel arch of High Bridge gracefully spanning the Harlem River, but it is not common knowledge that it takes the place of four granite arches that originally supported the bridge.

High Bridge, constructed in the 1840's to carry Croton drinking water from the Bronx mainland over into Manhattan, was a favored promenade for many decades. Edgar Allan Poe often strolled its length and admired the view, and hardly an important visitor from Europe ever came to New York without taking a carriage trip or steamboat trip to see the famous High Bridge.

The Harlem River, in those days, accommodated sculling crews, fishermen, excursion boats, sloops, canal boats, tugboats and barges and all of them had to thread their way past the granite pillars of High Bridge. The narrow passage and the strong tides were the subject of mounting concern, and when the twentieth century river traffic increased in volume, so did the length, width and tonnage of its shipping.

Numerous nautical mishaps occurred at High Bridge, and the various shipping firms petitioned the Federal Government to raze the entire bridge. Newspapers of the day carried heated arguments from New Yorkers protesting such a drastic solution, and so the petition was shelved.

Almost 25 years were to pass before sufficient pressure was brought upon the federal government to have the four hazardous pillars replaced by a single arch. Today, motorists on the Major Deegan Expressway can see both the steel arch, and the older granite arches that remain on the Bronx side of the bridge.

Old Jerome Park Reservoir Gave Name to Boro Avenue

Every biography of Winston Churchill mentions his American mother, Jennie Jerome. Her father was Leonard W. Jerome who, along with financiers Travers, August Belmont, and his own brothers, founded the American Jockey Club. Shortly thereafter, in 1866, Jerome Park Racetrack was laid out. A large portion of it is now Lehman College grounds, and the rest is beneath the waters of Jerome Park Reservoir.

Leonard Jerome was once known as the "King of Wall Street." He helped found three different racetracks, was a patron of the arts, established the Academy of Music and sponsored several singers. One of them was a Wakefield girl named Adelina Patti, who went on to operatic stardom.

Old maps show the forerunner of Jerome Ave. to be a plank road laid out in 1874 at a cost of $375,000 and labeled Central Ave., as it led northward from the Central Bridge (now Macomb's Bridge). It attained prominence once the Jerome Park Racetrack went into operation, and by 1888 it was paved its entire length.

The broad treelined boulevard leading up to the gates of Jerome Park was to be re-named in honor of an Alderman, but the matriarch of the Jerome family, Kate Hall Jerome, had other ideas. At her own expense, she had costly bronze street signs cast, hired a crew of laborers, and personally supervised the posting of the signs that read "Jerome Avenue." The local authorities discreetly forgot their plans to honor the Alderman — whose name is never given — and Jerome Ave. it remains to this day.

Today, the avenue is almost wholly in the shadow of the subway line, with no vestige of its former charming aspect. It serves as the dividing line between East Bronx and West Bronx, although the Grand Concourse is geographically more accurate, and the Bronx River historically more correct.

If Leonard Jerome, noted turfman and owner of splendid horses, could revisit the scene he would find not a trace of a horse on the entire length of Jerome Avenue — and earthly visitors would not find one of the bronze street signs, either!

Section 6

BELMONT, BRONX PARK,
BRONXWOOD, WEST FARMS

yright 1905 by the Rotograph Co.

A 102b. The Conservatory, Botanical Gardens, Bronx Park, N. Y.

The Conservatory in Bronx Park. A 1905 postcard shows the ambitious plans of the Parks Department and the New York Botanical Garden after it had acquired the Lorillard estate. (The Bronx County Historical Society Research Library)

Department of Highways — Webster and 180th Street, 1910. The Webster Avenue trolley tracks are in front of the horsedrawn carts. (The Bronx County Historical Society Research Library)

West Farms Square. Shades of 1940! Once a Bronx River port, a stage coach transfer point and, when this scene was taken, an important street car junction. Within eight years, buses would supersede this westbound trolley and the stores would be razed. (The Bronx County Historical Society Research Libarary)

First Bronx Phone Demonstrated in Wray's Hall 107 Years Ago

Where Boston Road meets E. Tremont Ave. once stood a three-storied edifice that was the social hub of West Farms in the last century. Known as Wray's Hall, it boasted of an auditorium that had the first gas lights to be seen in the Bronx. It also was one of our earliest communications centers and there, telegraph lines running from all parts of the Bronx were terminated. When you realize West Farms was a thriving river port with facilities for passenger boats, coal yards, flour mills, dyeworks and lumberyards, the need for such communication was obvious.

William Tarbox, a Bronx historian of note, once told this writer the first telephone was demonstrated in Wray's Hall in 1877 before a group of incredulous merchants. That same year his grand uncle, Charles Tarbox, became the proud owner of the first telephone in the Bronx. It was installed in his home at 1887 Washington Ave., and was connected with the Harlem Central Office at E. 125th St. and Lexington Ave.

In 1889, Catholics held a meeting in Wray's Hall to organize the parish of St. Thomas Aquinas, according to Stephen Wray who wrote historical sketches of West Farms, and who was a grandson of the original owner of the hall.

Around the turn of the century Wray's Hall had been converted into a hotel and there are old photographs showing it as The Trolley Inn, facing West Farms Square and a procession of early streetcars. Today, the site is occupied by a grassy plot and a parking lot belonging to the E.T.N.A. Houses—the initials standing for East Tremont Neighborhood Association.

The Bronx in Prehistory: "Rocking Stone" in Park

Visitors to Bronx Park who view the Rocking Stone there find themselves looking at a souvenir of the Ice Age, one of the Bronx's most treasured relics, and an attraction from prehistoric times til today. A rough cube of pinkish granite, resting on a granite base, with a height of 7 1/2 feet and a breadth of 10 more, it has a (calculated) weight of 30 tons.

Probably everyone from the cavemen, through the Indians, to Jonas Bronck and Messrs. Jessup, DeLancey and Lydig has tried to rock it, and with strong pressure at its most northern angle, the huge mass can be tilted—a scant two inches. Aside from its geological interest the rock also has served as boundary marker, for it was the northern limit of the tract that made up the 12 original West Farms.

Like all ancient landmarks, the Rocking Stone bears legends, and one of them concerns a wager made between a neighboring farmer and a foreman of the Lydig Estate, upon which the Rocking Stone stood, that 24 oxen could not dislodge it. That the stone is still in position proves the oxen did not move it. Incidentally, the foreman of the Lydig Estate was a Thomas Messer who drowned in The Bronx River in the winter of 1855. His cottage was quite close to the Rocking Stone.

That such an event involving 24 oxen ever took place is doubtful, as the Bronx was not suitable for such beasts. The soil, being of a rich, light character and easily worked, could be plowed easier and cheaper by horses or mules.

Secondly, the Lydigs would never have permitted such an outlandish wager, for the Rocking Stone was a natural curiosity, to be pointed out to visitors and guests. It would have been sheer vandalism to dislodge such a phenomenon. The DeLancey family, who had owned the land now Bronx Park before the American Revolution, always invited distinguished guests to see the Rocking Stone—and, before them, the Indians regarded the glacial leftover with superstitious awe.

The Rocking Stone was cherished and guarded by the landowners of bygone days, as it is by the Park officials of today.

DeLancey's Pine, 122 Feet Tall, Long a Landmark

The annals of Revolutionary warfare along the Bronx River frequently mention DeLancey's blockhouse, which was situated on the west bank of the river, at about present-day E. 179th St.

Colonel James DeLancey had sworn allegiance to the British crown, and he and his Tory troopers were the scourge of that region. Many times the rebels scouted their way through the forests (now Bronx Park) in an effort to capture the wily Colonel, or to destroy the blockhouse.

A favored vantage point was high up in a towering pine tree on the eastern bank of the Bronx River, and legend has it that sharpshooters would wait patiently for days, hidden in its branches, for a chance to shoot the Tory officer. However, the Colonel survived the war — but suffered banishment to Nova Scotia when his lands were confiscated.

The tree, known as DeLancey's Pine, was once the most famous landmark of the Bronx, standing more than 122 feet high and having a girth of more than 11 feet. It was of the Pinus Strobus or White Pine species and was over 250 years of age.

Around it had passed Indian chieftains, colonists like Richardson and Jessup, and Revolutionary personages — George Washington, Lord Howe, Generals Heath, Putnam and Parsons, Aaron Burr, Colonel DeLancey, and later, the Lydig landowners. Some of the older inhabitants of West Farms would never mention DeLancey by name, and referred to the tree as the Sentinel Pine.

Very few Bronxites remember DeLancey's Pine. The tree was cut down in 1913 by the Parks Department, after it had died and was judged a hazard.

Monterey Ave. Named for Battle In Which Bronx Officer Fought

Regarding Spanish names on Bronx streets, Yolanda Martinez wrote a question. On Monterey Avenue, "Would you know why a street in the Bronx would be named for a city in Mexico?"

The reason has to do with a Samuel Ryer, whose family farmed a tract of land north of Crotona Park since Revolutionary times. In 1846, when the United States was at war with Mexico, Samuel Ryer served as an officer in what was termed the Mexican Campaign. He won a commendation in the battle of Monterey, and when he returned to a peaceful life on his lands, he named the estate "Monterey" to remind his neighbors of his war experiences.

An 1866 map shows his property was bounded by Third Ave., E. Tremont Ave., approximately E. 182nd St. and Hughes Ave. When the property was acquired for city streets and building lots, there were three streets that were probably named at the request of the former owner: Samuel St., Ryer Pl., and Monterey Ave.

Samuel St. became E. 180th St. when the numbering system was introduced, and Ryer Pl. was absorbed by Belmont Ave. However, Monterey Ave. remains, to add to Tremont's Latin flavor.

First Newspaper Published Here (1812) Put Out by Matthias Lopez

A query from Luis Melendez regarding Hispanics in the Bronx led to some interesting facts on that subject. The first newspaper in this territory was published by a Matthias Lopez in 1812. Prior to that time, journals and colonial newsletters had been the meager means of reporting events, with post riders delivering the packets to subscribers. Lopez' small newspaper, in English, was called *The Westchester Patriot* and was printed in West Farms. Copies are still in existence.

Many of us know of Innocencio Casanova, Cuban importer and ardent proponent of freedom from Spain, whose mansion was situated on Hunts Point. His name was given to a street in that neighborhood. Another Cuban, Fernando Yznaga, sugar importer, has his name on Yznaga Place near Ferry Point Park.

If there were Argentinians in the 19th century Bronx, they were most likely horse trainers, grooms and coachmen for Edward Faile, another Hunts Point squire. He imported his thoroughbreds from Argentina (transportation alone costing $1000 each) and his correspondence mentions payment to hostlers with Spanish names.

As far as can be determined, there was a small colony of Puerto Ricans at the lower end of Willis and Lincoln Aves. in the late 1920s. It was just prior to World War II (1940) that noticeable numbers of Puerto Ricans settled around Prospect Ave. and Southern Blvd., and found work in the numerous factories in nearby Port Morris and Oak Point.

Since then, there have been many other Latin communities in all parts of the borough, the new Bronxites coming not only from Puerto Rico but from other Caribbean islands, and Central and South America as well.

Carpenter of West Farms Devised Looms Which Popularized Carpets

Anyone who owns a carpet should be thankful Halcyon Skinner devised a power loom that enabled carpets to be bought by the average housewife. Before his time, rugs were regarded as luxuries and were sold accordingly.

The settlement of West Farms on the Bronx River boasted — back in 1830 — several flour mills, bleacheries, coalyards, a sawmill and some wharves. Mechanics gravitated to this river port and one of them, named Joseph Skinner of Massachusetts, found employment in John Copcutt's sawmill. A typical New Englander with an inventive flair, Skinner had devised a contrivance for cutting thin slips of wood for violins, and this machine he enlarged and modified to cut veneers in the sawmill. Copcutt allowed Skinner to build and maintain his own workshop on sawmill property, and Skinner's family moved down from Stockbridge. A son, Halcyon, aged 14, began work in the sawmill.

On his 21st birthday, Halcyon's world caved in: the Copcutt sawmill went up in flames and, with it, the Skinner workshop and all the machinery. Discouraged, the elder Skinner took his family out to Ohio, and Mr. Copcutt moved his business to Yonkers. Young Halcyon remained in West Farms and worked as a carpenter until, four years later, an incident occurred that changed the entire course of his life.

Another young man, Alexander Smith, had been running a country store in West Farms, but in 1845 bought a small carpet factory that operated 20 hand looms. He had some original ideas, and one involved the devising and construction of an apparatus for particoloring yarns for ingrain carpets. Alexander Smith sought out the young carpenter about this problem, and Halcyon came up with a satisfactory machine that boomed the business and made it expand to utilize 100 looms. Skinner was hired by Smith as general mechanic, and he stayed with the firm for 40 years. After five years of success, Mr. Smith looked into possibilities of a power loom for weaving Axminster carpets which, until then, were produced by hand. Halcyon, despite crude tools and no formal schooling in mechanical construction, somehow designed machinery from which a fabric was woven, although the product was imperfect at first.

In 1856, a joint patent was procured, and in the spring of 1857, a complete Axminster loom was set up to turn out fine carpets. The Civil War forced the firm to manufacture Army blankets but by that time the former carpenter had become a business representative in London, exhibiting fine rugs throughout Europe.

Twice the carpet mills were visited by fire, and the second one caused the owner to relocate to Yonkers. From that time onward, the names of Alexander Smith & Sons, and Halcyon Skinner were identified with the industrial development of Yonkers. West Farms remained for a time a small port on the Bronx River, and has ceased to be that.

Letter and Tomb Commemorate Fallen Officer of Civil War

A century ago, the Pierce family of the village of West Farms owned a modest tract of land overlooking the Bronx River—a part of their property now being occupied by P.S. 6 on Tremont Ave.

A son, Samuel, fought in the Civil War and in the battle lulls, wrote home to his parents about the trials and tribulations of a sergeant's life in the Union Army. These letters, preserved by a grand-nephew, Lt. Col. Bolton Pierce (retired), reveal a flair for description and an eye for impressions during the hectic hours of warfare.

One letter from Cedar Creek, Virginia, is especially interesting for it has a sequel in the West Farms of today. Sergeant Pierce wrote home that his unit was nearly encircled by the Rebels but managed to fight their way out, suffering heavy losses. "Shortly after occupying this position," he wrote, "Lieut. Rasberry received his death wound—two or three of the boys took hold of him but he expired instantly."

Samuel Pierce survived the war and lived out a useful life in his beloved West Farms. The patriotic townspeople erected, by subscription, the West Farms Soldier's Monument and a burial plot adjoining the Presbyterian Church graveyard on E. 180th St. and Bryant Avenue. It was in this military cemetery that Samuel Pierce was buried, oddly enough, when E. 180 St. was known as Samuel St.

A nearby tombstone marks the resting place of his former commander, listed as a Captain and not as Lieutenant Rasberry. Today's visitor can read the legend:

"William J. Rasberry, Captain Co. C, 6th Heavy Artillery, Killed Oct. 19, 1864 at Cedar Creek, while leading his men up the hill."

150 Inventions Work Of Charles Tarbox

Perhaps a record in residence was achieved by Charles Wakefield Tarbox whose family moved to upper Morrisania when he was two years old. He lived 74 years in the same house on Washington Ave., during which time upper Morrisania became Tremont Village and eventually The Bronx. His father was Postmaster, and the Tarbox property ran from Washington Ave. to Railroad Ave. (now known as Park Ave.) and a business office, the post office and a paintshop fronted on this busy street. In those days, Morris St. (E. Tremont Ave.) was the main thoroughfare. Mott St. is now E. 176th St.

The boy clearly inherited his father's mechanical genius for, while still a teenager, he secured a patent on his first invention! With no tutor but himself, he mastered engineering, and in his lifetime perfected more than 150 mechanical, hydraulic, pneumatic and electrical devices! Little did he dream that, 100 years later, his pleasant home and gardens, his workshop and carriage house would be covered by the concrete playground of P.S. 58.

The name, Tarbox, seems an odd one, but it was an old and honorable one in New England. Charles was ninth in descent from a John Tarbox who settled in the Bay Colonies in 1600, and counted Miles Standish among his ancestors.

As active as his father, Hiram Tarbox, was in the Republican party of Tremont, Charles was just as widely known as a worker in the Democratic cause. He labored for the election of good, honest and capable men to public office, although he, himself refused nominations to office several times. He was a member of the Schnorer Club and also of the Fordham Club, and lived a full and active life past 80 years of age.

Busy Dr. Becker (Bronx 1903): Farmer, Banker, Realtor

In this age of specialization, it is refreshing to read about a 19th Century Bronxite who wore four hats, and all of them were financially rewarding.

C. Adelbert Becker did not begin life in this Borough but was born in a farming family in upstate New York, where he mastered every aspect of agriculture while still in his teens. The Civil War had just come to an end, and young Becker decided he wanted to be a physician, so for a few seasons he hired out as a farmhand, and saved his earnings.

He paid for a course in medicine and entered New York University Medical Department from which institution he obtained his degree. He became an ambulance surgeon (horse and wagons in those days) at Park Hospital but later was house surgeon in full charge of the hospital where he was known as "The Boy Doctor." In the 1870's the Bronx was changing from large estates and farms to small villages, and Dr. Becker decided to enter private practice up in Tremont.

A century ago, Tremont Ave. (then called Morris St.) was scarcely more than a narrow, unpaved country road, with the business section confined to Park Ave. (which was then called Railroad Ave.) In 1876 the young ambitious doctor settled on Merchants' Row and during his carriage trips on housecalls, he saw numerous lots to his liking. Soon he owned parcels of land scattered here and there but none large enough for the farm he dreamed of. Finally, in Westchester County, he did buy a 300-acre tract and there he ran a farm, using all his agricultural know-how and business acumen. A dozen hired hands operated the tractors and harvesters, and the doctor had easy access to his farm, thanks to the New York & Harlem Railroad.

He added his third hat around 1890 by becoming a successful Tremont realtor, and in 1903 he entered the banking business, becoming vice president and then president of the Bronx Borough Bank.

Dr. Becker's activities in the banking field soon increased to the point where he had to give up one career, so he reluctantly retired from his medical practice. However, to the end of his long and busy life, he was always addressed as Doctor Becker. If ever there were a Mrs. Becker, there is not a word concerning her. It may well be that the doctor/farmer/banker/realtor had no time for marriage!

Arthur Ave., in Belmont, Named for U.S. President

In the mail was a query from an obviously young reader, but his name is not mentioned here for diplomatic reasons. "I live in Belmont and my friends say Arthur Ave. is named for a famous Italian musician and director named Arturo Toscanini. I didn't believe them so I asked my father and he said there was a man who worked for the city and was a surveyor, and his name was Arthur Hoffman. Next to Arthur Ave. is Hoffman St., so is he right?"

Arthur Ave. was named many years before Maestro Toscanini came to America, where he eventually lived in Riverdale — and a diligent search of City records has never turned up a surveyor named Arthur Hoffman . . . so both tales can be catalogued as Bronx folklore.

Belmont was once part of the extensive Lorillard lands, and that wealthy family bequeathed their mansion to a religious society to house St. Barnabas Hospital. A niece, Catherine Lorillard Wolfe, inherited the property which, in the course of the city's expansion, was divided into streets and avenues. Miss Wolfe was an ardent admirer of the President of the United States, Chester A. Arthur, and in Madison Square — where the Lorillards once had a town house — there is today a statue of President Arthur that was donated by the heiress in the 1890s.

So when she requested that one of the new streets in Belmont be named in President Arthur's honor, the City fathers had no objection to her wish, for, in a long philanthropic life, she had funded many worthwhile civic causes and municipal charities.

And that's the story behind the name of Arthur Avenue.

Bronx Zoo's Dr. Ditmars
And His Snakes Recalled

Ask most Bronxites where is the New York Zoological Park and chances are they won't know, but if the unofficial name the Bronx Zoo is used, there is instant recognition. This world-famed zoological park was chartered in 1895, but it was not until 1898 that actual construction began.

A young reporter from the *New York Times* was dispatched by his editor to interview the director, Dr. William Hornaday, soon after groundbreaking. The reporter, Raymond Ditmars, had been interested in reptiles all his life and he so impressed the director with his experience and knowledge that, a few weeks later, the director offered him the post of keeper of reptiles. Ditmars was delighted to accept, so in July of 1899 he was hired as assistant curator of reptiles—and for over 40 years thereafter, his reputation as a herpetologist grew, until his name and that of the Bronx Zoo were known around the world.

The Ditmars family lived on Bathgate Ave. near E. 173rd St., but when the reporter-turned-curator married, the couple moved to Union Ave. There the young naturalist gained neighborhood fame by driving a second-hand Rambler to work—and in 1906 horseless carriages were rare indeed.

The young couple also went off on motor excursions to Sullivan County to hunt snakes, but the word expedition would be more appropriate, considering the dirt roads, almost total lack of gasoline pumps, and the slow and clanking gait of those early machines.

One Bronx episode was related in a book on Mr. Ditmars by L.N. Wood wherein the curator, his wife and two small daughters were returning from a long trip, laden down with luggage, insect-boxes snake-cages and even a maple tree in full leaf. They had been plagued by flat tires, clutch trouble and then an argument on the Nyack ferry where a guard had protested their cargo of snakes. Just as the weary travelers turned on to Webster Ave. from Tremont Ave., the car hit a bump and a cage of harmless snakes crashed to the cobblestones and burst open. Snakes slithered off in all directions, as passersby fled. Patrons of a corner saloon, hearing the crash, came out and immediately retreated to the safety of the bar, calling for the police.

Two policemen, wishing for St. Patrick's help, appeared and began to round up the fugitive snakes. With the aid of the four

Ditmars, all the reptiles were captured—and that episode lived on in Tremont folklore for many a year.

Throughout his lifetime, Dr. Ditmars wrote many nature books, hundreds of articles, lectured to countless organizations and traveled all over the world to enhance the Bronx Zoo with exotic animals and snakes. It was a loss to the world when Dr. Ditmars died of pneumonia in May 1942, but he left his mark on the Reptile House in Bronx Park.

Van Zandt Murals in Zoo Adorned Old Lion House

Visitors to our Bronx Zoo invariably are impressed by the scenes painted on the walls of the cages, for they faithfully reproduce the natural surroundings in which the animals once lived. According to an oft-told story, the backdrops in the snake house are so authentic that serpents there tried to enter the painted crevasses in the painted rocks — and there were other instances of animals being similarly fooled.

Some of the earliest examples of this art were painted 'way back at the turn of the century, and were an innovation at that time. A Bronxite named Meyer Van Zandt gained prominence with the African scenes he painted on the walls of the lion house, and his work attracted so much attention that many artists visited the Zoo, more to see his murals than to look at the animals.

Mr. Van Zandt did not limit himself to backgrounds of jungles, swamps and deserts, but painted many of the rare animals themselves, and was given a studio in the Zoo.

He was fortunate in being recognized in his own lifetime, but his private life was not a happy one. He and his wife had been separated for years, and he lived alone in a single room in a boarding house on E. 180th St. On an April morning in 1908, his landlady smelled gas and traced it to Van Zandt's room where he was found to have committed suicide. Police reported that the wall of his room were literally covered from floor to ceiling with paintings of animals, all of whom he had perpetuated in oils while, he, himself, was destined to disappear from the Bronx scene. Somewhere, even after 70 years, there must be some of those paintings still in existence.

Southern Blvd. Planned
In 1870s "Annexed District"

Some Bronx streets evolved from animal runs, through Indian trails to Colonial footpaths to 19th century carriage roads, eventually to become our paved roads of today. Southern Boulevard was not one of these: It was a drawingboard creation, planned by the Engineering Department of the Annexed District (the western half of our Bronx) sometime in the 1870s, to be a grandiose thoroughfare sweeping up from E. 133rd St. and Third Ave., cutting through the wide estates of the East Bronx, bypassing Crotona Park and Bronx Park and terminating at the Botanical Garden.

A latterday engineer once told this writer the name was first suggested when the countryside was still under the jurisdiction of Westchester County and the proposed boulevard was to be the southernmost of the County. Upon annexation in 1874, the name was still applicable as the boulevard did originate in the South Bronx.

It was laid out across the original Jonas Bronck farmlands which later became the holdings of the Morris family, and then cut a swath through the lands belonging to the Leggett, Fox, Simpson and Tiffany families. Longwood Park, property of wealthy squire S. B. White, had its wooded eastern section condemned, levelled and cut through, and only Longwood Ave. remains today to remind us of a far different era.

Southern Blvd. became the boundary line of the Minford, Woodruff and Lydig estates, the last-named becoming Bronx Park. It also cut off part of the academy grounds of St. John's (now Fordham University) and a Jesuit cemetery had to be relocated in 1889 to a more central place. This burial ground can be seen today in the northwestern section of Fordham campus.

The lower end of Southern Blvd. was settled first and became industrialized early in the 20th century whereas the upper end, near Hunts Point and running to Bronx Park, was a more attractive residential area.

Rockefeller Zoo Gift
O.K.to Mention Now

South of Fordham Road, through the Bronx Zoo's remarkable Rainey Memorial Gates, one comes upon an open plaza leading to the sea lions' pool. The center of this imposing plaza is beautified by a three-tiered marble fountain, dating back to early 18th century Italy. Mermaids, tritons and other allegorical fantasies bemuse the visitors, and prepare them for the aquatic display where the sea lions sport.

This priceless work of art was a gift of William Rockefeller to our borough sometime after 1910 when his nephew, Vice President Nelson Rockefeller, was only a boy. This alone makes it worth mentioning that the Rockefeller tradition of endowments was already well established back in those far off years.

Incidentally, the Rainey Memorial Gates, mentioned earlier, are a lavishly ornamented bronze portal stressing a jungle setting, with flora and fauna in stylized motif. Sculptors and designers have acclaimed it as the most handsome gate in New York City. Paul Manship was the artist, as booklets on the Bronx Zoo attest—but the names of the Italian mastersculptors are not known with certainty. Their masterpiece is generally and simply called the Rockefeller Fountain.

Chinese First Came to Bronx in 1890s and Kept to Selves

Every Bronxite must have noticed and remarked upon the increase in Oriental people in our borough, but they are not all Chinese. From available records, including the recollections of our oldest citizens, it appears there were already Chinese here in the 1890s, but earlier than those years, no mention is made of them in town records, directories or voting rolls.

Very few had wives or families, and they had little or no contact with their neighbors. Their recreation was a weekly trip down to Chinatown to socialize with fellow countrymen.

These early arrivals had but two trades: laundrymen and restaurateurs, and there was hardly a neighborhood without that traditional combination. Bronxites were fascinated by the mysterious East as expressed in the decor and unfamiliar foods of the chop suey joints which, incidentally, invariably served cheaper meals than their American counterparts.

Small boys liked to "take the laundry to the Chinaman" for the man might give them a few lichee nuts. Some Chinese had entered New York, not from California, but from Cuba—and had relatives back on that island. Seasonally, the laundrymen would receive a shipment of sugar cane and, if a boy were lucky enough, he was given a section, several inches long, to suck on. Some laundrymen were quite dexterous with a machete and could lop off a piece of sugar cane in any length.

Little girls, on the other hand, were reluctant to bring in the laundry for they had heard wild tales of White Slavery and the horrors of opium dens. These rumors were hardly true, for the Chinese were hard workers with a respect for the law. This is borne out by the fact that, in years of reading old police blotters, this writer has never encountered a Chinese name.

Old Roadhouse Yarn Wakes Half-Century Recollections

Retired Inspector James Cotter had a long and varied career in the New York Police Department, but prior to that, was a deliveryman for the Ward Baking Company, more than 50 years ago.

Mention of the Hollywood Gardens roadhouse on the Shore Road jogged his memory and he writes: "I had a restaurant route, and worked seven days a week. That was the job, and you understood that when you took the route. I delivered in the upper Bronx and had stops that later might be considered to be of historic interest as, for instance, the Woodmansten Inn off Williamsbridge Rd., the Castillian Royal and the Pelham Heath Inn on Pelham Pkwy. and Eastchester Rd., and the Clason Point Military Academy.

"The three roadhouses did good business if the size of the bakery order was any indication, and the Academy cadets sure had hearty appetites!

"There was a restaurant inside Bronx Park called the Rocking Stone Inn and that stop was one that always made me a bit nervous. I had a key to the Boston Road gate, and this entry gave me access to the footpath leading past the cages. I delivered at 3 o'clock in the morning and what a commotion this would cause in the zoo! The nocturnal animals would scurry around, giving squeaks, barks or hisses according to their nature—and this would rouse the bears, lions and bigger game. I used to wonder what would happen if an animal were loose at the time of delivery.

"Many a time I thought of a fellow-worker who made a delivery in the middle of the night to the Central Park Zoo with stale bread for the animals. He ran into an elephant that had been chained outdoors, and the animal leaned on the truck and broke the windshield. I was in the office that morning when the driver was making out an accident form. To the question 'To whose responsibility, if any, was the accident due?', he wrote in, 'the elephant's.' "

Section 7

FORDHAM, GUN HILL, KINGSBRIDGE, NORWOOD

Chateau Thierry Army Base Hospital and Columbia War Hospital, c. 1918. Medical department of U.S. Army, Ambulance and Stretcherbearer Corps on parade on Gun Hill Road. Camp Seuss, its unofficial nickname, was located in the vicinity of Gun Hill Road and Kings College Place, and served the injured veterans of World War I. (The Bronx County Historical Society Research Library)

NEW-YORK AND HARLEM RAIL ROAD,
DAILY.

FALL ARRANGEMENT.

On and after TUESDAY, OCTOBER 10th, 1848, the Cars will run as follows, until further notice.

TRAINS WILL LEAVE CITY HALL, N. Y., FOR

Harlem & Morrisania		Fordham & William's Bridge.		Hunt's Bridge, Underhill's & Hart's Corners.		Davis' Brook, Pleasantville, Chappequa, Mount Kisko, Bedford, Mechanicsville, Purdy's and Croton Falls.	
7 10 A.M.	12 M.			9 A.M.	5 30 P.M.		
8 "	2 P.M.	7 A.M.	3 30 P.M.				
9 "	3 "	9 "	5 30 "	*T'kahoe & White Plains*		*dy's and Croton Falls.*	
10 "	4 "	12 M.	6 30 "	7 A.M.	3 30 P.M.	7 A.M.	3 30 P.M.
	5 30 "			9 "	5 30 "	9 "	
	6 30 "						

NOTICE.

Passengers are reminded of the great danger of standing upon the Platforms of the Cars, and hereby notified that the practice is contrary to the rules of the Company, and that they do not admit any responsibility for injury sustained by any Passenger upon the platforms, in case of accident.

RETURNING TO NEW-YORK, WILL LEAVE

Harlem & Morrisania		Hunt's Bridge.		White Plains.		Bedford	
7 08 A.M.	1 40 P.M.	7 50 A.M.	3 16 P.M.	7 15 A.M.	2 45 P.M.	7 55 A.M.	1 55 P.M.
8 "	3 "	*Underhill's Road.*		8 35 "	5 "		4 25 "
8 20 "	3 45 "	7 40 A.M.	3 06 P.M.	*Davis' Brook.*		*Mechanicsville.*	
9 "	4 "	*Tuckahoe,*		8 26 A.M.	2 35 P.M.	7 45 A.M.	1 45 P.M.
11 "	5 "	7 35 A.M.	3 03 P.M.		4 55 "		4 15 "
	6 "	8 50 "	5 15 "	*Pleasantville.*		*Purdy's*	
Fordham & William's Bridge.		*Harts Corners.*		8 18 A.M.	2 20 P.M.	7 35 A.M.	1 35 P.M.
6 45 A.M.	1 15 P.M.	7 25 A.M.	2 50 P.M.		4 48 "		4 05 "
8 "	3 25 "			*Mount Kisko.*		*Croton Falls.*	
9 10 "	5 40 "			8 A.M.	2 P.M.	7 30 A.M.	1 30 P.M.
					4 30 "		4 "

The TRAINS FOR HARLEM & MORRISANIA, leaving City Hall at 7, 10, 8, 9, 10, 12, 2, 3, 4, and 6.30, and From Morrisania and Harlem at 7.08, 8, 9, 11, 1.40, 3, 4, 5 and 6, will land and receive Passengers at 27th, 42d, 51st, 61st, 79th, 86th, 109th, 115th, 125th and 132d streets.

The 7 A. M. and 3.30 P. M. Trains from New-York to CROTON FALLS and the 7.30 A. M. Train from Croton Falls will not stop between White Plains and New-York, except at Tuckahoe, William's Bridge and Fordham.

A Car will precede each Train 10 minutes, to take up passengers in the City; the last Car will not stop except at Broome street, and 32nd street

FREIGHT TRAINS leave New-York at 9 A. M. & 12 M.; leave CROTON FALLS 7 A. M. & 8 P. M.

On SUNDAYS an Extra Train at 1 o'clock P. M. to Harlem and Morrisania.

Nesbitt, Printer.

New York Harlem Railroad Timetable, c. 1848. This railroad ran at ground level along the present-day Park Avenue. (The Bronx County Historical Society Research Library)

How Poe's Cottage Was Saved From Demolition in 1895

There are many stories about the naming of Bronx streets and they range from documented records to mere whimsical folklore. This writer is always intrigued by the handed-down stories, so it was with a thrill to learn how Poe Park was named—with due process of law, petitions, minutes of the meetings, votes and final acceptance all included.

According to Irmgard Lukmann, of The Bronx County Historical Society, it came about on a May day in 1895. Edgar Allan Poe's cottage, standing on the East side of Kingsbridge Road, near Valentine Ave., was slated for demolition, as Kingsbridge Road was being widened.

Two men, members of a literary society, were standing in perplexity and gloom in front of the cottage, deploring the imminent loss of a literary shrine. They were Albert Frey, a Fordhamite, and Dr. Appleton Morgan, of the Shakespeare Society. Mr. Frey later recalled: "I suppose that it was by a sort of mutual inspiration that we both exclaimed that here was an appropriate work for our Society to preserve the cottage. I remember that just opposite was a wooded tract, partially an apple orchard, and on the plot were piled the contractors' and workmen's tools."

"There!" exclaimed Dr. Morgan, "would be the spot to move the cottage to, and we could call it Poe Park. That, so far as I know, was the first suggestion of a Poe Park."

Dr. Morgan presented a bill to the New York State Legislature to lay out a public park there, and in May of 1896 the so-called "Poe Park Bill" was approved by the Governor. All was not clear sailing, for another literary society wanted the 2.3-acre plot called Poets' Park to honor a number of other poets as well. Mayor Strong followed Dr. Morgan's original plan and signed the bill, and that's how Poe Park received its name. Hats off to Mr. Frey and Dr. Morgan!!

Nieuw Harlemites Grazed Cattle on Bronx Meadows

Nieuw Haarlem (New Harlem) was founded by the Dutch in 1658 on a tract some 3000 acres in area. The first settlers broke ground near the foot of 125th St. and the Harlem River and laid out their individual holdings. For security of the settlers, all of whom were required to carry arms, ten regular soldiers from the fort at Nieuw Amsterdam were furnished. The Indians withdrew to the upper end of the island but were a common sight on the Harlem River as they paddled their canoes down to Nieuw Amsterdam.

The farmers also pastured their cattle on the salt meadows opposite, on the mainland—a section we Bronxites know now as E. 134th St. below the Willis Avenue bridge. The use of these meadows was later challenged by farmers who purchased the land, but for years the Dutch of New Harlem contested it in court.

Opposite the north end of the island, the Town of New Harlem claimed additional land on the mainland—later called Kingsbridge—and whenever the Fordham landowner, John Archer, let his cattle graze there, he was charged with trespassing. The English Governor, Lovelace, recognized the Town's claim and fined Archer, who refused to pay. The Harlem authorities promptly locked his cows in the pound. Eventually Archer pled that his children were lacking milk, so the courts relented and released his cows. But Archer continued to be a thorn in their side, and in those of his neighbors as the blotter of the court attested:

> 1671—Complaint of David Demarest against John Archer for mowing grass in his meadow at Spuyten Duyvill.
>
> Complaint of Martin Hardewyn of Fordham against Archer for breaking down his fences.
>
> Complaint of Marcus du Sauchoy of Fordham against Archer for throwing his furniture out of doors.

All in all the good old days were not peaceful ones!

Rose Hill Name Arises From Madison Square

Rose Hill Park can be found at the intersection of Fordham Road and Webster Ave., and no one could be faulted for assuming that, perhaps a century or more ago, there had been a hill there, covered with roses. In reality, the tiny park is only a vestige of a far larger estate once called "Rose Hill" by its owner, John Watt. His lands covered a tract now occupied by Fordham University and additional territory extending to the present day Botanical Garden.

In 1775 Squire Watt married Jane DeLancey, whose family lived on the adjacent estate that is now Bronx Park. She was one of 12 children — no rarity in those times. Prior to his marriage, John Watt had lived on an estate in Manhattan near what is now Madison Square (E. 24th St.) which he named "Rose Hill" after the family seat in Scotland. The Watts then transferred this name to their manor-lands in the countryside of a forested Bronx.

These lands were kept intact after the Revolution, and it was not until 1839 that the estate and manor house were purchased by the Catholic Church to establish St. John's College — later to be renamed Fordham University.

So, the name "Rose Hill" was transferred from Scotland to Little Old New York, and then brought up to our Bronx over two centuries ago. And it still survives in a whittled-down parcel of land of less than an acre in size.

Fordham Manor Church Set Up by 1684 Bequest

Readers are indebted to Mrs. M. Olsen of the Fordham Manor Reformed Church who sent in a thumbnail history of "the first church in the Bronx with a regular ministry." Recently, the church celebrated its 275th anniversary with special ceremonies, a choral presentation, and worship service.

In 1664, the English took Nieuw Amsterdam away from the Dutch and named it New York and a few years later John Archer (actually, a Dutchman with an Anglicized name) was granted the first of the great Manors — the Manor of Fordham.

Archer soon lost his heavily-mortgaged manor to Cornelius Steenwyck, who in 1684 willed the entire Manor to the Reformed Protestant Dutch Church of New York. The first Church Charter upon which was set the seal of King William III of England described the Manor as north of the Harlem River and stretching from the Hudson to the Bronx River. In 1696, the Fordham Manor Reformed Church was established, and the church was erected in 1706 on what is now Devoe Park, opposite Andrews Ave.

September 29th, 1753, saw the beginning of an action which has since caused many regrets, for on that day the Church began the sale of the Manor of Fordham — more than five square miles of it. The Fordham Manor Church was left with about an acre of ground.

Fordham Manor suffered severely in the Revolutionary War. The church was destroyed, and its third minister, Dominie John Peter Tetard, went off to the wars as a chaplain.

In 1802, a new church was erected near the Kingsbridge Rd. and since that time three edifices have stood on this site, the second being built in 1849, the last in 1940. The bell cast for the church in 1823 is still being used by the congregation each Sunday morning.

Names associated with this ancient church have a ring of history to them: Jacob and Stephen Van Cortlandt, William Dyckman, Nicholas Bayard, Lewis Morris and Isaac Varian, Charles Devoe and Mrs. Edgar Allan Poe, Brant Schuyler and Walter Briggs. The Fordham Manor Reformed Church is important in Bronx history.

Villa Ave. Reminders of Jerome's Racetrack

A biography of Jennie Jerome, mother of Winston Churchill, was published a few years ago, and in it were some references to the area north of Kingsbridge Rd. and west of the Concourse, when it was still part of Westchester County and known as the Bathgate Estate. The tract is now partially occupied by Villa Ave., subway yards, Harris Park and the Jerome Park Reservoir and, today, gives no hint of the glamorous events of a century ago.

The financier, Leonard Jerome, purchased 230 acres of the estate to establish a racetrack to elevate the horse race from the rowdy to the social. On this estate he built the most elaborate racetrack in the country, sporting a grandstand seating 8000 people, a luxurious clubhouse with a glittering ballroom, dining room and facilities for such diversions as polo, trapshooting, sleighing and iceskating. Jerome also built a villa near his racetrack where his family could spend winter weekends. He had an area frozen and flooded, so that his daughters could waltz on the ice while a band played in the cold air.

All the girls were accomplished riders and ice-skaters, as noted in the newspapers of the day, and one can imagine the Jerome daughters gracefully skating on the ice to the accompaniment of an orchestra, on a wintry night. Their cottage has long since disappeared, but its memory lingers on in the name, Villa Avenue.

Landowner N.P. Bailey
Ruled Roost, Century Ago

If ever there was a big frog in a little pond it might well have been a 19th Century Bronx landowner by the name of Nathaniel Platt Bailey, whose property covered a sizeable area of what we call West Fordham today.

According to maps of the 1870's, the Bailey lands extended roughly from Fordham Road, to Kingsbridge Rd., and from Bailey Ave. to University Ave. His mansion, situated overlooking the Harlem River, was described as commanding a view to the west that included the New Jersey Palisades.

"N.P." as he was called by his servants, (but not to his face) was not just a country squire but an urbane businessman whose name frequently turned up in newspaper accounts of horse racing, lavish lawn parties, church-related activities, and social events that took place in Manhattan.

The Protestant Episcopal Church of St. James, adjoining St. James Park, listed him as vestryman a century ago, and at one time (1884), he was elected president of the aristocratic St. Nicholas Society of the City of New York.

Came the 20th century and N.P. Bailey departed this earthly plane, and his scenic estate was subdivided into streets and avenues, with the main portion kept intact to become the grounds of the U.S. Veterans Hospital.

Only Bailey Ave. remained to remind following generations of a once-prominent civic leader. But does it? Sad to say it does not—for practically everyone in that Fordham-Kingsbridge neighborhood thinks the avenue honors P.T. Barnum's circus partner. This is a classic case of misconception that became folklore and as a result of this, N.P. Bailey is a forgotten man today.

Old Edison Studios Were Birthplace of Cartoon Films

The Gramercy Boys' Club building, which is being constructed on Decatur Ave. and Oliver Pl., stands where the old Edison Studios stood — a movie-making center for many years.

What is not generally known about the landmark is that the first animated cartoon films in color were made there. Prior to 1934, cartoon films such as "Koko the Clown," "Felix the Cat," "Oswald the Rabbit," and even Disney's Mickey Mouse series were in black and white. In 1935, Terrytoons (operated by the Terry brothers) experimented with a short film which had to be entirely hand-painted. As each second on the screen accounted for 16 frames to be painted in opaque colors, the reader can readily understand that thousands of separate drawings were required. The cartoonists (called animators), the photographers and most of the opaquers who colored the film, were Bronx residents (including this writer) and the experiment turned out to be a financial success. Efficiency experts from the Disney Studios had watched the operation closely in all its stages and, at its completion, hired many of the key personnel.

This writer also recalls the five-minute scenes, paid for by theatrical agents to publicize their clients. A camera crew, some musicians and scenery painters were hired, a studio room rented and an aspiring singer or dancer would have his or her act recorded on film. The reel would then be shown to prospective producers, or financial backers.

One time a crew of carpenters worked all night to have a giant-sized clock ready for a morning's song session. Ethel Merman, then a relatively new songstress, perched on the clock and sang "Time on my Hands" time and time again, until the director was satisfied.

Another young and hopeful comic used to come to the Edison Studios, and run through his string of jokes. "Some old, some new, many borrowed but none blue," he used to boast, and referred to himself as "The Thief of Bad Gags." This brash youngster, named Milton Berle, eventually became TV's Uncle Miltie.

The residents along Decatur Ave. never knew when a Broadway or Hollywood personality would walk by, but that's all in the past, now.

Actor Frank McGlynn, of the Bronx, Had Notable Lincoln Screen Career

Around 1910, when the motion picture industry was in its infancy, the Bronx had two silent film studios — the Biograph Studio near Crotona Park, and the Edison Studio in Fordham. At times, local children and adults were hired as extras, and this led to screen careers in some cases.

One family, then living on Marion Ave., had both a father and a son who found employment in the Edison Studio. Frank McGlynn was already in the movies thanks to his height and resemblance to Abraham Lincoln, and he played this role on stage in various theatres across the country. From people who had actually seen and heard Lincoln, he learned of mannerisms and gait that won their praise. He had parts in Civil War silent films and continued on into the early talkies so that, today, he is occasionally seen in film revivals.

One Decatur Ave. resident once told this writer of an amusing incident involving McGlynn and the Edison Studio which was situated on the corner of Oliver Pl. The actor was to appear at a benefit performance of a Tremont church, and did not bother to remove his makeup. Passengers in a Webster Ave. trolley were astounded when the tall, bearded man in stovepipe hat and old-fashioned clothes came aboard, and calmly paid his fare.

His son, Frank, played parts in some early movies, including "The Luck of Roaring Camp," that was partially filmed in the Bronx.

"Ye Wading Place" in Time Came To Bear Present Name of Fordham

A visitor from England, named Fordham, was intrigued that a neighborhood, an important avenue and a university carried his name, and wondered if one of his ancestors had been a landed proprietor in the remote past.

His genealogical fancy was dashed when he learned Fordham was the title of a 1250-acre tract owned by a Jan Arcer in the 1670's. Arcer rendered his name in various spellings, but, having an English wife and the territory having been transferred to British rule, he called himself John Archer. The name he gave to his manorlands was Fordham — "The Home by the Ford." This ford . . . or wading place . . . led over the shallow Spuyten Duyvil creek to the Bronx mainland in the general vicinity of today's Broadway and Kingsbridge Road. Archer was given permission by the English authorities to settle 16 farming families "near ye wading place at ye passage commonly called Spiting Devil."

The small rural settlement was practically wiped out during the Revolutionary War when marauders from both sides drove off the cattle and tore down fences and houses for firewood.

It was only decades later that the Manor of Fordham was once more settled, but on the eastern side — the area from University Ave. to the Bronx River. Fordham Road was laid out, St. John's College was renamed Fordham University, and the commercial life radiated out from the railroad depot on Webster Ave.

Of the original village of Fordham on the western side there is no trace, and even "Ye Wading Place" over Spuyten Duyvil Creek has been filled in, to disappear from memory.

Kingsbridge Kids in '16 Found Washington's Cannonball Hoard

Jean Guthrie Knowles writes of a charming Bronx that is hard to believe in, but which certainly existed not many years ago.

She writes: "Before World War I, my father and mother looked for property in the Kingsbridge section. There they found few houses, but much woodlands, narrow dirt roads and green fields and, to their pleasant surprise, maples, elms, oaks and some evergreens. They came to Giles Place, named for the family who had owned the area, once the site of a Revolutionary fort, and decided to buy a part of the estate. Trees and shrubs must have been important to the Giles family, for mother and father found they had had fallen heir to lovely varieties of plant life: the European purple beech, several kinds of elms, Osage orange trees, snowball bushes, hydrangeas, smoke trees and lilac and rose bushes. We children fell heir to something even more exciting.

"It was during the period of World War I that the families in that area became historians. It happened one day in 1915 when my brother and I were playing (war) with our playmates and decided to dig trenches. A likely spot was an open field off Sedgwick Ave., and we dug and dug, using shovels, picks and trowels borrowed from the respective family cellars. Soon we hit something very solid — not rock, but iron. It was a huge cannon ball. Another one turned up, and another. The pile grew: all sizes of balls, some barshots and a few chainshots. That evening we told our parents. So did our friends.

"The adults gathered to take a look and, as interest grew, soon everyone was rolling the heavy cannon balls down Giles Place. The news spread and finally it reached historians and people in authority. It was ascertained the cannon balls were some buried by General George Washington when he left Fort Independence to go north. They were several hundred in number and some ended up in private homes. The bulk, however, were gathered together and in time were distributed to various museums, such as the New-York Historical Society, the Jumel Mansion, the Dyckman House and the Van Cortlandt Mansion.

"In honor of the (find) the Park Department established a small park near the spot and it was an event of great neighborhood importance when the dedication day was set. Lawns were mowed and paths scraped. A small grandstand was built for the occasion, a suitable tablet was placed on the gatepost and a flagpole was set up inside the park.

"It was Saturday, May 6, 1916, and there were soldiers, and a band, and dignitaries and speeches, and patriotic songs. We children had a definite role in the program. We all were introduced and one of us told the story of the find. Another unveiled the tablet and still another opened the gate. One child helped a soldier raise the flag—a large one that almost carried the youngster up in the sky when it was caught by a gust of wind.

"The event was even printed in the downtown newspapers, and there were proud parents in Kingsbridge that night."

Jerome Park Race Track Gave Tone, Excitement to Old Bronx

A large oil painting, done in black and white, hanging in the New York Athletic Clubhouse, Manhattan, holds a good deal of historical interest for Bronxites. Neglected for years and hidden in an obscure corner, it was discovered by a member of the Club's art committee and carefully examined. It was a race track scene, and over the arch of the entrance gate was found the name "Jerome Park." The painting was executed around 1885 by an artist named E. Sanguinette, but who gave the picture to the New York Athletic Club and when, is not now known.

The founder of the Park was Leonard W. Jerome who sought to revive racing, which had been halted during the Civil War. He purchased the Bathgate Estate, located in Fordham, and with the aid of other rich men, organized the Jerome Park Club. The race track was regarded as the "Daddy of Horse Racing in the United States" when it held its first meet in September 1866.

The club had a membership of 1300 and the first president was August Belmont. Other members were William Vanderbilt, James Gordon Bennett and Francis Morris, who later was connected with Morris Park Racetrack.

The club house was noted for its spacious dining room and magnificent ballroom. The track itself was of the loop design, and any member who had a stud and raced his horses was especially esteemed. In the winter, sleighing parties came up from the city; trapshooting and skating were also enjoyed, and in later years, polo became the rage.

Jerome Park flourished until 1894, when the Club held its last meet and disbanded, ending a colorful chapter in Bronx history. The site is now occupied by Jerome Park reservoir, and nothing remains to remind Bronxites of its existence except the name Jerome Ave., and the oil painting in the New York Athletic Clubhouse. Some people say Minerva Pl. next to the reservoir, was named to recall a statue of that Roman goddess where she once graced the lawn of Jerome Park.

Lorillard Bros. Advertised Snuff And Segars 'way Back in 1787

We tend to think of advertising as a fairly recent craft until we learn that the Lorillard brothers—who established a snuff mill on the Bronx River—are credited with using the earliest known advertising campaign. Their father had had a tobacco shop "near the Gaol" in Colonial New York but during the occupation by the British army, he was slain in a quarrel with Hessian soldiers. The widow and her two young sons, George and Pierre (Peter) then moved to the comparative wilds along the Bronx River in 1792 and there built a home and mill. "That never failing stream, Bronck river" as they called it, turned the wheels of their snuff mill, and business flourished.

The brothers Lorillard advertised their chewing tobacco, snuff and "segars" by printing broadsides and mailing them to every postmaster in the United States, for they knew post offices were usually in general stores—the centers of community life. Hundreds of postmasters handled Lorillard sales, with profit to themselves. This was 'way back in 1787 and the advertisement featured an Indian smoking a long clay pipe as he leaned against a hogshead marked "Best Virginia."

Cigarettes were unknown at that time, so the names of the snuffs and "chaws" are completely strange to us, today: common kitefoot, hogtail, pigtail, ladies twist, Maccuba snuff and Irish high toast.

After the Civil War, the firm moved to New Jersey where, incidentally, it became the first company to introduce an industrial baby sitting service when it hired (in 1885) sitters for children of their women workers.

The stone mill on the Bronx River fell into disuse, presenting a melancholy picture to visitors from nearby Botanical Garden. In the 1950s, however, the P. Lorillard Company financed the restoration of the snuff mill so that today it constitutes an attractive historical landmark, as well as a restaurant and meeting place for us latterday Bronxites.

Stagecoaches Rumbled Over Old Bronx Roads

Stagecoaches were not used exclusively in the Far West, but were part and parcel of life in the Old Bronx, a century ago.

A twice-daily stagecoach system connected West Farms with Morrisania, from where the commuter could board a steamer bound for Peck Slip. In 1856, the *Westchester County Journal* carried the following notice to its readers of Fordham, Tremont, Melrose and Morrisania:

"New Stage Route—Lewis' Line of Stages, to connect with the Steamer 'Slyvan Shore' will on and after April 27, 1856, run as follows: Leave West Farms for Harlem, 9:30 A.M., 1:40 P.M. via Boston Road Seventh Street (E. 169th St.) Fordham Avenue (3rd Avenue)."

A stagecoach timetable, provided by reader Joseph Duffy, of the Bronx Old Timers, sets forth the running times of the Union Stage Association in 1859, signed by John Murphy, of Tremont, secretary.

The timetable lists coaches connecting Tremont and Harlem, where travelers embarked on the New York boats, at 8c per trip, 16 trips for one dollar. The first trip to Harlem was at 5:15 a.m., and 11 trips were scheduled to 6:15 p.m. Return trips to Tremont were made when the New York boats docked at Harlem.

Stage service also was provided from Fordham to Harlem, three times daily. The trip between Fordham and Tremont was 3c.

A note at the bottom of the timetable read: "Waiting rooms will be found at the office of the [Union Stage] Association, Sutton's Hotel, near the Railroad Depot, Tremont, and at Mrs. Shay's Newspaper Depot, Fordham."

Valentine-Varian House
Survived 1777 Warfare

One of the few pre-Revolutionary houses left in The Bronx can be seen on Bainbridge Avenue and E. 208th St., adjoining Reservoir Oval. Called the Valentine-Varian House, it stands alongside what was once the old Boston Road, for this path led from Spuyten Duyvil eastward to the Long Island shore and on up to Boston.

It was sometime around 1750 that the Valentines built this fieldstone cottage and cleared the land for farming. A map of the lands of Fordham Manor was made by Samuel Willis, a surveyor, and it clearly shows a house and two buildings at that location. The map was dated 1756. The first written mention was in a litigation between Peter Valentine and the Dutch Reformed Church that inherited the ownership from John Archer, founder of Fordham.

After the start of the Revolutionary War, Washington retreated to White Plains. The house was occupied by Hessian and British forces into 1777, but then General Heath with 250 patriots came up the valley (Mosholu) and past Fort Independence (Sedgwick Ave.) and captured the house and some of the troopers. A pitched battle took place around the house, but it miraculously escaped destruction.

In 1791, some 260 acres were sold to Isaac Varian. This tract included the Jerome Park Reservoir and up to the Bronx River, and cost $7,500. One grandson of Isaac Varian became the Mayor of New York from 1839 to 1841.

In 1905, the property was sold at auction and it passed to the Beller family. A son, William C. Beller, donated the house to The Bronx County Historical Society in 1965, and today it is the Museum of Bronx History.

Old Jesuit Cemetery at Fordham One of Dozen Small Ones in Boro

Ask any Bronxite what cemeteries there are in his native Borough and he will name St. Raymond's and Woodlawn Cemeteries, forgetting that there are at least 12 more "God's Acres" tucked away here and there, behind churches, in public parks and on islands.

One is a Jesuit cemetery on the grounds of Fordham University in a little square surrounded by a privet hedge, but no burials have been held there for more than half a century. Originally Fordham University began existence as St. John's College, back in June 1841, by Bishop Hughes, under the direction of Jesuits who had come from Kentucky at his invitation.

In those far off days, the grounds of St. John's stretched from what is now Webster Ave. eastward to include today's Botanical Garden and Bronx Park; and in a wooded grove in the vicinity of present day Southern Boulevard, a small cemetery was located. Here, not only were the Jesuits who died at St. John's, but all those of the other Jesuit homes in the metropolitan district were buried.

In 1889 the property beyond the Boulevard was sold to the Parks Department, and the little cemetery was moved to its present location next to the auditorium and contiguous to the Church. The last Jesuit buried there was the Reverend William Pardow, S.J. who died in 1909.

Section 8

FIELDSTON, KINGSBRIDGE HEIGHTS, RIVERDALE, SPUYTEN DUYVIL

View from the Hudson River in the 1880s of the College of Mount St. Vincent. Fonthill Castle is located on the right, the administration building is in the center. (The Bronx County Historical Society Research Library)

Spuyten Duyvil on October 1, 1928 looking west toward proposed bridge site. The railroad swing bridge at the water level is in the center background. The waterway is the Harlem River ship canal. The peninsula in the center was the site of the Johnson Iron Foundry. (The Bronx County Historical Society Research Library)

Broadway at Mosholu Avenue in 1899. The Riverdale Inn on Broadway faced Van Cortlandt Park. This was a classic example of a roadhouse that was first accessible only to diners who arrived by horse and carriage, but then became more democratic when the trolleycar system was installed on upper Broadway. The rails were laid out on opposite sides of the road. (The Bronx County Historical Society Research Library) 138

Mounted Fire Chief
Faced Perils of Irate Bulls
as Well as Flames

The Westchester District, north of the Harlem River and west of the Bronx River, was annexed to the City of New York in 1874, and the Tenth Fire Battalion, with eight paid companies, was organized to replace the volunteer firemen in the towns of Morrisania, West Farms and Kingsbridge.

According to FDNY Historian Clarence Meek, the General Order organizing the Tenth Battalion specified that "the Commander shall be mounted." This command was obeyed, for an early account mentions "the fast grey horse used by the Chief" and a budget item reads: "feed for one horse."

An entry in one of the journals of 1870 records: "an accident to the Chief of 10th Battalion—while crossing field to make short cut, responding to call from Spuyten Duyvel [Duyvil] Village." The injuries to the Chief were caused by being chased by a bull who evidently resented a horseman cutting across his pasture!

By the 1890s, the officers graduated from saddle horses to lightweight carriages, but Chief Croker, whose name is well known to all firemen, purchased his own shiny black Locomobile and made headlines in 1901 by runs to fires in his newfangled horseless buggy. However, he played it safe by keeping his horse and rig in service to transport him whenever his Black Ghost developed motor trouble.

Today, whenever a bright red Fire Chief's car speeds past, this writer invariably thinks of the long departed Chief in helmet and uniform madly galloping down a meadow in Spuyten Duyvil Village, pursued by an irate bull.

Spuyten Duyvil Creek Rich in Ancient Lore

Spuyten Duyvil Creek has figured in Bronx history ever since the days of the Indians who had to cross it to reach the island of Manna-hatin.

The creek was a swift and torturous one, with a current that was affected by the ebb and flow of both the Harlem and Hudson rivers. Because of this double tide, the Indians called the region "Paparinemo" (place of false starts, or double tide) and the name was attached to the creek. Some historians insist the true name is "Muscoota" (where the cattails grow). The Dutch name of Spuyten Duyvil was superimposed on the winding creek by the early settlers, for a 1653 deed mentions "Papparinemin, byde onse Speit den duyvil gesaght" (by us, called Speit den Duyvil).

The true meaning of the Dutch name is vague. Popular legend has it that a messenger was dispatched from Fort Amsterdam to the Bronx mainland for reinforcements, but high tides and treacherous current swept him away and he lost his life. It was the Spite of the Devil that prevented the messenger from completing his mission.

More likely is a 1647 reference to a gushing fountain of fresh water that poured into the creek. The Hollanders called it the Devil's Spout "Spuit den Duyvil." This Dutch name gave the British army engineers much trouble, for on their military maps of 1777 and 1778 the name was rendered into Spike & Devil, and also Spiten Divil. The Hessians were no better: in the German diary of Lt. Von Krafft he referred to "Spakent Heill!"

Later, the name was anglicized to Spitting Devil and, sometimes, Spouting Devil. It was spanned by the King's Bridge (W. 230th St. and Kingsbridge Ave.) and for the next century the little stream carried the alternate name of Kingsbridge Creek.

River traffic was hampered by the winding creek, so in 1895 the Harlem River Ship Canal was cut through to eliminate the curves and shallow water. After that, there was little or no traffic on the creek. In 1897, an excursion boat, "The Black Bird" did venture up Spuyten Duyvil Creek from the Hudson River to pick up a party of picnickers from St. Stephen's Methodist Church, but spent most of the day trying to turn about and free itself.

The creek's days were numbered, and by 1916 it and the historic

King's Bridge that spanned it were buried under tons of fill to bring the area up to city grade. Today, all traces of the old waterway have disappeared under Broadway and W. 230th St., but on the West side of Marble Hill there is still evident the dried-up channel of what was once Spuyten Duyvil Creek.

Bronx's Fort Independence Didn't Live Up to Name

Two hundred years ago three divisions of American troops converged on Fort Independence (Giles Pl.) which had been captured by the British. One column advanced down the Albany Post Road from Yonkers, another marched down from New Rochelle and the last division tramped in from Scarsdale, bypassing the Valentine farmhouse on today's Bainbridge Avenue.

In the chilly dawn, mounted British sentries spotted this last column on Gun Hill Road and raised the alarm. The small Redcoat garrison in the Valentine farmhouse (now The Bronx County Historical Society's Museum of Bronx History) fled westward to Fort Independence, alerting their Negro allies in the Negro Fort (atop today's St. George's Crescent, near the Concourse).

General Heath, in charge of the American troops, advanced to Kingsbridge and demanded the surrender of Fort Independence. Hessians and Queen's Rangers, supplemented by the garrisons from the Negro Fort and the Valentine farmhouse, refused, and Heath opened fire with field pieces (guns on wheels) that had been hauled down from Westchester. The cannonading proved ineffectual, especially when a hidden cannon began to rake the Americans who tried to storm the fort from the south.

This attempt to recapture the important fort failed, and one of Washington's thorniest problems remained. Fort Independence, built by the Americans and named by them, stayed in British hands for the next three years, but the occupying forces called it simply Fort No. 4 and so it appears on their field maps. Today, a visit to Giles Place and nearby Cannon Place will give the visitor a good idea of the strategic importance of the fort that once dominated Kingsbridge.

"Henry Clay" Steamboat Disaster of '52 Preceded "Slocum" Tragedy

The "General Slocum" steamship disaster which took place off the Bronx shoreline in 1904 is conceded to have been one of the worst marine catastrophes of the 20th century. The "Henry Clay" steamboat fire that also occurred along the Bronx shoreline on July 28, 1852, gives our Borough the doubtful distinction of having one of the worst disasters of the 19th century as well.

Carl Carmer, in his book *The Hudson* describes the event.

Up to that time, the Hudson River, from Albany down to New York, had been a race-course, as rival steamboat lines urged their captains and crews to greater speed in an effort to capture the cargo and passenger trade. This particular summer's day it was evident that the "Armenia" officers meant to reach New York before their arch-rivals on the "Henry Clay." The latter ship had cost $38,000 to construct, and its 206 feet length was designed for speed. More than 300 passengers had come aboard, and they lined the rails as the two ships raced downriver, trailing thick clouds of smoke and showers of sparks. Both ships quivered from the enormous thrust of the paddle-wheels, and a few of the passengers grew alarmed and begged the captains to slow down.

Just below Yonkers, the "Henry Clay's" boilers blew up and the pilot swung the blazing ship to the east bank. It plowed up on the shore of a Riverdale estate, knocking over its smokestacks and throwing the passengers about like tenpins. A solid sheet of flame roared to the stern, where hundreds of people were trapped. Scores jumped over the side and drowned. Others tried to fight their way forward to reach the bow, and perished in the flames.

The "Armenia" stood by, and her lifeboats sped to the rescue. On shore, a New York Central train was halted on the embankment and the passengers hurried from the coaches and assisted in the rescue work. Even a Newfoundland dog named Neptune was seen, bearing a child ashore.

Not all was noble and heroic: river pirates were seen rowing through the floating debris, robbing helpless drowning victims and, later, other small craft carrying plunderers appeared on the scene. The ship burned fiercely so that by nightfall, only the bow was left, burning slowly "like a warning beacon" while the dead were laid in rows along the shoreline. More than 80 corpses were counted by the stunned survivors.

Charges of criminal murder against the owners and the officers of the "Henry Clay" were set aside by Judge Edmonds in Westchester County (of which Riverdale was then a part) and the defendants were acquitted.

But a few months later the Steamboat Inspection Act finally put an end to steamboat racing on the Hudson River.

Stature Added to Henry Hudson Statue by Sculptor Karl Bitter

There are many statues in our Borough familiar to generations of Bronxites, and most of them have interesting histories.

One of the better known is that of Heinrich Heine at E. 163rd St. and Grand Concourse. Another is the World War I "Doughboy" at the top of Edward L. Grant Highway. On Mosholu Parkway, there is a grouping of soldier statues at Hull Ave.

The "Old Soldier" that stands in the Bronx River at Gun Hill Rd., is matched by the Civil War sentry in West Farms Cemetery, and his brother-in-arms atop the Oliver Tilden Post shaft in Woodlawn Cemetery. Another statue in the latter cemetery is the Arctic explorer in parka and boots that guards the tomb of George Washington DeLong. Lesser known is the statue of Archbishop Hughes on the Fordham University grounds.

These are all overshadowed by the 16 foot statue of Henry Hudson which stands on a Doric column, 100 feet in height, at Spuyten Duyvil, where he can be seen from New Jersey and from many parts of the West Bronx as well. Created by Karl Bitter, the statue depicts in seafaring costume, Hudson seemingly braced against a strong wind. Although Henry Hudson Park was dedicated in 1909, the statue was not hoisted to its lofty stand until the 1930s.

This writer once asked Karl Bitter which man had served as a model for the explorer. Three men, said the sculptor, posed for the statue and they were all over six feet tall, although research indicated Hudson had been a stocky man below five feet, six inches. This was done so that the image would be in better proportion to the shaft, and its height from the ground.

The first model was the janitor of the studio, who obligingly stood for the preliminary casting. His name Mr. Bitter had long since forgotten, nor did he recall the name of the college athlete who took the janitor's place. Another collegian posed for the finished product and he, too, has been anonymous these 30 years.

Most, if not all the men who posed for the poets, soldiers, clergymen and explorers must have died long ago, but their graven images stare out over the Bronx scene in eternal stone.

Claflin Ave. in W. Bronx
Named for Quaker Tycoon

Occasionally a Bronxite realizes he has been living on a street for years without the faintest idea why it was given its name. A neighborhood librarian might have the answer, or an oldtimer may pass on some folklore but, in the main, the momentary curiosity dies off without satisfaction.

Of sterner stuff is young Harvey Pearlmutter who writes: "My father says our street is named after a famous man, but my teacher never heard of him. The man in the drugstore is sure it was named for a woman who ran for President. We live on Claflin Avenue."

Claflin Avenue in the West Bronx indeed was named after a famous man who, although a Brooklyn resident of a century ago, maintained a summer estate above Kingsbridge Road when that region was a peaceful countryside. It was subdivided and sold in 1903, and the City laid out the avenue in 1922 that was named for the former owner.

Horace B. Claflin established a dry goods business in 1843 and, after the Civil War, became the city's largest wholesaler. His portrait hangs in the Chamber of Commerce of the State of New York at 65 Liberty St. and is one of the very few that is not bareheaded. Quakers, he said, bared their head to no man. However, when he died, his widow hastened to the painter and insisted the hat be painted out and put in his left hand. This was done.

A decade later, his son John, also a member of the Chamber of Commerce, commissioned another painter to copy the original, but with a hat firmly restored to his head! Today, both portraits (in different rooms) can be seen.

The son, John, was an extensive traveller, for in 1877, with a single companion, he crossed the South American continent at its widest—that is, from Peru on the Pacific coast east through the Amazon jungle of Brazil to the Atlantic Ocean.

"The man in the drugstore" doubtlessly knew of two sisters named Victoria and Tennessee Claflin who were sponsored by Commodore Vanderbilt when they opened a Wall St. brokerage house. In 1872 Victoria Claflin Woodhull was a presidential candidate of the Equal Rights Party. The women were daughters of a Buckman Claflin of Ohio, and not related to the Quakers.

That Unlucky Friday the 13th When 8 Were Killed in Crash

One January afternoon in 1882, the crack Atlantic Express left Albany bound for New York. Due to a snowstorm, it was late and the engineer was making up for lost time. There were 13 cars in the train, six of them sumptuous parlor cars and these were occupied by some 70 politicians celebrating the adjournment of the State Legislature. Speeches, songs and cheery conversation accompanied the wining and dining, and everyone was in a jovial mood as the Express thundered into Riverdale.

That it was Friday the 13th and there were 13 cars had no special import at the moment, but later on, the coincidence was highlighted by the fact that another train, the Tarrytown Express, was exactly 13 minutes behind the Atlantic Express.

As the train emerged from the Spuyten Duyvil cut, a tipsy passenger apparently pulled the emergency cord, and the double-header screeched to a halt. A doubleheader was a term denoting that two locomotives, in tandem, were hauling the train. Trainmen could find no danger, but the brakebar, connecting the two locomotives, had broken and the air cylinders were inoperative. Recharging the cylinders would take at least 15 minutes so the conductor ordered a brakeman, with two signal lanterns, back to the cut to stop the oncoming train.

The Rev. William Tieck, Bronx Historian, records the fact in his book, *Riverdale, Kingsbridge and Spuyten Duyvil*, that the brakeman did not go far enough to flag down the Tarrytown Express in time, but had loitered to watch the train crew at work. The Tarrytown Express sped out of the cut before the engineer could slam on the brakes, and his engine plowed into the stalled train in an explosion of wooden cars, flying glass, steam, passengers and baggage. The crash reverberated down the Harlem River valley, and the fiery glare startled the inhabitants of Kingsbridge. They hurried to the scene where, for lack of water, they rolled huge snowballs down to the tracks to fling them on the flames. Eight people died, and scores were injured.

In the later court proceedings, it developed that the brakeman was unfamiliar with the manual of procedures. He was illiterate, but claimed his wife read the rule book to him, from time to time! Both the brakeman and the conductor were indicted for manslaughter in the fourth degree, but later were exonorated. History records eight people died, but local lore had it 13, to conform to the date and the number of cars.

Kingsbridge to Lose Landmark, Ahneman & Younkheere Building

Kingsbridge lost one of its landmarks recently when the firm of Ahneman & Younkheere closed its doors and ended a 75 year lumber and hardware business.

Back in the more leisurely days of coaches, mansions and gaslight, a carpenter named Charles Ahneman bought land in rural Kingsbridge and began to build a house. A cabinetmaker from Detroit, Disry Younkheere, volunteered to help him, and their sparetime work soon attracted the attention of some neighbors. The two young men soon found themselves with contracts to erect homes in nearby Spuyten Duyvil and Riverdale and so, in 1892, the firm of Ahneman & Younkheere was established.

Their modest carpenter shop on Broadway and 236th St. soon became too small, so in 1905 the building was built on Bailey Ave. From time to time, it, too, was expanded. One addition, still on the spot, once served as a stable of the old Jerome Park Race Track and on its wooden side can be seen the dim lettering: Lager Beer 5 Cents.

The lifelong partnership came to an end when Charles Ahneman died in 1924. Disry Younkheere died in 1938, but sons of both men had grown up in the business and took over the management. The decline of private houses in the community and a desire to retire led the second generation Ahnemans and Younkheeres to close down.

The Kingsbridge residents miss the bulletin board and window displays, for George Younkheere continually displayed maps, Indian relics, Revolutionary cannonballs and 19th century bric-a-brac.

Another diversion was the exhibition of misspelled envelopes addressed to: Adam & Young Cheese, Ahenman & You Cheers, and even Akueimian & Yaiurkhiew!

The buildings and the land have been sold to a large real estate operator, and soon a tall apartment building will stand where once Disry Younkheere parked his bicycle and Charles Ahneman cranked up his model T.

Valentine Family, Father Zeiser Both Figure in History of Bronx

The Valentine family with its numerous branches has always been prominent in the history of Fordham, but Valentine Ave. is the sole reminder of this well-known family. Valentine's Hill, Valentine's Spring and Valentine's Brook exist now only in old dusty records and scarcely anyone knows where they once were.

Valentine's Brook originated west of St. James' Park, north of Fordham Road and flowed westward into the Harlem River. The northern rim of Devoe Park shows the curve of this ancient waterway, accounting for the graceful arc of what was W. 188th St. Today, this street is known as Father Zeiser Pl. and honors a priest of nearby St. Nicholas of Tolentine Church.

Blasius Zeiser was born in Mauch Chunk, Pennsylvania, in 1878, attended Villanova College and then decided to enter the Priesthood. He became a member of the Augustinian Order in 1903 and was ordained four years later. (No need to look for Mauch Chunk on a map, for the name has since been changed to Jim Thorpe, Penn.!)

The young priest was assigned to St. Nicholas of Tolentine parish from 1908 to 1912 as assistant to the pastor, but after a short sojourn in Philadelphia, returned to St. Nicholas to serve as pastor. Father Zeiser remained as pastor from 1917 to 1946 and during those three decades built the present "Cathedral of the Bronx" on the corner of Fordham Rd. and University Ave. Through his efforts, the necessary sections of the parochial grammar school were added, and a high school department for boys and girls was opened.

He pioneered in dramatics, choral activities, socials and favored athletics, and thus was brought into close personal contact with his parishioners. As he grew older, they grew older and a mutual reverence developed, so that he became one of the legends of Fordham Heights.

In 1951, Father Zeiser returned to Villanova, where he died. He was so beloved, it took two buses to transport mourners from the Bronx to Pennsylvania for his funeral. After his death there developed a grass roots demand for some official recognition of his work, and the renaming of W. 188th St. to Father Zeiser Pl. was the result.

This writer is indebted to Father Hurley of St. Nicholas of Tolentine Church for the foregoing biography.

Hudson Memorial Bridge
Plan of '03
Just Didn't Get Across

Have you ever heard of the Hudson Memorial Bridge? No? It was a Manhattan-to-the-Bronx span, designed in 1903 by a bridge engineer named Alfred Pancoast Boller. Scheduled to be finished to coincide with the Hudson Tercentennial Celebration of 1909, marking the 300th anniversary of Henry Hudson's arrival in the New World, the bridge was planned to pass over the Harlem River at Spuyten Duyvil, where Hudson's ship, "Half Moon," had anchored.

Boller planned the approaches to be a series of graceful Roman arches leading to a steel arch over the river, and his sketches so captivated the City administration that one million dollars were funded to further the project. It was such a certainty the bridge would be built that picture postcards of the span were printed by the thousands from Boller's sketches. Today, few such postcards exist, and these are regarded as collectors' items — for the bridge was never built. The Art Commission vetoed the concept without publicly stating its objection, although editorials of the day speculated that majestic Roman archways were inappropriate in such a forested area. In any event, the Boller plan died.

It was not until the 1930s that a bridge was built from Spuyten Duyvil to the Bronx and was called the Henry Hudson Bridge. The architect, David Steinman, who referred to himself as "a Lower East Side boy," stipulated the bridge be painted a dark green to harmonize with the woodlands of Inwood and Riverdale, but in the ensuing years, aluminum paint has been used.

In engineering circles, the names of Steinman and Boller are honored ones, but by some quirk, it was Boller who has had his name affixed to a Bronx Avenue — an Eastcheser street that is quite distant from the bridges he did build.

Riverdale "Jumbo's Corner" So Called for Innkeeper

Whenever this writer sees circus posters appear in the Bronx to herald the approach of Spring, he invariably thinks of Jumbo, the out-sized African elephant immortalized by P. T. Barnum, back in 1882. So widely publicized by the newsmen of the day was this giant pachyderm that the very name "Jumbo" became a synonym for anything larger-than-life, and as a result the word has become part and parcel of the English language.

Why W. 258th St. and Riverdale Ave. once carried the nickname of "Jumbo's Corner" has plagued this amateur historian for many years, nor could he find any connection with that particular intersection and P. T. Barnum, or even its use as a seasonal circus lot. Then, as so often is the case, the solution came about through a chance remark and an old photograph.

The old photograph showed an outing of the Anvil Club sometime around 1900, and one of the mustached gentlemen was identified as Charlie Zorn "the Clambake King." At his shoulder was an immensely fat man named William Olms, but better known as "Jumbo." This good-natured elephant of a man, an Alsatian by birth, was the proprietor of the Riverdale Inn and its location was found to coincide with Jumbo's Corner. So well known was Mr. Olms that local citizenry did not even refer to his tavern as the Riverdale Inn, but as Jumbo's Hotel and although the Inn has since changed names, the nickname of its location remained for many years afterward.

The Anvil Club was a fraternal organization of Westchester County farriers, but gradually the membership rules were relaxed to admit blacksmiths, too. Next, horse trainers, carriage makers and racetrack officials gained admittance. Then politicians, hotel keepers and some wealthy squires were given honorary membership in the club until eventually the charter members were outnumbered by their friends; but, judging from the merry faces and contented poses of the gathering, the good times were democratically shared. So, thanks to the old photograph, the mystery of Jumbo's Corner was solved!

Buffalo Once Roamed Home At Van Cortlandt Park, 1907

Following the quiz on "The Bronx that was," several readers inquired about the herd of buffalo that once grazed in Van Cortlandt Park. *Animal Kingdom*, official publication of the Bronx Zoo, has had articles about the animals and some old photographs show the bisons (their real designation) peacefully feeding in the vicinity of Vault Hill.

Around the turn of the century, buffalo were rapidly disappearing as a result of indiscriminate slaughter by hunters. Dr. William Hornaday, a director of the Bronx Zoo, had foreseen the eventual consequences, and had managed to acquire a few buffalo, which he pastured in Bronx Park. Calves were born the following year, and the herd slowly increased while, out in the Far West, the wild buffalo were almost extinct. Finally, Congress established a reservation in the Wichita Mountains of Oklahoma, but the problem was to acquire enough buffalo to keep the breed alive.

By this time (1907) the Bronx herd had increased so much they exceeded the Zoo range, so seven bulls and eight cows were transferred to Van Cortlandt Park, preparatory to being shipped off to the Oklahoma reserve. In October of the same year, the herd was sent West — a six-day trip by cattle cars — accompanied by some Oklahoma cowhands and two employees of the Bronx Zoo named H.R. Mitchell and Edwin Sanborn. That was over 60 years ago, so there are some 10 generations of western bison descended from the Bronx herd. They are roaming the plains from Montana to Texas, from the Rockies to the Mississippi, thanks to the foresight of Dr. Hornaday, whose name lives on in Hornaday Place.

Two Bronxites, now deceased, often told this writer of the "thundering herd" that awed the boys of Kingsbridge and Woodlawn Heights, and gave them the urge to emulate Buffalo Bill.

Mt. St. Vincent College Once Actor's Estate

At the extreme northwestern corner of the Bronx is Mount St. Vincent, a Catholic college staffed by the Sisters of Charity of St. Vincent de Paul. The grounds and the impressive granite tower had belonged, in the 1850's, to the wealthy actor Edwin Forrest who once described his home overlooking the Hudson River as "a make-believe English Cathedral looking like a church turned into a drawing-room by a crazy bishop."

He and his wife, Catherine, took as their model an 18th century castle in England known variously as Fountell, Fontel and finally Fonthill "because of the abundant springs that gushed from the side of its hills." Forrest's property, on the slopes of today's Riverdale, also was enhanced by a few springs so that he adopted both the architecture and the name.

On the Fourth of July, Fonthill was an ideal spot for Forrest's observance of the holiday. Atop the high tower, which was described as Norman-Gothic, his flag caught the warm winds that swept up from the valley, and proclaimed that the master of the estate was asserting his patriotism.

Originally, Forrest intended his mansion and estate to become a home for "decayed and superannuated actors and actresses of American birth" when he and his wife died. However, legal problems ensued, and the actor eventually sold most of the property to Archbishop Hughes. This eminent churchman acquired the picturesque spot for the Sisters of Charity, and it has remained in their hands for over a century.

One of Tallest Bronx Landmarks Isn't Visible from This Borough

One of the tallest landmarks of the Bronx can only be seen from Manhattan. A gigantic letter C, painted on the rocky face of Spuyten Duyvil Hill, it faces out over the Harlem River and so cannot be seen from any point in the Bronx; so that it is Manhattanites and out-of-town visitors who ride the round-Manhattan sightseeing boats who see this 60-foot high letter.

The story of how and why it was painted has already collected variations even though the Big C is of very modern vintage. The most common tale is that it was painted in a single night by daring collegians of Columbia University. This writer cannot vouch for the truth of the single night's work, but a Kingsbridge merchant, George Younkheere, did sell an uncommon amount of blue paint to Columbia undergraduates.

The letter was painted in near-professional dimensions, giving rise to the idea that it was the assignment of an engineering class. The students surveyed the rocky face from their campus in Manhattan designed their C on drawing boards and then, with the aid of long ladders and a bo'sn's chair, proceeded to finish their assignment.

Although its paint has faded somewhat, the Big C will remain there for many years to come, intriguing the passing mariners and adding its bit to Bronx folklore.

Shad Fishing Started
With Early Dutch

Each year the number of shad fishermen on the Hudson River diminishes, but along the shoreline above Spuyten Duyvil one can still see their nets, anchored to poles, during the month of March.

The early Dutch settlers had a quaint custom regarding the fish that swam into our waters at regular times of the year: they gave numbers to each kind of fish in the order they made their annual appearance. So, the fish we know as the shad was called "elft" (11th) by the Dutch and they were 11th to appear in the Hudson River from the ocean.

If we can believe the legends, these fish always arrived on the 11th of March, off Sandy Hook. Among the fishermen, it was their custom to present the first shad of the season to the Governor, and it was "planked" to his taste: the fish was split and fastened to a piece of birchbark and cooked, Indian fashion, over glowing embers. Then, still on its birch plank, it was served at the Governor's table. Towards the end of March, the 12th fish arrived — the sea bass. The Dutch called it "der twaelft" not only because it followed the shad, but also because of its stripes, six on each side.

A missionary who visited our city in 1679 reported: "The waters of the Sound, the Harlem and the Hudson and of the numerous brooks and streams supplied the settlers with fish; so that of food there was an abundance, even upon the tables of the poorest; while upon the tables of the well-to-do there was such a variety and profusion as to arouse comment of such Europeans as visited the colony."

An official of the Dutch West India Company was astounded at the amount of fish caught in the rivers, and composed a long poem which he sent back to the authorities in Amsterdam. In it occur these lines:

> "Ook Elft, en Twaelft niet schaars
> Maar overvloedig."
> or
> Also 11th (shad) and 12th (bass)
> Not scarce, but in overflow.

If our metropolitan waters receive the benefits of a long range sewage disposal system, perhaps those lines written so long ago will become a reality once again.

Riverdale's Arrowhead Inn Drew Cafe Society of 1930s

Riverdale, in the 1920s and 1930s, was a region of wooded estates, a few small settlements and two or three prestigious roadhouses. Well known to the wealthier set was Ben Riley's Arrowhead Inn, high above the Hudson River, with a stunning view of that historic waterway and the New Jersey Palisades.

One story is that Indian arrowheads had been found on the site when the land was cleared for construction of the inn, and that tale is as good as any.

Its isolation gave the Arrowhead Inn an exclusive atmosphere, and it was a favorite spot for Broadway luminaries and high society, especially since the orchestras were top-notch groups and Ben Riley was a discerning host who carefully screened his guests. Summer nights were enhanced by an outdoor dance floor that was cooled by the breezes from the Hudson Valley—and if Prohibition was in effect banning the sale and consumption of beers, wines and liquors, somehow the Arrowhead Inn was in a world of its own.

Unfortunately the Arrowhead Inn suffered a disastrous fire almost 40 years ago and was never rebuilt—and Ben Riley, debonair host and gourmet, died in the fire.

Ploughman's Bush Really Exists — But There Wasn't Any Plough

If readers could snort in disbelief, by mail, then it would be possible to register their skepticism that such a place as Ploughman's Bush exists in the Bronx. Short of leading a safari of Doubting Thomases over to the Hudson River in the Riverdale sector, this writer will merely pinpoint the settlement to the satisfaction of taxi drivers, delivery men and those casually interested in Bronx street names.

Riverdale, once devoted solely to vast estates and fine mansions, has been gradually becoming urbanized and invaded by skyscraping apartment houses. Still, quite a few estates exist with only here and there a small tract given over to subdivisions. Such an area is Dodgewood, part of the Dodge estate, a community of winding lanes and prosperous homes.

Alongside this secluded section is an even smaller, more rustic settlement of a dozen houses called Ploughman's Bush.

It is reached by a short private road, just north of W. 246th St. and Independence Ave., and is identified by a hand-painted sign. It was the property of a Robert M. Field who, around 1930, subdivided his land and gave it this fanciful name. His son stated that it had no historical or family connection, but that Mr. Field Sr. just decided on an odd name.

It is so listed in the Postal Guide and, of course, in the telephone book.

Section 9

CASTLE HILL, CLASON POINT, PARKCHESTER, SOUNDVIEW, UNIONPORT, WESTCHESTER SQUARE

Phil Dietrich's Restaurant & Tavern in 1918. This business was located on Soundview and Gildersleeve Avenues in Clason Point. The sign on the right reads "Greetings to our Mayor Hylan from the Staff of Phil Dietrich." (Seifert Collection, The Bronx County Historical Society Research Library)

Bailor's Hotel located at the former Avenue C and Ludlow Avenue in 1900. The old Hotel is now Joe & Joe Restaurant on Castle Hill Avenue and Bruckner Boulevard. Note the bicycle racks behind the hydrant. (The Bronx County Historical Society Research Library)

Fixing a flat on Ludlow Avenue and Eastern Boulevard in 1921. Eastern Boulevard is now Bruckner Boulevard in the vicinity of Unionport. Photographer, Donald Braithwaite. (The Bronx County Historical Society Research Library)

Indian Craft Used Pugsley Creek, Then Sloops, Now, the Tugboats

Pugsley Creek has always marked the boundary between Cornell's Neck (now Clason Point) and Cromwell's Neck (now Castle Hill Point). This historic old stream was an Indian waterway long before the coming of the white men, and continued in that role for the schooners and sloops of the early settlers. The creek originally reached well inland from the East River almost to the Westchester Turnpike, and was called (in the 1600's) Cromwell's Creek.

During the American Revolution, it was mapped as Wilkins' Creek after the 18th century proprietors of Castle Hill, and at a later date, 1820, the winding stream was called West Creek. The Pugsley family owned large tracts of land, including a portion of what is now Parkchester, and their Cow Neck farm was accessible to water traffic, thanks to the creek. Their farm produce and cattle were taken aboard sloops from a dock once located near present day Lafayette and White Plains Avenues.

Since Civil War days, the creek has carried the name of the Pugsley family, and until recent times was the haunt of muskrats, raccoons and herons. The vast, swamp region was first crossed by Ludlow Ave. (now Bruckner Blvd.) and landfill blotted out the inland reaches of the creek. Next, Lacombe Ave. was laid out athwart the waterway, and tons of landfill covered the creek and Pugsley's dock, all the way back to Bruckner Boulevard.

Today, only a short distance of Pugsley Creek is left for water-borne traffic, but it is the very stretch once used by the Indians to reach their village on Clason Point.

Park Versailles Naming Traced To Influence of Lewis Guerlain

Park Versailles is the name of the neighborhood directly west of Parkchester but it is seldom used in identifying the area. A frequent question is: "How did it ever get that name?"

The principals of the real estate venture being long since dead, it can only be surmised that the evenly laid out avenues, lined with trees, suggested Versailles in France, a park noted for its planned landscapes.

The French influence harked back to 1796 when Lewis Guerlain purchased 174 acres (now part of Parkchester) on which he built an attractive chateau. Guerlain Avenue and Mansion St. are reminders of that period. In later years, the Mapes family, who were related to the Arnows (Arnaux), owned the land and it was during their proprietorship that the land was surveyed, subdivided and sold. At that time the U.S. Ambassador to France was a man named Merrill and this may account for Merrill Place.

The grid pattern of streets might well have influenced the realtors in naming the main street, St. Lawrence Avenue. Frank Wuttge, an avid student of Bronx street-naming patterns, suggests the connection with St. Lawrence himself, a holy man usually depicted holding a miniature gridiron; for it was on such a torture rack that he met a martyr's death.

The French touch is apparent in Theriot Avenue, for Ferdinand Melly Theriot was one of the bankers interested in the venture, and an Albert Theriot bought land in 1893 from the Mapes family. Yet another place in Park Versailles has a French ancestry although the name has figured prominently in Revolutionary history and is classified as an Early American name, and that is "Guion."

Today, the only thing French about Park Versailles would be a shop advertising itself as a French bakery.

Dominick Lynch Name Once Locally Famous

Dominick Lynch is a name connected with early Bronx history for, through him, Clason Point was the scene of the first authenticated Catholic services held in what is now our Borough.

Directly after the American Revolution there is record of the firm, Lynch & Stoughton, merchants, at 41–42 Little Dock St. (now Water St.), and Mr. Lynch lived at No. 16 Broadway. He was a wealthy man and one of the witticisms of his day was that he was the only Irishman ever to bring money to America.

In 1798, when New York suffered from a plague of yellow fever, some 2,000 inhabitants died. The merchants donated money or merchandise to the stricken families, and Dominick Lynch was listed as giving one ox, two pigs, two lambs, 80 chickens and 16 bushels of potatoes. According to another old book on merchants, Dominick Lynch was one of the leading Irishmen of the city, and an officer of the St. Patrick Society from 1790 to 1804.

As was the custom in those days, merchant princes bought lands in the surrounding countryside, there to build estates and summer residences. The western half of Cornell's Neck was purchased by Mr. Lynch, while the eastern side became the property of Isaac Clason. On his side of the peninsula, Mr. Lynch built a handsome stone mansion (vicinity of Seward and Soundview Aves.) with a fine view of the Neck and the Bronx River. Carrara marble graced the mansion, and it was there that the devout Catholic died in 1825, the last rites being administered by Bishop Connolly.

Five years later, his executors sold the land to the Ludlow family, who later sold it to the Schieffelins. Finally the Christian Brothers of the Catholic Faith bought the mansion and property and used it as a school. Then, in 1883 it was changed into the Sacred Heart Academy and still later became the Clason Point Military Academy. Many Bronxites remember the academy, before it was razed for a housing development.

It is interesting to speculate why Isaac Clason's name has lived on to gain official recognition on city maps, and not the name of Dominick Lynch, who shared the Neck with him.

Old Westchester Village Was Home For Some Colorful Sea Captains

Westchester Village (now Westchester Square) was located on the creek of the same name, and the importance of this creek in the life of the old settlement is shown by the number of sea captains who lived there — and many old sea yarns have lived on in the memories of their descendants.

Captain William Bowne took the first ship out of New York after the War of 1812.

Captain Elnathan Hawkins sailed to the Far East in 1824 and brought back the flowering quince. He also transported the first ailanthus tree, which is called the Tree of Heaven.

Then there was Captain Watson Ferris who sailed to California in 1851 with a cargo of shovels, wheelbarrows, boots, overalls, pots and pans for the Forty-Niners. The ship, the "John Stuart," was gone two years for its voyage led around Cape Horn, up to California and out to China. In Panama, Captain Ferris contracted yellow fever and died — and his body was placed in a hogshead of rum. His son took command and continued the voyage, returning to Westchester with a load of California redwood — the first lumber of its kind to be seen in these parts. Captain Ferris' body was perfectly preserved and was interred in the family vault behind Westchester Square.

Another colorful sea captain was Andrew Arthur, a Nantucket skipper who visited Westchester village to see his sister, Mrs. Cornell Ferris. Ashore, he was quite jovial and when he invited three village boys to ship out on a voyage to China, they gladly signed on.

Aboard, Captain Arthur ran his ship with an iron hand and tolerated no friendliness. The village boys visited the captain who asked them what they wanted.

"Oh, just to talk."

"Well, you are beyond Sandy Hook now, and at sea the captain talks to no one. Get below, and don't ever come up here again."

Months later, near Cape Horn, a terrific storm came up and the three boys were huddled together at the rail when the captain came along. Realizing their terror, Captain Arthur remarked "Well, boys, did you ever see a blow like this on Westchester Creek?"

These were the only words he spoke on the entire voyage!

First Boro Catholic Church Was on Bear Swamp Road

The first Catholic church to be built in the Bronx stood at the junction of Walker Ave. and Bear Swamp Road. The parish had already been formed in 1842, so that this Fall the present-day parishoners of St. Raymond's Church are celebrating the 140th anniversary of its founding.

An Italian priest, the Rev. Felix Villanis, had been teaching philosophy and Italian in the Seminary of St. John in Fordham (now Fordham University) and he was assigned by Bishop Hughes to be the first parish priest. From 1842 to 1845 the parishioners had been meeting in a wooden barn on the acre of land purchased by the Bishop, so his first task was to obtain enough contributions to erect a fairsized church. In those three years, the zeal of Father Villanis brought about the church.

By 1898, the original church stood with the present day Church of St. Raymond being built behind it. Later the smaller church was razed. Walker Ave. had become E. Tremont Ave., and the name of Bear Swamp Road changed to Bronxdale Avenue.

Unionport (Parsonage) Rd. Was Site of Black Workers' Church

Near the intersection of Unionport Road and Westchester Avenue, there is a concentration of no fewer than four funeral homes. It is just mere coincidence that an 1868 map of the same junction shows an African Church and Cemetery facing Unionport Road, which then had the alternate name of Parsonage Road.

Speculating who might have been the parishioners of that long-vanished church and who were the occupants of the burial ground, this writer can only think of the Morris family of Throggs Neck, and the diZerega land-owners of what is now Ferry Point Park. Both wealthy families had Black coachmen, household help and horse trainers, and these servants would be most likely to attend services there. Possibly other servants on the Huntington estates (now part of Pelham Bay Park and Throggs Neck) also were the churchgoers.

The Morris family retainers were Blacks from Texas and Louisiana, while the diZerega Blacks were West Indians from the Virgin Islands in particular. Incidentally, the latter are buried in the diZerega family plot in Woodlawn Cemetery.

A later (1872) map shows the same church and cemetery, but sometime in the 33-year gap to 1905 they disappeared. The next map in a 1907 atlas depicted the Charles Koterba wagon repair shop and yard at that location.

Today, the land is occupied by stores and a restaurant on Unionport Road, and nothing remains of the early Black burial ground and house of worship.

Unionport Hotel

This being the traditional month for Oktoberfests, a Unionport landmark comes to mind. Almost a century ago, a squarish frame hotel, topped by a conical tower, stood on what had been called Lowerre's Lane but which had lately been changed to Ave. B. The region was one of rural isolation and the people in the neighborhood were mostly of German stock, engaged in farming.

The Unionport Hotel was a popular resort as it featured a beergarden during the summer and fall months, and fraternal organizations "from the city" drove up in coaches for clambakes, corn roasts, picnics and beefsteak parties. Baseball was just becoming popular in that era and was usually one of the features of the outings.

Around the turn of the century, and Ave. B being renamed Havemeyer Ave., a Martin Hoffmann was the proprietor and for decades his place was known as Hoffmann's Casino. It went through a decline during Prohibition (1919–1933) but its loyal patrons never missed the Oktoberfests even though the beer was not legally brewed nor tasted as well.

In the 1930s Huber's Casino became its name, and the tavern passed through several ownerships and renovations, becoming Castle Garden and, since 1962, the Castle Harbour Casino. Stephen Deutsch, host for the past twenty five years, still welcomes the German-American clubs to the traditional Oktoberfests where the songs ring out, the dancers fill the ballroom and the beer flows as in the days of yore. Prosit!

Zerega and Castle Hill Aves. Touch Twice at Their Ends

Zerega and Castle Hill Aves., although parallel streets, touch twice — a geographical oddity that is not found elsewhere in the Bronx. The avenues meet near E. Tremont Ave. at one end, and at Castle Hill Point Park at the other.

From the Point back to Lafayette Ave., an extensive estate once existed but just beyond Squire Screvin's land was a cluster of small factories facing Westchester Creek. There was a boatyard, a stonecutting establishment and Howell's bottling plant, with small truckfarms behind them.

Brohmer Brothers were the owners of the stonecutting studio, and their workforce was recruited from nearby Westchester Square and environs. In the 1890's, the firm had a contract with the New York Zoological Park — popularly known as the Bronx Zoo — to make various animal statues to grace the buildings that were to be built there.

Power tools were not in general use in those days, so it is easy to visualize the workmen, using only handtools, slowly and carefully shaping the bears, elephants and buffalos from the granite blocks, as the leisurely Westchester Creek flowed past their workshop. The imposing lions at the entrance to the Lion House were chiseled by two residents of Westchester Village (now the Square) using the age-old technique and traditional hand-tools that artisans have used for centuries. They were a nephew and an uncle named Holt, and some of their grandchildren still live in the neighborhood of Westchester Square.

World War Changed Things For Odd Fellows Orphanage

At one time more than 100 orphans were lodged in the Odd Fellows Home, and they were educated in the nearby PS 36 on Castle Hill Ave. Subsequently the Boys' Band became a wellknown unit at all parades and was much in demand up to World War I.

By that time, the term "Orphanage" was dropped as no children were kept in public institutions under a new policy of the Board of Charities. The orphans were sent to private homes and away from the German atmosphere. The teaching of the German language was discontinued and the Grand Lodge scrapped Article 1 which had stipulated its use at official meetings. In 1919, the name of the home was changed to United Odd Fellows Home.

The Unionport home was maintained by Odd Fellow Lodges and the metropolitan membership — of almost 30,000 — changed composition over the years from German to Jewish. This turnover was reflected in the Home, where a dietary kitchen and a synagogue were added.

During World War II, residents of Unionport and passing motorists saw the acreage put to good use in the form of Victory Gardens, and many of the residents turned out to be surprisingly good farmers. Part of this land was lost when E. 177th St. was widened to form the Cross-Bronx Expressway. In the late 1950's, a modern wing was added and such innovations as a solarium, gym and swimming pool enhanced the living conditions of the Odd Fellows.

In 1970, the turrets and blue-stuccoed building of the second Home were razed, and now the third most modern Home is there. The cornerstone, reads I.O.O.F.

The HOME and ORPHANAGE 1886–1891 sign was salvaged, and was incorporated in the new building.

Oddly enough (no pun intended), the cornerstone was a solid block of granite, for this writer had hoped to find some memorabilia in a hollow space. However, when the cornerstone was raised, five Annual Reports were found underneath it in a poor state of preservation. Dated 1887 to 1891, and written in German, the reports tell of the activities, difficulties and stresses that took place when life was much slower and in many ways simpler.

Castle Hill Point Has Designation–From Ancient Greece and Rome

It is said parents affect the lives of their children by the names they give them. An unusual first name is a strong factor in the subsequent behavior of an individual, as is borne out by many studies on the subject.

Solon Frank is a good example of this school of thought, for evidently his parents hoped he would be as wise, honest and judicious as the original Solon, an upright legislator of ancient Greece. All we know of Solon Frank today is that he became a successful real estate dealer when the Bronx was still a semi-rural territory. In the years 1885–1910 Castle Hill Point had been the property of John Screvin, whose father-in-law, Gouverneur Morris Wilkins, had been the previous proprietor. Screvin sold the property in variously-sized plots, and one of the largest was purchased and developed by Solon Frank.

Very much aware of the classic origin of his first name, Mr. Frank lost no time in naming the new streets after famous Romans and Greeks of antiquity. As a result, passersby near Castle Hill Ave. will find a Caesar Pl. (Julius Caesar "the noblest Roman of them all"), a Cicero Ave. (Marcus Tullius Cicero, orator and statesman whose literary style was regarded as faultless), Cincinnatus Ave. (the plain-living general who was called from his plough, to lead a Roman army), Virgil Pl. (the most illustrious of all the Roman poets), Homer Ave. (the epic poet of Greece who wrote the Odyssey), and Solon Pl. (the Athenian sage), which also memoralizes a go-getter of the early Bronx.

Open Trolley Ride Led to Finding Indian Village

As late as 1917, the remains of a large Indian village were discovered on Clason Point by an archeologist connected with the Museum of the American Indian. Oddly enough, the discovery resulted from a pleasure trip on a summer's day when Alanson Skinner, passing Leland and Soundview Avenues on an open trolley noticed oyster shells on a large sandbank. Realizing the shells marked the site of an aboriginal settlement, Skinner went to A.P. Dientz, a representative of the Sound View Improvement Corporation owning the site, who granted permission for excavating. Samuel Riker, Jr., a trustee of the Museum, financed the subsequent dig which produced numerous relics pertaining to the Indian mode of living three centuries ago.

Seventy Indian lodge sites, with their refuse heaps, were unearthed. These lodges contained hundreds of fish hooks, bone awls, arrowheads, bits of harpoons, carved bowls of tortoise shell, and some antlers. Several dozen clay pipes were also found. Evidently the Siwanoys carried on a trade with the white settlers for, in addition to their native pipes, there were found churchwarden pipes that were made in Holland.

In several pits of yellow sand, were found the bones of dogs, deer and wolves covered with charcoal and shells, denoting the pits had been used as places of sacrifice. This custom is mentioned by the early Dutch writers.

The natives sold the land, called by them Snakapins, to Thomas Cornell in 1643 and the Dutch authorities granted him a Patent in 1646, but soon after the Indians burned his house and killed some of the family. Cornell escaped but later returned, backed by the military might of the Dutch governor, Kieft, and reclaimed his holdings.

The relics uncovered on Clason Point were removed to the Museum of the American Indian, Heye Foundation, 155th St. and Broadway, where they can be seen today.

Oldtime Milkman Trashes Police Booth

Although he has been retired from the Police force for many years, Jim Cotter never fails to chuckle when passing the corner of Unionport Road and E. Tremont Ave. There was once a police booth located at that corner of the Catholic Protectory grounds (now Parkchester) with a steep drop behind it, and it figured in a bizarre episode.

"In those days of the 1930's," said Jim, "home deliveries of milk in bottles was a profitable business, and one milk company, Borden's, was located on nearby Bronxdale and Van Nest Aves. The rival company, Sheffield Farms, was at E. 180th St., near the Bronx River.

"E. Tremont Ave. was a cobblestoned street and it was rough riding in a wagon. The trolleycar tracks were a solution to the problem for, when no streetcars were in sight, the milkmen would steer their wagons onto the car rails for a smoother ride. Sometimes, in the dawn hours, it looked like a chariot race with the rival drivers striving to get onto the rails.

"One early morning, a Sheffield Farms milkman was unable to manage his runaway horse. At the aforementioned corner, the horse, wagon and its frantic driver jumped the track, mounted the sidewalk and crashed into the booth and tumbled it into the hollow. Luckily there was no policeman in the booth at the time, and it was so thoroughly demolished that it was never replaced. But you can imagine the broken bottles, spilled milk and wrecked milkwagon that the driver had to account for. Around that time, milkwagons were being replaced by delivery trucks, so using the trolleycar tracks was no longer practiced by the milkmen."

Kane's Park Resort Recalled
By Oldtimer of Clason Point

From Florida, a Clason Point oldtimer, Charles Jones, sends in some early memories of days when there were summer tent colonies and an amusement park "out on the Point."

"During the summer my entire family camped at Higgs' Beach, which later on was called Harding Park," he writes. "My uncle, Jim Bridges, set up the first tent there. We later lived on a houseboat, named 'Indian' on the edge of Kane's Park, which was a resort that boasted of a large casino, restaurant, dancehall and picnic area. We children had just a short walk to the scenic railways, shooting galleries and rollercoasters of Clason Point Amusement Park — where Shorehaven is now located.

"If we had enough money, we'd swim in the outdoor pool, but most times we swam in Pugsley Creek. I graduated from PS 69 and then spent a short time in James Monroe HS, but left to work in Con Ed for the next 45 years. I well remember the Gibson brothers, Charlie and Harry, who also lived on a houseboat. They were daredevils who used to ride a motorcycle inside a large steel mesh, but what they did when the season was over I never knew.

"When Holy Cross R.C. Church was organized, the parishioners attended Mass in the basement of Kane's Casino. If the sermon was too long, we would hear the orchestra begin practicing upstairs, or else the waiters might start carrying up trays and tablecloths. By the time the parishioners were singing the last psalm, Kane's men were rolling the beer barrels — and that was the final hint. Happy days those were!"

Catholic Protectory Boys Didn't Run Away Sundays

Oldtimer Leo Weigers sends on his memories of the N.Y.C.P. near Van Nest. You don't know these initials? They stood for the New York Catholic Protectory that stood on the land now occupied by Parkchester.

"It was run by the Christian Brothers, numbering about 30 teachers. The boys were all sent there by Court commitment, principally for truancy, and their ages were from 12 to 16. The boys were all well informed on the various batting averages of their local baseball heroes, but their scholastic interests left much to be desired; but, after all, this shortcoming had brought on their truancy in the first place.

"A popular semi-pro team, the Lincoln Giants, rented the Protectory ballfield and every Sunday there was a double header, pitched by the redoubtable Joe Williams. They played such teams as the Cuban Stars, House of David and the Jersey City Allstars.

"Certain picked boys acted as vendors for soda pop, candy and hot dogs while the Protectory Band supplied lively music. All the boys could come to the games and it was very rare that a boy would run away on a Sunday. The Protectory hired two private plainsclothesmen who went to the homes of the boys who had absconded, and brought them back. There were several shops wherein the boys learned carpentry, painting, signpainting, tailoring (all the Protectory uniforms were made there) shoemaking (every pupil had two pairs) and printing."

This shop printed school programs and a local monthly called *The Suburban News,* a newspaper that to date has eluded members of The Bronx County Historical Society who want a copy for their archives. Do I hear an offer?

Our Lady of Solace Catholic Church

"Recently I read where Our Lady of Solace Catholic church in Van Nest was having a fund-raising affair," wrote oldtimer Jim Cotter. "This church held an annual Fourth of July carnival on the grounds of the Catholic Protectory where Parkchester stands today. What wonderful times were had! A durable platform was constructed for dancing and jigging. There was more than a fair share of Irish-Americans in attendance."

This writer remembers that not only parishioners came, but people from the farm communities of Middletown and Throggs Neck. A large contingent from Schuylerville (Bruckner Blvd. and E. Tremont Ave.) always arrived in haywagons, and enjoyed the Old Country dances which included "The Siege of Ennis" and "Stack of Barley."

A wide lawn, lined with shady trees facing E. Tremont Ave., was set aside for these yearly picnics, and there were games for the children, baseball for the adolescents and barrels of beer for the adults. Throughout the day, boys fired off firecrackers, and a few adults could be counted upon to bring along small, brass cannons that were fired in honor of the Fourth.

The Catholic Protectory maintained its own farm where many boys learned to be farmers. There was a sizeable pigsty and the meadows now covered by Metropolitan Ave. supported a large herd of cows, and on the Fourth of July these animals retreated to their sheds, for the uncommon noise, music and fireworks made them nervous.

"I worked in the Bronx Gas & Electric Company in those days," ended Mr. Cotter. "And the Line department had the job of setting up the wiring for lights over the dance floor—and later on, to remove them. How many persons are still around who had such a good time at those affairs?"

No Working Farm Vehicles Left In Bronx, Crops Are Shrinking

A recent news item stated the Bronx was the only county in New York State without a working farm vehicle (Even Manhattan had three licensed tractors!). But this is not to say the Bronx has no commercial farms. Right now, three farms along Eastchester Rd. are winding up a final crop of lettuce, zucchini, stringbeans and carrots. But their days are numbered, if rumors are to be believed, with a religious order negotiating to acquire the land.

Ever since Jonas Bronck cleared land for his plantation, three centuries back, the Bronx has been a region of extensive farming. Old maps show most of the farms were east of the Bronx River, where the fertile countryside sloped to that stream and Long Island Sound. The West Bronx was much hillier, with rockier soil, and so the tillage there was not as productive.

In the late 1800s there were the Bathgate farms, the Powell farm of Belmont and many truck farms on Clason Point, Castle Hill and Wakefield. In our 20th Century, oldtimers remember the Koch farm of Middletown, and the Coster and Delayo farms on Throggs Neck. Some motorists, as they drive to the Bronx Whitestone Bridge, might recall that both sides of the Hutchinson River Parkway once were lined with farms. It might surprise residents of Parkchester to learn that extensive farmlands were situated there when there was a Catholic Protectory in existence. Many Protectory boys were taught agriculture and eventually were hired by local farmers, or acquired their own homesteads.

One by one these rural holdouts disappeared, as streets were laid out and homes were built. So it will be with a sigh of regret when the last farms in the Bronx yields its final crop and becomes just a memory.

"Great Race Track Fire of 1910" Is Recalled in Detail by Woman

Who remembers the great Race Track Fire of April, 1910? Mrs. Beatrice Stalter did, and her vivid description is a pleasure to pass on to readers, for it brings back an exciting chapter in the history of Parkchester's neighborhood.

"On April 10, 1910, the ball game was just over at Cannon's at Tremont and Castle Hill Aves., opposite St. Raymond's Church. I was a little girl, clinging to my father's hand, homeward bound, when we noticed smoke over the 'track' as we referred to the Morris Park Race Track grounds.

"My father suggested going over to see what it was, and over the N.Y.N.H. & H. tracks we went. We trudged through the fields, not making much progress because the wind was blowing a gale. Pretty soon we heard the clang of the fire engines and, turning around, we beheld the most spectacular sight I have ever witnessed. Moriarity's house was a sheet of flame that seemed to reach to the very heavens. Our own house on Poplar St. was almost directly opposite that blaze and instinctively we started for home.

"When we reached there, my mother was frantically trying to account for the family—and there were eight of us children. The firemen ran through the streets calling to each householder to play the hose on his roof. I can still see my father and brother pouring pails of water over the roof.

"There was so much to watch as to exceed the Ringling Brothers' Circus for diversified interest, and for the first time I had a box seat at a big show. It was a three-alarm fire. Engines came from Belmont Ave., and that was quite a distance away. The only way to get the hose near the blaze was across the railroad tracks, and all trains had to be halted which added to the excitement.

"The steeple of the Westchester Methodist Episcopal Church on Tremont Ave. caught fire. Not much damage was done to the church, but the water just about ruined its new green carpet. Word got around that PS 12 was burning. Young hearts beat high, hoping it would burn to the ground, but it was only the school fence that burned!"

Section 10

CITY ISLAND, CO-OP CITY, COUNTRY CLUB
FORT SCHUYLER, THROGGS NECK

Aerial view of Freedomland shows the contours of the United States. The $65 million outdoor family entertainment center opened in the summer of 1960. The New York Thruway is now the New England Expressway. The site is now part of Co-op City. (The Bronx County Historical Society Research Library)

This automobile accident occurred in a trench for a new sewer. Eastern Boulevard (now Bruckner Boulevard) north of LaSalle Avenue, April 1, 1918. Note auto in center of picture. (The Bronx County Historical Society Research Library)

Indian Trail in Silver Beach, c. 1920s. Atop a high bluff, this 1929 post card shows Indian Trail in the private community of Silver Beach on the East River. Today, the residents enjoy spectacular views of The Bronx-Whitestone, and Throgs Neck Bridges and the skyline of Manhattan. Starting in 1923 two developers, Mr. William Peters and Mr. Emil Sorgenfrei rented out tent and bungalow sites. Gradually the 400 bungalows became permanent homes and in 1972, the community became a cooperative when the residents purchased the land. (The Bronx County Historical Society Research Library)

Hot Horse Races Developed On Old E. Tremont Ave.

We don't think of E. Tremont Ave. as a race course for impatient squires, but at one time — in the horsedrawn days — many a spirited race was waged on that country road. Of course, around 1905, it was called Fort Schuyler Road and, sometimes, Walker Avenue, and was in a very sparsely settled area.

From Throggs Neck in to Westchester Square, the road ran past many fine estates, owned by gentlemen who prized horses and fine carriages. Some of them drove to the railroad station daily for the trip downtown, and it became their custom to race each other. Partly from friendly competition but also from a desire not to eat dust would the wealthy landowners whip up their horses and attempt to get ahead of the other team.

Oldtimers of "the Village" (Westchester Square) remember some mornings when twin columns of dust could be seen from a distance, and then two squires would dash in, sometimes standing upright in their urgency, and cracking their whips over the horses' sweating rumps. John A. Morris (of Morris Park fame), Archer Milton Huntington, Frederick deRuyter Wissmann, Frederick Jackson, Matt Colford and the Adee brothers hated to be passed, much less eat dust, so some of their races along the dusty road, now known as E. Tremont Avenue, were downright dangerous.

Old Stream Recalled By Weir Creek Park

A weir is a dam across a stream, or an enclosure of twigs and vines for catching fish, and the Indians along our Bronx shoreline were quite adept at this method of fishing. They took advantage of the numerous creeks that flowed in from the Harlem and East Rivers, and the Long Island Sound, by stringing their woven nets across the mouths of such creeks and, as the tide ebbed, the fish and eels were trapped on the mudflats, or in the net itself.

The early settlers on Throgs Neck noted the strategy of their Siwanoy neighbors, and called one stream the Weir Creek. This creek wound its way through the swamps from Dewey Ave. north almost to Middletown Rd. (using present-day directions) while a southern branch curved around Edgewater Park and reached a point at Lawton and Kearney Aves. On an English military map of 1779, the creek was labelled Middle Brook, probably because it was navigable to small boats up to the village of Middle Town. In some 1840 deeds, it was referred to as Wire Creek, and for a while in the 1880s, it carried the name of Turnbull's Brook, after a landowner near Lafayette Ave. But the old name of Weir Creek persisted.

Four wooden bridges crossed the stream — at Miles Ave., Lafayette Ave., Layton and Waterbury Aves. — but by the turn of the century the Middletown stretch that ran through farmlands, had degenerated to a ditch. Fishermen and canoeists could still reach Lafayette Ave. on the north, and small boys on rafts could pole their way South to the hummock of land at Lawton and Kearney Aves.; but all this was changed with the coming of E. 177th St. and several avenues that spanned the creek. Only a short distance remained open to boats and even that was drained off and filled in by the Throgs Neck Bridge approach.

Plans call for a park to be laid out where once Weir Creek flowed, so The Bronx County Historical Society submitted the name of Weir Creek Park to the City officials in an effort to preserve some local lore. It was accepted. [However, in 1976, during the Bicentennial celebration, the park was renamed Bicentennial Veterans' Park.]

Ancient Locust Point
"New Found Passage"

Locust Point has figured largely recently in *Press-Review* news, due to its location in the path of the Throgs Neck Bridge. Elsewhere, the reader can read of its future, but here we delve into its past.

We know the region at the foot of 177th St. [now known as Locust Point Drive] was an Indian fishing camp for centuries before the coming of the white man. It was occupied chiefly during the warmer months when fishing and hunting were favorable, but when winter came the braves retreated to their villages inland. Researchers have found stone urns, bone weapons and scraping-knives used by the men, but nothing to denote the presence of their squaws.

In 1619, the first English explorers sailed cautiously around the tip of present-day Fort Schuyler and ventured into the Sound. But when the land was ceded to the English, it was called "New Found Passage," as it was an alternate seaway to the ocean.

In 1667, Colonel Nicolls, the Governor of New York, granted to Roger Townsend "a certain parcel of land . . . at ye South east end of Throgmorton's Neck, commonly called New Found Passage, containing 15 acres, and also a small neck thereto adjoining called Horseneck, being about the same quantity of land, which is not in occupation." Horseneck, then, is a very ancient name of Locust Point.

In pre-Revolutionary days, the land was owned by an Edward Stephenson who lived on Frogge Point (Ft. Schuyler) but whose son cultivated five acres on Horse Neck. During the Revolution, a British officer — Major Blaskowitz — drew a military map of the area, on which the name — Locust Island — was noted for the first time. A stand of locust trees along present-day Tierney Pl. accounted for the name. The island was surrounded by marshes and practically inaccessible at high tide.

Thereafter, a Captain Wright gained title to the land. Legend has it that Captain Wright had been a pirate, and bought his island with some of his booty. Also, that some of his pirate treasure is still buried there. Another version is that the Wrights were merchants who secretly financed piratical ventures, and shared the loot on a businesslike basis. At any rate, for the next century it was known as Wright's Island, and the tip on which the Yacht Club stands, was charted as Locust Point.

Living like barons, the Wrights enjoyed fine orchards and trotting horses, and employed farmhands, shepherds, a coachman, gardener and other help. Their home was located approximately at 177th St. and Glennon Pl., and the barns, dove-cotes, shearing-pens and stables were on the area now occupied by the tollbooths of the Throgs Neck Bridge. The Wrights had a causeway built to connect their estate with the mainland. It led across the marshes in a half-circle to the junction of Harding and Pennyfield Ave., the junction being known as Wright's Corners for many years.

During Prohibition, rum runners found the lonely waters off Locust Point an ideal anchorage and many cases of illegal liquor were smuggled ashore in the dark of night. Eventually the Wrights sold out, and the land was divided into city streets. From World War I onward, Locust Point became the official name of the entire peninsula. The marshes were drained. The Cove was widened and deepened, and the Point became the pleasant little community it is today. [The Throgs Neck bridge, opened in 1961, eliminated the eastern side of the community but did not change its character.]

Devil Moved in Old Bronx On "Belt," Stepping Stones

Much publicity has been engendered over the so-called Devil's Triangle, a vast expanse of the Atlantic Ocean touching Florida and Puerto Rico, with Bermuda as its apex. Sinister tales of sunken ships and missing planes have given the Triangle a reputation verging on the supernatural.

According to Colonial history, the early inhabitants of what is today the Bronx had a strong belief in the Devil, and this is borne out by the fact that, in the 1600's, two natural features had names that bespoke supernatural aspects.

Long Island Sound, in Colonial times, was known as the Devil's Belt. "Belt" did not mean a leather strap, but denoted a strait of water, and, due to the sudden storms and destructive Nor'easters of the Sound, the colonists soon took to attributing its ownership to the Devil.

On early maps of this Devil's Belt were charted the Devil's Stepping Stones — a cluster of mussel-covered reefs within sight of City Island. These reefs owe their name to an Indian legend that Habbamoko, an evil spirit, was fleeing from the Indians of Connecticut, and used the reefs as stepping stones to reach the safety of Long Island.

The name persisted into the latter part of the 19th century, but it proved too cumbersome for mariners' charts when a lighthouse was erected on the reefs in 1876. However, the name lived on in local usage for a few more decades, for this writer remember a fish peddler who used to land his boat on the Throggs Neck beaches, blow his horn to summon the housewives, and shout: "Fresh fish — right from the Devil's Stepping Stones!" We youngsters used to stare at his catch with superstitious awe.

Anne Hutchinson Home Site Is Still Debated

The Hutchinson River, flowing down from Westchester County and emptying into Eastchester Bay, was named after Anne Hutchinson, one of this Borough's pioneers. According to historical record, she and her family fled religious persecution in the Massachusetts Bay Colony and, in 1638, made their way to a wilderness north of the Dutch colony of New Amsterdam.

Historians are not sure of the exact location of her cabin but do know the Hutchinson holdings were located in the vicinity of Boston Road and the Hutchinson River. Ancient deeds speak of Black Dog Brook and Ye Hutchinson Meadowes and this has led researchers to the conclusion the pioneer family lived on the west bank of the river.

Others believe Anne lived near the Split Rock in Pelham Bay Park which is on the east bank of the Hutchinson River. A bronze tablet once was affixed to the Split Rock attesting to the settlement "near this spot" but there is some scholarly doubt that the statement is correct.

In 1643, Anne Hutchinson and her family (she was a widow) were massacred by Siwanoy Indians, with the lone exception of one daughter, Susannah, who was carried off into captivity. Later she was returned to her relatives in Massachusetts where she regained a command of English and the ways of civilization.

Famed Cedar of Lebanon Toppled by 1944 Hurricane

The Bronx lost one of its best-known landmarks, when the famous Cedar of Lebanon was toppled by a hurricane on Sept. 14, 1944. The majestic tree was more than 75 feet high and more than 150 years old, and for many decades had been used by East River mariners as a guidepost along the Throggs Neck shoreline.

Its origin went back to 1790 when Philip Livingston, a wealthy landowner, returned from a pilgrimage to the Holy Land with a small sapling and some soil from Lebanon. The cedar was planted near the present day southeastern corner of E. Tremont and Schurz Aves. and subsequent owners of the property — the Posts, Mitchells, Van Schaicks and Huntingtons — all were deeply interested in arboriculture and horticulture, and saw to it that the imposing tree was protected.

When E. Tremont Ave. was extended to the East River, the cedar was directly in its path and seemed doomed to be cut down, but Borough President Cyrus Miller, who doubled as Bronx Historian, came up to Throggs Neck and had the street line resurveyed. This time the Cedar of Lebanon was bypassed. Though saved by man, the tree was not spared by Mother Nature, and an inspection by members of the New York Botanical Garden in 1938 showed it had died.

The towering gaunt skeleton remained as a landmark for a few more years until the hurricane brought it down. There it lay like a fallen giant, gradually being whittled down by nearby residents.

In the 1950's a workcrew from the Botanical Garden brought back a large section of the trunk — still aromatic with the scent of cedar — for the museum. A few years later, the remainder of the Cedar of Lebanon was salvaged by members of The Bronx County Historical Society, and some cubes, paperweights and gavels were cut from it as gifts to Bronx dignitaries. Members of the Society also benefitted: this writer is the proud possessor of one such gavel, and the aroma of cedar is still apparent.

The Time That a Shell, Fired To Warn Ship, Hit Fort Schuyler

Every ship coming to New York harbor via Long Island Sound had to stop at City Island and pick up a pilot who would guide the vessel past the forts, into the East River and to a berth somewhere in the metropolitan harbor. The time was 1917.

The stories differ as to the reason the captain of a foreign freighter did not halt at City Island to take on a pilot of the Hell Gate Pilots' Association. Some say he was a Norwegian, unaware of the wartime precautions. Others say it was a Hollander unwilling to pay the pilot's fee for guiding the ship through treacherous Hell Gate, but in any event the coast artillerymen in both forts were alerted that a ship was steaming their way without proper clearance. A wireless message to halt was ignored, and soon the freighter was at the entrance to the East River.

The gun crew on Fort Totten fired a shot across her bow, and the captain hastily ordered the engines in reverse. The shell, intended to intimidate the foreign seamen, ricochetted off the water and hit a corner of Fort Schuyler, where it exploded. Luckily, no one was in the immediate vicinity and there were no casualties, but the accidental hit generated much excitement among the wartime garrison, and a variety of stories developed from the incident.

Some 10 feet above ground level, in the shadow of the Throgs Neck bridge that passes overhead, is a granite block in the wall of Fort Schuyler. If any cadet of the New York State Maritime School knows why that particular corner is damaged, he is a rare one.

No Tunnel Ever Connected
Two East River Fort Sites

A bit of Bronx folklore that apparently will never die out is that there is a tunnel under the East River connecting Fort Schuyler on Throggs Neck with Fort Totten on the Queens side. Periodically that question is asked of this writer, whose unvarying answer is that there has never been any need for such a tunnel, nor sufficient manpower or mechanical equipment for such an undertaking in the 18th or 19th century.

There were two different locations that might have been mistaken for tunnel entrances. Captain Charles Ferreira, once the lighthouse keeper at the tip of Fort Schuyler, long ago showed this writer a square pit outside the fort walls which, he said, was an abandoned ammunition dump. Among the World War I soldiers stationed there, it was barracks gossip that the pit really was an entrance to a tunnel under the river.

Eugene Just of Unionport once was conducted around the fort by the lighthouse keeper whose title of Captain was purely honorary. He was shown a small room inside the fort itself and Captain Ferreira said a similar room existed in Fort Totten, opposite. In this stone chamber was a pit in which a steel cable was wrapped around a revolving drum. The cable was stretched, underwater, between the fort and a floating mine was attached to it, to deter any unauthorized ship that might slip past during the night. Daytimes, the mine was towed to Fort Totten by means of a winch, and ships passed through the strait under the supervision of City Islanders who belonged to the Hell Gate Pilots' Association.

Either pit might have started the story of a tunnel, and so the legend will go on and on, for it is a more interesting tale then the real one.

Ancient Eastchester Covenant Set Rules for Rattlesnake-Killing

Rattlesnake Brook still trickles through Seton Falls Park, a reminder of the times in centuries past when that region was a haunt for those feared reptiles.

When the early settlers of Eastchester "sett down at the Hutchinson River" they found many wild animals, some of them an asset and the others not desirable at all. Deer, raccoon and rabbits were plentiful, so were game fowl and all manner of fish. On the other hand, there were dangerous species of wildcats, wolves, bears and rattlesnakes.

The original ten families of Eastchester, to govern themselves in orderly fashion, wrote up a covenant which they all signed. There were 27 paragraphs they adopted, the second being "that we indeavor to keepe and maintayn christian love and sivell honisty.", and the twenty-first: "That one day, every spring, be improved for the destroying of rattlesnake."

Old records, as late as 1775, tell of a rattlesnake being killed near the brook, measuring some six feet in length!

The colonists had one method of keeping themselves safe from these snakes. If they had to go through an area known to harbor rattlesnakes they would drive several hogs in front of them. Hogs find snakes a delicacy and will eat all they encounter, whether they be poisonous or not. A porker, with his thick lining of fat and his coat of bristles, hardly feels the fangs of a snake and so is more than a match for the rattler.

Some readers have reported seeing small snakes in the Hutchinson River area, but none — to this writer's knowledge — has encountered a rattlesnake.

Palmer Cove Bears Name Of 1740 Bay Lands Owner

Palmer Cove, a small inlet on Eastchester Bay extending into what is known as the Spencer Estate, was referred to many times in records dating back to the Revolutionary War. On a current map of the Bronx, it is bounded on the north by Griswold Ave. and by Radio Dr. on the south. At one time it extended inland almost to Kennelworth Pl., and oldtimers recall ice-skating its length "when the Sound froze over."

John Palmer was the proprietor of all the lands fronting on Eastchester Bay in the 1740s, and on a military map of 1777, his home is shown due west of the cove (at approximately Ohm Ave. of today.)

Palmer Cove figured in many deeds of a century ago, as it served as a reference point and boundary marker, and on old charts it was noted as the sole "port of call" along that shoreline. Yachts and yawls, fishing smacks and oyster-boats made a run for the cove whenever a storm caught them on Eastchester Bay, and various landowners the Furmans, Campbells, Waterburys, Bayards and the latterday Spencers and Lorillards — maintained a suitable dock for their naptha launches and sailboats.

When the Country Club and Spencer Estate were subdivided into building lots 50 years ago, a fisherman named Ed Morris bought the dock at auction for $1200 and built a fishing shack on it. On fullmoon tides, Ed would have a foot of water in his shanty, and if a Northeaster blew . . . and they usually blow for three days . . . Ed would sleep in an upper bunk, with three feet of water flooding his home.

A colorful character, he fished, clammed and speared eels in Eastchester Bay all his life, and no one ever saw him without his fisherman's boots. He paid his taxes to the Dock Department down in New York City, and always made the trip in boots. He would clump into the Dock Office and announce himself "Ed Morris of Palmer Inlet!"

The dock, now augmented by concrete pilings, is still there; but Ed and his shanty have been gone these many years.

Volunteer Fire Departments Still Keep Vigil in Waterfront Areas

The oldtime villages of the Bronx once depended entirely on volunteer firemen, until these hamlets were annexed to New York City. Then paid firefighters took over the fire houses and a colorful phase of the oldtime Bronx passed into history.

However, on the fringes of the growing city where people found themselves remote from fire houses, the Volunteers were resurrected in what were called summer colonies such as Orchard Beach, Edgewater Camp, Silver Beach and Harding Park. Pails of sand hung outside each summer bungalow, and fighting a blaze was a community affair. Later on, each Company graduated to hand-drawn carts, then to ancient Model T Fords or obsolete taxicabs, and finally to Army surplus trucks or modern fully-equipped vehicles.

When Orchard Beach Camp was demolished to make way for the present bathing beach and pavilion of the same name, the Bronx lost one of its Volunteer Hose Companies. The other summer camps became year-round communities, and each has its own Hose Company, ever ready to respond to a local blaze, organize a dance, or march smartly in a Labor Day parade.

There is still a small-town atmosphere in the Volunteers' quarters, a faint lingering air of an earlier Bronx that is no more. The oiling of the leather buckets has been replaced by the polishing of the high-pressure nozzle, and the checkerboard has given way to the TV set, but there remains a carryover from the past century in the smell of freshly-brewed coffee on a cold night, the thump of a bung driven into a beer barrel, and the excitement and urgency of a fire alarm.

Monorail Line to City Island Derailed on First Run

An oldtime newspaper, that vanished in 1925, was *The Bronx Star,* and one of its 1908 news items conjured up a fantastic mind image of a monorail system that would operate in various parts of the Bronx.

The Public Service Commission had recently granted permission to the Pelham Park & City Island Railroad Company to substitute a monorail system of transit, operated by electricity, instead of the antiquated horsecars then in use. The company had not become a reality until it was shown that the monorail, which was a German idea, was practicable. This firm, the American Monorail Company, planned a four-mile run from Bartow railroad station (near the Shore Road) to the Southern end of City Island.

The *Star* reported: "If the monorail proves a success on the City Island route, it is intended to introduce it on White Plains Ave. to E. 242nd St., on Westchester Ave. to Pelham Bay Park, and also through Unionport, giving residents of those sections the most up-to-date system of electrical traction."

Work began in 1909 and by the summer of 1910, a shiny new monorail car was ready to transport passengers from the railroad station to the City Island bridge. The extension onto the island and down to Belden's Point was to follow.

The excursionists jammed themselves into the car, dangerously overloading it, and on its first run it tipped over. No one was killed but some passengers were injured and the system was promptly shut down. The horsecars and jitney-buses remained in business, while repair crews bolstered the overhead structure and strengthened the foundations of the monorail. The "mile-a-minute" car was immobilized for the rest of the Summer.

There was intermittent service of this line until 1914, and then it was replaced by electric trolleycars. So the highflown plans of 1908 and the expectations of the residents of Westchester Ave., White Plains Ave. and Unionport never materialized. Alas, for those dreams of aerial trains whizzing along over our Bronx thoroughfares!

Historic Little High Island Sold To NBC for Transmitting Base

The dream of owning a little island is universal and not confined to any particular century, for records of our Bronx past reveal that all the wealthy land owners, whenever they could, purchased islands off the Bronx mainland.

One Benjamin Palmer once wrote: "In the year 1761 I bought an island in the Manor of Pelham, in the County Westchester and the Province of New York in North America, commonly called Mineford's Island for £2,730, and divided it into 30 equal parts." This was the eighth time City Island changed hands since Thomas Pell had purchased it from the Indians.

Like an anchored satellite, little High Island was attached to City Island by a sand bar, and a year later — 27th of November, 1762 — reference was made to an island in the Sound, commonly called High Island, the property of Captain John Wooley. High Island, with sheer rock walls on the northeast, a flat and sandy shore on the southwest, and only six acres in extent, has remained in private hands ever since, Elisha King was its owner in the 1830s, along with a plot on City Island (now King St.) to give him wharfage.

The little isle abounded in Indian artifacts, and later became popular for its excellent swimming and fishing. For the past 80 years it has been the private island of the Miller family of City Island and the summertime vacation spot for some 150 campers. The wintertime population dwindled to a few hardy souls who acted as caretakers. The sand bar to City Island was covered at every high tide, so in 1928 a wooden footbridge was built to surmount this watery obstacle.

This well-known landmark gave way to a span capable of supporting trucks and heavy equipment, as progress invaded the island: The National Broadcasting Company purchased the isle as a transmitting base.

Dynamite Johnny O'Brien Was Noted Pilot, '90s Filibuster

City Island, a colorful part of the Bronx, has never lacked colorful characters, most of whom were of a nautical cast.

The Pelham Cemetery (located on the Eastern shore of the island and not in Pelham as the name would suggest) is the final berth for some of them, and an oldtime Hell Gate pilot, James F. Horton, once wrote:

"Resting in the graveyard is Dynamite Johnny, a true islander. O'Brien was his name and he sailed the fast schooners that went to the West Indies. He was a Hell Gate pilot and was buried about 1915. The Cubans gave him a great funeral because he had been a gunrunner in Cuba's war for freedom against Spain."

Paul Miller, once of Throggs Neck, adds to the saga of Dynamite Johnny: "He was a famous filibuster back in the 1890s who smuggled guns and explosives to the rebels in Cuba. He became famous on one run in a converted yacht when the cargo of dynamite started to shift during a storm. Everyone else was scared to touch the stuff, so O'Brien went down into the hold and lashed the crates back in place, even though there was so much electricity in the air from the storm that sparks danced around on his hair! That's how he got the nickname of 'Dynamite Johnny.'

"He was a symbolic hero of the era, and when the wreck of the battleship 'Maine' was raised in 1912 from Havana harbor, it was O'Brien who was given the honor of going aboard the hulk when it was towed out to sea. He opened the valves to ceremoniously scuttle her, and she went down with flags flying."

It was the sinking of the "Maine" that brought the United States in conflict with Spain, precipitated the Spanish-American War of 1898, and the resultant freedom and independence of Cuba.

Co-op City Was Once a Cucumber and Pickle Farm

Looking at the towering building of Co-op City from Connor St., it is hard to imagine that a thriving cucumber farm and pickle factory once was situated there. Nathan Johnston, formerly of Utica, had purchased in the 1870's some 25 acres of land fronting on Boston Road and running on either side of Connor St., then known as Town Dock Road. Since Colonial days, schooners, barges as well as small steamboats had docked there on the Hutchinson River, hence its name.

All this was gleaned from an autobiography of a grandson, Herman Weiss Johnston, who wrote: "My earliest memory is of a crowd of Italian laborers that walked down from New Rochelle two and a half miles every morning to hoe and pick cucumbers for the pickle factory. This was in 1893.

"Hoeing required a great amount of hand labor. The picking baskets were of woven hickory that workers shouldered, and the cucumbers were dumped into barrels at the end of each row. When the barrels were full, they were loaded onto wagons and hauled off to our salting sheds. The vats were 8 ft. high and 16 ft. in diameter.

"By 1895 N. Johnston & Son were operating their own factory that steamed the pickles after they were stored in brine. Some were shipped by steamboat that made three trips a week from the Town Dock to an East River pier in downtown New York. Others were bottled by trained girls, labeled, placed in sawdust in boxes made on the spot, and shipped to a warehouse in New York for distribution to wholesale grocery houses. The rest were bottled and exported to Cuba and these had to be dyed a vivid green — but even in those days, the law prevented such practice in New York."

From Cucumbers to Strawberries at Co-op Site

In addition to their own farm (now part of Co-op City), the Johnston family bought the crops of nearby farms that, in 1895, became Bronx territory where Westchester County ceded some land to New York City. A year later, Nathan Johnston died of a heart attack while driving his buggy. His horse, being blind, followed the scent of water and waded into a fresh water pond patiently stood there for two days until two boys spied the horse, carriage and dead man.

William Johnston inherited the farm and business, but a plant blight made cucumber growing impossible, so he closed out the enterprise and concentrated on raising strawberries for the local market. That venture prospered and the crops were widely distributed in lower Westchester County for many years. During the harvest season, local boys came at 4 a.m. from Mount Vernon to pick the berries. At 8 they had to walk home, change their clothes, eat breakfast and be in school by 9 a.m.

Grandson Herman Johnston, who wrote these memoirs, was a rarity: a farm boy with a college education. In 1908, he attended City College and that meant a daily trip on the Westchester and Boston Railroad from Dyre Ave. to E. 180 St. and then the subway to Lenox Ave. and E. 135 Street — over two hours each way.

As early as 1918 there was a marked deterioration in the strawberry crop and by 1929, "nematodes" (worms) spelled the end of the strawberry business. A few years later, the land was sold to the Curtis Wright Aircraft Co. for an airport that never materialized, but left the Johnstons financially well fixed. A racetrack was next contemplated for the land that had once been the Johnston cucumber farm, but nothing came of that plan either. In 1960, Freedomland, a theme park modeled on Disneyland, was built along the Hutchinson River on landfill that included the former farm. And this entertainment center in turn was replaced by the upper end of Co-op City by 1967.

Freedomland

Freedomland is a name that can conjure memories for most any Bronxite over the age of 35 and no doubt many an album has photographs of the educational-amusement park that was to be the Disneyland of the East.

In the 1950's a vast marshy tract alongside the Hutchinson River in the Northeast Bronx was eyed for development. Earlier plans had envisioned a racetrack there and once it had been considered for an airport. But while these ambitious blueprints were gathering dust in some engineering office, William Zeckendorf of the real estate concern of Webb & Knapp promoted a venture that would entertain and educate the American public on a scale that would outdo Disneyland. Two hundred and five acres of wetlands were filled in and Freedomland, in the shape of the United States, was built at an estimated $65 million.

The promoters predicted an annual attendance of five million people and in the spring of 1960 the extravaganza opened. Visitors rode horsecars and stagecoaches, paddlewheelers and replicas of San Francisco's cablecars. They saw re-enactments of the Great Chicago Fire, the Pony Express and other exhibits of American history but, as one reporter succinctly put it, "people don't go to amusement parks to be educated."

In its first season only 1,500,000 people came through the turnstiles and the following years were equally disappointing. Apparently, what was not taken into consideration was our northeastern climate which limited Freedomland to function only five months a year, whereas Disneyland, in California, never closed. Five summers after it opened, Freedomland—one of New York's most expensive misadventures—closed down. A year later, plans were underway to build Co-op City on the same site, and this time the story had a happy ending.

Section 11

BRONXDALE, MORRIS PARK, VAN NEST

The Morris Park Racetrack and Grandstand in 1899. It became the most fashionable landmark of the newly annexed part of The Bronx, after the Jerome Park Racetrack closed down in the 1880s. The grandstand covered present-day Bogart and Van Nest Avenues, and the clubhouse was located at Van Nest and Fowler Avenues. (The Bronx County Historical Society Research Library)

The Morris Park Racetrack Clubhouse. Located at Van Nest and Fowler Avenues, with five stories of opulent furnishings within and Pompeiian villa style without, it was the costliest and most elegant resort in America. Officially opened in August 1899, and named after the John A. Morris family of thoroughbred owners, it dwarfed the small communities of Van Nest and Morris Park. (The Bronx County Historical Society Research Library)

Morris Park Race Course Drew Crowds, 1890-1904

In pre-Revolutionary times, the meadows and farmlands belonging to the Fowler families stretched westward from the road to Williams' Bridge to an Indian trail that had been gradually widened for the carts of the early colonists. This rough path was called the Bear Swamp Road.

Over the years, parcels of land changed hands and in the 19th century deeds occur the familiar names of Hunt, Pearsall, Pierce and Sackett. On an 1850 map, the road skirting Bear Swamp carried the alternate name of Snuffmill Lane as it led from the village of Westchester (now Westchester Square) to Lorillard's snuffmill. This mill, restored and maintained by the Parks Department, stands in today's Bronx Botanical Garden alongside the Bronx River.

By 1880 Williamsbridge Road had become a well-travelled highway, while Bear Swamp Road was once more widened and paved—in sections—for it linked the villages of Westchester and Bronxdale. The level acreage between the roads attracted John A. Morris, a wealthy member of the American Jockey Club, who envisioned a fine race track to be laid out there. It was not until 1888 that his syndicate—the Westchester Racing Association—acquired all 152 acres, and work began on the stables, oval track, grandstands and clubhouse. The grounds extended from Sackett Avenue to Pelham Parkway, and from Williamsbridge Road to Bear Swamp Road (since renamed Bronxdale Avenue.)

The towering clubhouse stood just off Bronxdale Avenue, within easy walking distance of the railroad depot—and the immense grandstand covered both present-day Fowler and Bogart Avenues. The first race was held in 1890, and the Park was a steady source of revenue and entertainment until it finally closed down in 1904.

Morris Park Track Was Site of World's First Airfield

The facts that make history are often unrecognized at the moment of their happening. A good example of this was the infant Aeronautic Society of New York, numbering less than 80 members, that leased a broad space of open land, near a subway terminus on the outskirts of our growing Borough in the year 1908. It was the abandoned Morris Park Race Track—and it was the first time in history that land was ever taken with the idea of flight.

Many years ago, gliders and monoplanes and helicopters whirred, sputtered, soared and crashed as the enthusiastic aeronauts experimented with an astounding variety of aircraft. In those far off days, no one thought it necessary to learn how to fly—it was assumed that if the machine could get off the ground the inventor would fly it, as a matter of course. Needless to say, accidents and mishaps were quite common!

At one time the largest dirigible in America was built on the former race track. John A. Riggs and Joel T. Rice utilized three propellers to steer their 105 ft. long gas bag. Underneath was suspended a framework of steel tubing, 100 ft. long, which supported the two men astern. All three propellers were bolted to the prow and two of them had a vertical pitch to raise and lower the craft which was named "The American Eagle."

The dirigible was housed in a huge canvas tent that cost the airmen $1200, and the cost of their attempts passed the $5000 mark. A gale later destroyed the tent, but Riggs and Rice managed to deflate the balloon and save it from serious damage. When winter came, the men stored their air vehicle there, but did manage one short flight—with Riggs and Rice, derbies firmly on their heads, directing the course.

Bat-Like Glider Used by Youth To Soar Over Van Nest in 1908

Back in the year 1908, the residents of Van Nest were startled to see a young man soaring overhead, supported by only two sets of bat-like wings. He was 17-year-old Lawrence Lesh, who had been invited by the New York Aeronautic Society to come to nearby Morris Park racetrack and demonstrate the art of gliding.

Young Lesh had already gained fame by using the air currents over the St. Lawrence River to make a flight almost six miles in length, towed behind a motorboat. Lesh then brought his glider to the Bronx exhibition and made a number of fine glides, towed first by a galloping horse and later by a speeding automobile. On his last flight he cut the tow-lines when he had reached sufficient height, and sailed out over the racetrack and the rural fields of Van Nest.

The excited crowds ran beneath him, impeded his landing and caused him to break an ankle. He was taken to Fordham Hospital where, it was reported, the fracture was badly set, and it became necessary to place the young man under the care of a specialist.

Eventually Lawrence Lesh regained the use of his foot and resumed his breath-taking pastime high over the racetrack of Morris Park.

Louis Chevrolet Raced Cars
At Old Morris Park Track

In Morris Park, how many drivers of Chryslers and Chevrolets have any idea that Walter Chrysler and Louis Chevrolet once raced cars over the same terrain?

An exhibition in Queens College, "The Swiss in American Life," contained the surprising news that both these men were once actively connected with car racing in The Bronx. From a collection of newspaper clippings, photographs, trophies and personal mementoes, this writer learned for the first time that Chevrolet, a young Swiss immigrant, came to New York at the turn of the century, aged 22.

A mechanic by trade, he began building racing cars and repairing others, and soon became involved in the dangerous sport as a driver. In the early 1900s, speed and endurance races were held at the Morris Park Racetrack, and these naturally attracted the young Swiss. Driving a Fiat for a mile record of 52.8 seconds, he once won a gold watch that was donated by Walter Chrysler. Young Chevrolet and his brother Gaston graduated to professional racing and both survived numerous crashes at the expense of fractured ribs and broken bones. An any rate, Bronxites of that era were familiar with Chevrolet and Chrysler as the names of two men, not cars. Marriage to an American girl and the death of Gaston in an accident made Louis decide to give up the dangerous sport, and in November 1911, he founded the Chevrolet Motor Company.

His business prospered until the infamous Wall St. Crash of 1929 that ushered in the Great Depression. Chevrolet switched to airplane motors and experimented with helicopters, but his efforts were to no avail. Suffering a cerebral hemorrhage, Chevrolet had to retire and passed his last years quietly in Florida where he died in 1941.

To find out if or where Louis Chevrolet ever lived in the Bronx during his racing days could be an interesting project for some amateur historian. Do we have a volunteer?

Bronx River Boundaries Caused 1884 Row for Bolton Family

The Act of 1884 condemning Certain Property for Public Parks to form the proposed "Bronx Park" is fully documented in our Borough archives, and Harvey Lubar of the Parks Department has unearthed an interesting document concerning the Bronx River.

Ann Bolton (deceased) had left her considerable estate outside the village of Bronxdale to seven children and an adopted son named William Birchall. Two sons and Birchall ran a bleach mill, print-works and a tape mill, all being powered by the flow of the Bronx River. When condemnation proceedings were begun by the City, the three partners were to be compensated for the mills and the machinery that had to be dismantled and moved.

In the seven years' negotiations that followed, the value of the land, mills, machinery, docks and homes rose, and the Bolton family petitioned the City for additional compensation. A further complication was the fact that the Bronx River formed the boundary between New York City and Westchester County, and some of the Bolton mills were on the west (New York) bank, with the private homes of the workmen and the tape mill on the east (Westchester) bank. White Plains, the Westchester County seat, was therefore involved.

Then a family split ensued when the brothers and sisters, who had not been consulted by the three mill operators, refused to pay the lawyers, as they had not hired them. The two brothers and foster-brother Birchall eventually settled with the Department of Public Parks, and the other heirs and heiresses "shared and shared alike" and apparently everyone was finally satisfied. The dry legal language made no mention of the millworkers and their families who then had to vacate their village, to find homes and work elsewhere. Their dwellings were dismantled and today Birchall Ave., Bolton Ave. and Bronxdale Ave. are the only reminders we have of the obliteration of a community that took place a century ago. And the Bronx River still flows serenely on.

Tangle Woods Often Searched By Boys Hunting "Kidd's" Treasure

Tangle Woods (sometimes spelled Tanglewood) was the name of a wooded tract bounded by Pelham Parkway on the south, Allerton Ave. on the north, Seymour Ave. on the east and approximately the Esplanade on the west.

Who gave it that descriptive name is not absolutely known, but a fair guess is that it was Captain Israel Honeywell Watson who was a landed proprietor there, more than 85 years ago.

Tangle Woods was a dense stand of timber bisected by a winding brook that flowed in a southeasterly direction from Gun Hill Road, eventually to empty into Westchester Creek. Where freshwater brook met saltwater creek is the area, now filled in, occupied by the New York State Mental Hospital.

The watercourse through Tangle Woods was called Stony Brook for most of its length, but where it wound through Abbott's land (now covered by Jacobi Hospital), it was mapped as Abbott's Brook.

At one time it was known as Kidd's Brook at its upper reach. The lads of the surrounding neighborhoods naturally thought in terms of Captain Kidd, and from time to time they would venture into the deep woods and dig haphazardly for an iron chest, full of doubloons, rumored to be buried there. If a king's ransom in jewels and gold pieces ever were dug up, no one has told of it.

Actually, a Harvey and Lucretia Kidd once had owned property on the northern end of Tangle Wood, but of this the village boys from Bronxdale, Van Nest and Wakefield were happily unaware — and so their dreams of buried pirate treasure were never exploded.

Gypsy Encampments Held by Bronx River Years Ago

Don DiMartin, once of the Bronx but now sojourning in Florida, asked this writer if he ever saw the annual Gypsy encampment that took place between the Bronx River and White Plains Road, along Pelham Parkway. It was a sizeable encampment, consisting of dozens of wagons and a few rundown trucks; and a conservative estimate of the number of Gypsies would be between 100 and 150 men, women and children in colorful garb.

The site selected was a good one for the purpose, lying close to Boston Road, being sparsely populated, containing grazing fields for the horses and ponies, and having a plentiful supply of fresh water in the Bronx River. The Gypsy women also washed their laundry in the stream which, around 1909, was relatively pure.

During the annual "Invasion," homeowners checked the locks on their chicken coops, and housewives kept a vigilant eye on wet wash hanging out on the clothes lines. Mounted policemen paid periodic visits to the encampment to "keep an eye on things." Oldtimers of Van Nest might recall the Gypsy men fanning out through the neighborhood, offering to mend pots and pans. The younger, prettier women went shopping along White Plains Road and Morris Park Avenue, meanwhile offering to read palms or tell fortunes with playing cards which they carried in their flowing, gaudy gowns. The teenaged boys kept watch over the herd of horses and hauled firewood and water, while old women tended fires that were set in stone pits, dug for that purpose.

Mr. DiMartin recalls the mixed curiosity and fear of the Wakefield and Van Nest youngsters who watched the activities from a safe distance. They had been warned by their elders not to venture too close to the Gypsy camp lest they be kidnapped — a common belief in those days.

Parade in Van Nest Bade Adieu To Old Volunteer Fire Fighters

Saturday night, May 14, in the year of 1910, went down in Van Nest history as one of the most glorious events of the past, as the nostalgic "Nesters" marked the disbandment of Van Nest Hose Co. No. 1. Fire Commissioner Rhinelander Waldo had notified the 75 officers and men who comprised the volunteer company that the newly-formed paid companies, Engine Company 90 and Hook and Ladder 41, would take possession of the new firehouse on White Plains Ave. at Morris Park Ave. — and the valiant "vamps" (with a record of 16 persons rescued from death by fire) were ordered to disband.

The people of Van Nest showed their appreciation to the volunteers by holding a parade in their honor, extending through Van Nest and a section of the McGraw Estate (part of Parkchester) and being fully a mile in length. There were fireworks and torchlight flares, fanfares and speeches, and the civic, political and fraternal clubs that took part formed an impressive sight. There were floats, and bands and volunteer fire companies from Westchester Square and Unionport. And baseball teams. And singing societies.

Eighteen hundred pupils — the entire roster of PS 34 in Van Nest — led the parade behind the Cathedral Band. Then followed the Foresters of America, the Red Men, Van Nest Taxpayers Association, Bronxdale A.C., Bronx Turn Verein and the Bronx Maennechor Corps and 200 cadets. Who recalls the Hayseed Club? They marched in farmer garb, and the Van Nest Turn Verein turned out in identical uniforms.

A half-century has elapsed but oldtimers still gather and recall the glorious, incredible, noisy, colorful night when the Van Nest Volunteers disbanded.

Recalled are Woodmansten, Pelham Heath Roadhouses

Motorists using Williamsbridge Road or Eastchester Road in the vicinity of Pelham Parkway have no idea they are passing places that were considered "out in the country" by earlier drivers. Shortly after World War I, motorists would stop at the Woodmansten Inn, off Williamsbridge Road and Morris Park Avenue — a noted roadhouse of its day.

A youngster named Jerry Lama used to walk over from Castle Hill Avenue to wait outside the Woodmansten Inn just to see the big name bands that played there. "I heard Helen Morgan sing there once," he wrote. "The other night club — or roadhouse as they were called — was the Pelham Heath Inn on Eastchester Road and Pelham Parkway. Top bands played there, and broadcast coast-to-coast. I played bass viol with the Fred Cola Orchestra, and also with Bill McCune in those days, and it was a sad day when the Pelham Heath Inn closed its shutters around 1953."

Playing in an orchestra was not all glamor and fame, as Mr. Lama goes on to mention the Depression of the 1930's: "I was a young man then, and the father of three children and the going was tough. I was playing the bass viol in orchestras but there were very few jobs to be had, and when you did get a club date you were lucky to get $4.00 for the night's work. Once we played for a Fusion Club during the La Guardia administration and we got paid off in vegetables. I had to lug the bass fiddle under one arm and a bag of potatoes under the other on the subway! (Who could afford a car in those days?) Some political clubs gave the musicians a ticket which when presented to the butcher, entitled them to five pounds of frozen beef. We did not have much in those days but we were happier as there was no such thing as a tax, and whatever you made was yours to do as you pleased with."

Historians Seek Source of "Woodmansten" Name

A charming old mansion, built in the times immediately after the Civil War and standing sturdily far into our twentieth century, was the famous Woodmansten Inn.

It stood, surrounded by an extensive estate, overlooking Williamsbridge Road, and was once the palatial home of Denton Pearsall. The estate was mapped in 1868 and included present-day Allerton Avenue, Eastchester Road, Sackett Avenue and Williamsbridge Road. In the atlas, the tract was labelled "Woodmansten" and was considered one of the finest in Westchester County. (This section of Westchester County was annexed to The Bronx in 1895.)

The estate was sold and subdivided in the years 1910 to 1917, and the house — much enlarged — was renovated into a roadhouse. With the advent of the auto, the fame of Woodmansten Inn extended well past its former boundaries, and big name orchestras and singers entertained the patrons.

Sometime around April 1930, a fire razed the structure and, so far as this writer knows, no souvenir or memorabilia were saved. Today, a row of brick homes facing Tomlinson Avenue and Alfred Loreto Park occupy the site.

How About That Bus Ride That Ended in '28 Arrest?

Sometimes a faded copy of the *New York Times* of 50 years ago will contain a news item that can still be of interest today — partly from its reference to a vanished Bronx landmark and partly from a mention of an entertainer.

This sequence of events began back in 1928 one wintry evening when some 100 people were dancing to the music of Vincent Lopez in the Woodmansten Inn, a noted roadhouse near the intersection of Williamsbridge Rd. and Morris Park Ave. Underneath the ballroom there were a dozen musicians and chauffeurs lounging in a room assigned to them, when a small man entered. Lending emphasis to his order to put up their hands, he fired a shot into the floor. Then he backed the dozen men against the wall and rapidly emptied some of their pockets, and ran out.

A bus, en route to Westchester Square, happened to be passing by, and the gunman hailed it. Boarding the bus, he pointed his pistol at the driver's head and ordered him to "step on the gas!" Six passengers had a wild ride down to Westchester Square, with some of the robbed chauffeurs in hot pursuit. One of the musicians had the presence of mind to phone the Police Station — which at that time was located at the junction of E. Tremont Ave. and Williamsbridge Rd. — and patrolmen and detectives rushed out just as the bus braked to a stop.

The gunman — a Joseph Sullivan — began to run, but Patrolman Haffner and Detective Connolly fired two shots, and Sullivan halted and surrendered. His loot consisted of $17. A woman passenger who had fainted was revived, and the cops-and-robber chase was over . . . right in front of the Police Station!

The Times reporter did not remark on the wild coincidence of a bus passing by during the holdup — or could it be Sullivan planned his crime, with the bus schedule in mind? We'll never know.

King's Road Trustee — MacAdam Built One in The Bronx, Too

The Bronx may well lay claim to having had the first macadam road in America. How? Read on.

John L. MacAdam, a Scotsman, lived in New York during the Revolution and amassed a considerable fortune in mercantile affairs. Although at war's end some of his wealth was confiscated, enough remained for him to retire to Scotland and buy a large estate. He was made Road Trustee by the king at a time when the roads in the United Kingdom were generally bad, dangerous to travel on, and costly to repair. MacAdam experimented with different types of surfaces, finally trying layers of stones, each weighing no more than 6 ounces, raised slightly above the adjoining land, and with drains on both sides. The layers were to be consolidated gradually by the passage of traffic on the road. By 1815, MacAdam's roadbuilding technique was adopted throughout the British Isles, and gradually his name was attached to the roads themselves.

His second wife was Anne Charlotte DeLancey, whose family were owners of what is today Van Nest, Bronx Park and Belmont. A persistent story is that MacAdam gave a demonstration to his father-in-law by having a "macadamized" stretch of road laid out from the DeLancey mansion to the highway (now E. Tremont Ave.) leading to Westchester Village. As the DeLancey mansion was situated alongside the Bronx River just above the waterfall at E. 180th St., this early driveway would have been eastward across Bronx Park and possibly in the bed of Adams Street.

According to historian, Frank Wuttge, the road was still visible inside the park in the 1930's, but was bulldozed during the following years when landscaping was introduced. No trace of MacAdam's road can be found today, but amateur historians need not despair, for there remains one way to determine if any stones, scattered along a line from the Bronx River to Adams St. are from the original macadamized road.

It seems MacAdam suggested that, in lieu of weighing every stone to keep to the six-ounce size, it would be faster if the workman would test for size by fitting the stones in his mouth. Stones too large were to be discarded. The story is that the foreman had no teeth at all, so the stones he used were far too big. This resulted in an inferior road, and was no credit to MacAdam.

Amateur researchers are advised by Mr. Wuttge to either bring along a small scale and look for 8-ounce stones, or else. . . . . yes, you guessed it!

Gen. Collins Recollects Boyhood in Van Nest

Alumni of PS 34 have winced at the piecemeal destruction of this once fine school, feeling its eventual demolition will take away another vestige of their childhood. With this in mind, Nicholas DiBrino, local historian of Van Nest and Morris Park, recently communicated with one of its most distinguished graduates and, with an Army career behind him, (ret.) General James F. Collins harked back to his boyhood.

In a letter, Gen. Collins wrote: "My parents were eager to get out of crowded Manhattan to bring up their children, so we moved to 1820 Unionport Rd. in 1909. It was a two-family house and we lived on the top floor. Our apartment was heated by a coal stove plus some portable kerosene stoves, but we put in a gas stove a few years later.

"Van Nest was a great place to be brought up in. It was in general a genial neighborhood despite the religious and ethnic prejudices of the times. I can still recall eating matzoth and drinking Jewish wine in Sammy Weinstein's home, and eating in Swiss, German and Italian houses. I remember going to the Morris Park Racetrack twice with my parents before it burned down.

"I attended PS 34 from 1911 to 1919 and it was a good school. Mr. Story, the principal, maintained strict discipline, and the teachers were excellent. The students were the usual mixture of German, Irish, Swiss, Italian and Jewish. One Negro family in Van Nest were the Yates, and their children attended PS 34, too. From there I went on to Regis HS, and then was appointed to West Point.

"After 37 years as an officer, I retired as a four star general. So you can see that PS 34 and my parents prepared me well for future life. God was good to me and always placed me in the right place at the correct time to advance up the ladder. Sincerely, James F. Collins."

Why Is Our Borough Called THE Bronx?

It is a paradox that with some two million people in The Bronx, there is not one of us who really knows why our Borough is THE Bronx. Many theories have been advanced, and today readers can pick and choose their favorite:

An old story is that settlers of Nieuw Amsterdam, when visiting the Bronck family, would refer to their trip as "going to the Broncks." Considering Jonas Bronck lived less than three years on his farm, how many visitors could he have had? And the language in use at the time being Dutch, the phrase is hardly creditable.

Another tale is that the first English settlers, hearing of Bronck's Land assumed "broncks" were some kind of hummock or bog. So they called the territory "the broncks" as we would refer, today, to "the flatlands" or "the barrens."

Dr. T. Kazimiroff, official Bronx Historian, theorizes it may be a corruption of The Bronx River, or The Bronx Kills as a geographical definition in use, after the Revolutionary War. In popular usage, it then became shortened to simply "The Bronx."

Politicians of the era (1874–1895) when our Borough was being brought into the City, were much influenced by the fact this countryside was known as the territory of the Bronx (River). People spoke of the Grand Canyon of the Colorado, the valley of the Shenandoah; not to forget the Civil War references to the Grand Army of the Potomac, and the Army of the Tennessee. For just that reason, it has persisted to this day.

Section 12

BAYCHESTER, EASTCHESTER,
WAKEFIELD, WOODLAWN

Gun Hill Road and Edson Avenue vicinity. This 1909 southeasterly view of Givan's Creek shows the last extension of Gun Hill Road being filled up. The temporary tracks on the right were used by the contractors to bring in landfill. In the background, a northbound locomotive of the New York, New Haven & Hartford Railroad emits a trail of steam. (The Bronx County Historical Society Research Library)

The End of Jerome Avenue, c. 1900. Fred Anderson on his dog cart by Van Cortlandt Park and the trolley tracks. Fred's father was in charge of the polo ponies and stables at Van Cortlandt Park. (The Bronx County Historical Society Research Library)

1860 Restaurant Attracted Artists, Writers to Boro

There was a time when such notables as Henry James, the novelist, Mark Twain and Bret Harte traveled to the Bronx to dine — in The Hermitage, a restaurant on the banks of the Bronx River favored by writers and artists of the period.

The proprietor of the spot, Baudoin Laguerre, was the subject of a book written by F. Hopkinson Smith, in *A Day at Laguerre's*.

Baudoin Laguerre came to the United States in the 1840's, almost penniless because of "marauding" of his native France by soldiers of Napoleon's armies.

In New York, he found employment as a dishwasher and a sign painter, and then opened a small restaurant in downtown Manhattan, with which he had success. He visited the Bronx to see a colony of Frenchmen he had heard about, in the Gun Hill Road area. He liked what he saw, and bought 18 lots along the Bronx River, for less than $1000.

The Hermitage was opened about 1860, and the meals and wines served out-of-doors when weather permitted, became locally famous. The restaurant's charms were enhanced by the presence of a daughter, termed "velvet-eyed" by Smith in his book.

Wide lawns ran from the eating place to the river bank, where rowboats were rented to Hermitage guests. Nearby was a colony of Frenchmen, silk weavers, formerly of Aubusson, living in well-kept cottages surrounded by gardens.

The restaurant was a victim of "progress" in 1906, when the Bronx River Parkway Commissioner condemned the building, which was razed. It is recalled only in Bronx folklore.

Long-Gone McLean Brook
Flowed in Family Estate

The late Joe Havender once took this writer on a leisurely ramble through Woodlawn Cemetery and that section of The Bronx due north of it, known as Woodlawn Heights. The well-known monument sculptor was on his "home grounds" and pointed out the various landmarks in passing, and as we walked up Katonah Avenue to the city line, Mr. Havender traced the path of a long-disappeared McLean Brook in which he had once fished for minnows.

An 1876 area map indeed shows a meandering brook, without a name, in what is now called Woodlawn Heights, originating just south of McLean Avenue, and ending in the Bronx River at about E. 233rd Street.

In 1971, the Woodlawn Heights Taxpayer & Community Association published a well-illustrated historical booklet on their area, and this writer is indebted to the editor, Raymond Leggiero, and his assistant John F. Murphy, for their information on this little-known Bronx rivulet.

The McLeans emigrated to this country in 1679 from Scotland, settled on Staten Island, and subsequently located in New York City around the Revolutionary War. George W. McLean was a direct descendant of that family, serving on the original Park Commission after the Civil War, and holding a seat on the stock exchange. He had a town house at 3 W. 34th Street, but had purchased a country estate outside the city. It was a 100 acre tract. Later he purchased an additional 6 acres south of his lands, which he converted into a lake. The lake, fed by natural springs, was used as an ice pond to supply ice to the mansion on the estate. Eventually the pond was stocked with fish, and became known as McLean's Lake. Its approximate location was along the Bronx-Yonkers boundary at Katonah Avenue.

In later years, children would fish and swim there. Rowboats were rented from a Mr. Thomas who also had a refreshment concession. A brook, about six feet wide, ran off from this pond south through the woods into Woodlawn Heights, and contained various small fish and frogs. It travelled down the west side of Katonah Avenue for about four blocks to E. 234th St. The waterway then entered Woodlawn Cemetery's northeastern corner, flowed out at E. 233rd St., curved again into the burial grounds, feeding a beautiful little lake along its easterly border, then continued to the Bronx River.

Wakefield's Black Settlement

Ever since Jonas Bronck's days in the 1600's, there have been Blacks in the various villages that were situated in what is now the Borough of The Bronx. But, according to century-old directories, they lived among their white neighbors and not in separate sections. Lately, some readers have written in, inquiring where the first Black settlements were.

It was only around 1890 that any cohesive Black communities came into existence, and all four were small, occupying at most two blocks each. Three settlements owed their inception to railroads, and were approximately a mile from each other, all west of Third Ave.

Another enclave was located in the Williamsbridge-Wakefield area which is east of The Bronx River and came about from other factors than the railroad. According to a 1976 study called "A History of the Black People in the Bronx," this pocket evolved from the availability of vacant land, improved transportation and the job situation.

Male members were either railroad workers, or coach drivers for the wealthy families of Mount Vernon and the North Bronx. Letter carriers and post office employees were among those early Black settlers, and they were organized in various social and civic groups. One such club was the "Coachmen Society" (organized in 1890) and another was a more recent (1930) "Benedicts."

Social life revolved around St. Luke's Episcopal Church, Butler Memorial Church and Trinity Baptist Church and the practice has continued to the present time.

Woodlawn Cemetery More Than a Burial Ground

The merry, merry month of May has always been this writer's favorite time to stroll through Woodlawn Cemetery, and it has been an unfailing source of wonderment to realize there are Bronxites who have never, in their entire lives, been to this unique place.

To begin with, there is nothing macabre or depressing about a visit to Woodlawn Cemetery, but instead there can be a rewarding experience in a leisurely walk, unhindered by traffic and enhanced by the magic of bird-song. Birdwatchers will find almost every species of birdlife in our hemisphere using Woodlawn as a temporary refuge or a permanent home, as it has been for over a century. For anyone interested in botany, there are well-tended plants and shrubs in profusion. There are sun-dappled lawns and shady, tree-lined lanes, and nature lovers will discover a small lake and even a murmuring brook that drops down the steep eastern slope.

Revolutionary War buffs can stand next to the rock marking the summit of Gun Hill in the southeastern corner of the cemetery, and overlook the Bronx River valley which the cannon emplacement once dominated and controlled. Civil War markers and Spanish-American war markers are scrupulously maintained, nor are World War I and II neglected, thanks to patriotic groups.

Students interested in art can have an instructive afternoon studying the sculpture, mosaics, stained glass windows and the many types of lettering employed. Even "rock hounds" whose interest lies in stones will be amazed at the variety of imported marble or granite to be seen, as well as local Fordham gneiss and Manhattan schist.

Readers interested in Bronx history will see mausoleums and tombstones relating to pioneer families whose names are found on today's street signs. Names of worldwide fame can also be encountered in almost every sector: Arctic explorers, railroad tycoons, merchant princes, operatic divas, admirals and clippership captains, painters, writers, actresses and actors, athletes and poets, African trailblazers and statesmen all have found a final resting place in this verdant unhurried tract of rolling hillside.

So, whatever interests the reader, he or she will surely find a responsive facet in the photogenic, out-of-the-ordinary retreat known as Woodlawn Cemetery.

Ill-Fated 1879 Explorer's Statue Adorns His Grave

In the first week of July, 1879, Lieutenant George Washington DeLong left San Francisco to find a passage through the polar ice, from Alaska to Greenland. The Jeanette Expedition, as the public called it, was followed with intense interest by the public coupled with the fact the ship JEANETTE was the first steamboat to use electric lights.

After passing the Bering Straits, the vessel was locked in the ice for two years, and was finally crushed by ice floes and sank in 1881. Of the 31 men, only a dozen survived after a gruelling trek to Siberia. Lieutenant DeLong was not one of them: he had died from the extreme cold, exhaustion and hunger. DeLong's body eventually was brought home, and was buried on Chapel Hill in Woodlawn Cemetery.

On July 4th, 1929 — a patriotic event took place on Chapel Hill which was attended by a large crowd, naval units and their commanders, local dignitaries and members of the DeLong family. An enormous statue of the Arctic explorer was unveiled, and the larger-than-life statue, in Eskimo parka and boots, was depicted facing the elements in front of the DeLong tomb.

Visitors to the northeastern corner of the cemetery can see this impressive statue of the polar adventurer and, in an area famous for its many unique monuments, Commander DeLong's is judged to be one of the most unusual.

"Sweet Adeline" Renamed To Honor Bronx Diva Patti

Although he was born in Somerville, Mass., Harry Armstrong came down to New York City around 1897 and settled where the rooming houses were cheaper than they were around Broadway — his real goal.

A good amateur boxer and an accomplished pianist, young Armstrong hoped to storm Tin Pan Alley with his songwriting talent. One song he wrote, "My Old New England Home," was melodious enough, but had no lyrics and the aspiring songwriter found it unanimously rejected by all the publishing firms.

To support himself, he played a piano in a honkytonk for his keep until one fateful day, Armstrong met a writer who agreed to fit words to Harry's song. The lyricist, Richard Gerard, changed the name of the song to "Sweet Rosalie" of whom he wrote: "At night dear heart, I pine for thee. You're the flower of my heart, sweet Rosalie." Still, the song was rejected.

At that time — about 1902 — Adelina Patti, a renowned singer who lived on Matilda Ave. in Wakefield, was widely acclaimed in operatic circles, and Gerard, noticing some of her posters, suddenly found his inspiration: "Sweet Adeline, for you I pine!" He hastily rewrote the lyrics and "Sweet Adeline" became the flower in the hearts of every barbershop quartet. M. Witmark & Sons published the song in 1903 and it has never lost its popularity.

Harry Armstrong signed over his rights to the tune for $1000 and never again managed to write a song so adaptable to harmonizing. Richard Gerard received $1600. What Adelina Patti thought of the song is not known, but it is certain the operatic star never sang it in public, if at all.

It's nice to know that two Bronxites, now long dead, had parts in the creation of one of America's best-loved songs.

Nieuw Haarlem Patentee Gave Bussing Ave. Name

Bussing Ave., running north from Gun Hill Road, is one of the most ancient paths of the Bronx having been an Indian trail that became the Colonial road to Boston. It has been travelled upon by marauding Indians, Colonial rebels under George Washington, a horseman named Paul Revere, French, British and German cavalrymen, and the squires and farmers of the 19th century.

As late as 1925 there was mention of a John Bussing in a local real estate transaction, but the name itself goes back to the earliest records of the Dutch founders.

A Bussing was one of the original settlers of Nieuw Haarlem — then a tiny village on the Harlem River at approximately 125th St. The year was 1658, and Arent Harmanse Bussing, "one of the most worthy of the Harlem patentees," came to the settlement from Westphalia with his friends Meyer and Dyckman. The farmers had to serve in the militia, and Bussing was one of the eight volunteers (Nieuw Haarlem's quota) sent to fight the Indians. Jan Dyckman was another.

They left by canoe, promising their sweethearts they would return as corporals. The Westphalians were so valiant in the Esopus campaign that they did get their promotions, and both did marry upon their safe return.

Bussing later was appointed magistrate of the thriving community, but he also concerned himself with adding to his original tract so that at the time of his death he owned 127 acres of valuable riverfront property opposite present-day Yankee Stadium. A grandson, Aaron, kept the holdings intact and when the Bronx opened up, the latterday Bussings sold out and located in Wakefield.

"Irish Fifth Ave" Lost Lace Curtains in 1930s

A little late for St. Patrick's Day, but still pertinent, is a glance back to the 19th century when the Irish were a main factor of Bronx life.

There was "Irish Fifth Avenue," once, a nickname for Alexander Ave. when it was a fashionable street, lined with trees and well-kept homes. Lawyers, doctors, some political figures of Irish descent, if not straight "from the Old Country," gave the street a genteel atmosphere, which it managed to retain until the 1930s.

Then there were the two separate "Irishtowns" of the North Bronx. The first was a nickname for the area of Woodlawn Heights, from Van Cortlandt Park to Oneida Ave. Irish laborers made up most of the population, and most of them worked on the nearby Croton Aqueduct while some found employment in the newly-activated Woodlawn cemetery. The nicknames were in use from approximately 1880 to the early 1900's, according to Woodlawn Heights' oldest inhabitant, a Mr. Bazzone who was nearing the century mark, when giving this information.

The second "Irishtown" was a settlement at W. 258th St. and Riverdale Ave. Some of the men were employed in the Johnson Iron Works at Spuyten Duyvil and cycled back and forth to work. Other menfolk worked on the Riverdale estates as coachmen, gardeners, laborers and farmhands; while the wives and daughters were the laundresses, maids and cooks. A localism for this settlement was "Coogan's Alley."

By far the largest Irish community was Highbridgeville where, as one inhabitant once remarked to this writer: "even the gulls on the Harlem River screeched in Gaelic!"

Awning Makers Became Early Boro Movie Moguls

Nicholas DiBrino sends along information on four theaters that were strung along White Plains Ave., together with the explanation for the odd-name of the B.B. Theater.

Herman Bolte is the protagonist in this saga of a German immigrant who came to New York directly after the Civil War, and found employment as a grocery clerk. Learning the language and the business, he eventually migrated to the Melrose section of the Bronx, there to be the proud owner of his own grocery store. That was back in 1884, and by the time he died in 1897, the business had prospered greatly. With their five children, his widow moved up to Williamsbridge in 1903, and two of the sons, Herman Jr. and John, became awning manufacturers on White Plains Ave. Up and down the avenue the concern was known simply as Bolte Brothers.

The startlingly new innovation known as motion pictures (or movies) was coming in, and the brothers opened a small theater in August, 1913, near E. 221st St. which they called the B.B. (Bolte Brothers.) How they made the transition from awnings and shades to the theater industry is not explained, but there is a definite link between their business and the need, in a theater, for a large screen. The B.B. attracted the citizens of Wakefield and Olinville to such an extent that the brothers enlarged the original hall, until it had a seating capacity of 599.

In 1926, upon the death of Herman, John Bolte erected the larger Laconia Theater at E. 224th St. just as silent movies were being enhanced by sound. In 1927, the Burke Theater was opened at Burke Ave. and a year after that, when the Wakefield Theater was inaugurated on E. 234th St., talking pictures had become a reality. In the meantime, the little B.B. closed down forever.

For many years thereafter John Bolte was a vital factor in the theatrical industry, and hardly anyone ever remembered the time "Bolte Brothers" meant awnings and screens, and not Hollywood films.

Bronxite Helped Carry Lincoln On Night He Was Assassinated

A few years ago there was mention in this column of a Wakefield resident who had been present at President Lincoln's assassination. William Withers and his three brothers and their father all served in the Civil War, from beginning to end, and all survived the war. William became an orchestra leader in Ford's Theatre in Washington, D.C. and on that fateful night he had gone backstage. His purpose was to speak to Laura Keene, a prominent actress, about a song he had composed, when he heard a pistol shot and saw a man leap from the president's box to the stage.

"I was in his path," said Mr. Withers in later years. "And I was struck a glancing blow by his dagger and knocked down. Spangler, a scene shifter, later confessed he was to turn out all the gas lights as soon as the shot was fired, and permit John Wilkes Booth to escape in the darkness. But I accidentally blocked his way, and the assassin was recognized."

In 1885, Mr. Withers bought a house on White Plains Road and lived there until his death in 1910.

Yet another local man, Isaac Walker Maclay, was in the audience that night at Ford's Theatre. He helped to carry the President's body from the theatre. Maclay later became a surveyor in the Department of Parks, and married one of the wealthy Havemeyer daughters. It is believed that Maclay Ave. near Westchester Square owes its name to him.

One wonders if Maclay and Withers ever met, and compared notes on that unforgettable night of their lives.

Wakefield & Joseph Conrad

Joseph Conrad is a name that evokes mastery of the English language, yet this Polish-born author of sea stories did not learn English until he was 21 years of age. Born Josef Konrad Korzeniowski, the young Pole became a British subject and used his first two names as author of the literary masterpieces he eventually wrote.

What has this to do with the Bronx? Read on. At the outbreak of World War I, Conrad and his family were stranded in the war zone behind the German lines, but managed to get into Austria although this too was enemy territory. As the United States was still neutral, Conrad requested help from the American ambassador, Frederick Penfield, and that gentleman managed to get them to Italy and safety before the Austro-Hungarian authorities were aware of it. Barely had the novelist and his family been aided over the border than ambassador Penfield was ordered by the Austro-Hungarian government not under any circumstances to allow the fugitives to depart. Penfield had to excuse his zeal, but meanwhile Conrad's party managed to sail off to England — and the writer often mentioned his gratitude to the ambassador.

Frederick Penfield was of a wealthy and cultured family whose estate overlapped Wakefield and Mount Vernon, in the previous century. Their gardens and orchards were showplaces, and the mansion reflected the prestige and taste of the landowners, who also maintained an extensive stable of thoroughbred horses. All the Penfields travelled extensively on the Continent and whenever European visitors came to Wakefield, the Penfields liked to take them to the French restaurants overlooking the Bronx River at Gun Hill Rd. Their mansion, which stood at approximately E. 242nd St. off White Plains Road, burned to the ground in May 1912 — and today only little Penfield St. is a reminder of the Bronx aristocracy of long ago.

Mystery of Buried Bones Solved by Capt. McKeown

Not all entries in police blotters are grim. Consider a report in the Wakefield stationhouse in the days of mounted patrolmen, bicycle cops and foot patrolmen, when a White Plains Road resident excitedly reported finding human leg bones in his back yard. He had been placidly tilling his vegetable plot when his spade turned up the remains of what might have been an unsuspected murder.

Patrolman Hylan was dispatched to the scene and, taking the spade from the shaken homeowner, went to work. After an unsuccessful hour's work to a depth of three feet, the policeman found nothing more so he reported back to the stationhouse with the bones.

As he was making out his report, Captain John McKeown came in and asked why Hylan was laboring over such a long report, when it concerned the leg and hip bones of a pig. Captain McKeown had had no medical training but he had been a cook at many a barbecue and most certainly recognized a pig's skeleton when he saw it.

Many a good laugh was had at the expense of Patrolman Hylan, but the jokes were tempered with good humor, for the men of that Precinct straightway planned to hold a pig roast. Naturally, Patrolman Hylan was the guest of honor but if the homeowner of 4137 White Plains Rd. was invited to the party it was not noted.

Havemeyer Ave. Named For Bronx "Sugar Kings"

Almost all New York's former mayors, from its Colonial beginnings to the late 1890s, have their names affixed to Bronx avenues. These avenues are particularly grouped in the Eastchester-Baychester area, but a few exceptions are found elsewhere.

One former mayor, Hugh J. Grant has a Circle named in his honor, outside Parkchester—and a Unionport avenue recalls three-time Mayor William Frederick Havemeyer, and his family.

Why Havemeyer Ave. is so far from the other streets has to do with a bit of local history. Whereas the other mayors have no historical connection with the Eastchester-Baychester area, the Unionport street does have a definite link with the Havemeyer family.

Their genealogy can be traced back to 1644 when a Hermann Hoevemeyer helped organize a bakers' guild in Germany. Dietrich Hoevemeyer, born 1725, was a master baker and served in the Seven Years War. With the name slightly changed, Wilhelm Havemeyer came to America in 1799 and learned sugar refining. His son and grandsons became known as "the Sugar Kings" and all of them owned fine estates on Throggs Neck. Another Havemeyer owned Silver Beach, and still another the property that includes Lafayette Ave. and Bruckner Junior High School.

After the Civil War, the town of Unionport was building up and Samuel Lowerre's farm was sold to the Odd Fellows who erected a Home. Lowerre's Lane was renamed Avenue B and, around 1900, received the name of Havemeyer Ave. to honor the family that had been so generous in its contributions to the Home.

First Bronx Schoolhouse (1683) Served Children of "Ten Farms"

What could be regarded as the first P.T.A. meeting in the Bronx took place on Oct. 15, 1683, according to the eminent historian, Robert Bolton Jr. Three centuries ago, this recorded meeting, attended by the inhabitants of "The Ten Farms" in Eastchester, resulted in the construction of a one-room schoolhouse "between the property of Richard Shute and William Haiden, and encouragement given to Mr. Morgan Jones to become the schoolmaster."

As the boundaries of the early farms were fixed by large trees, stone walls, small rivulets and sometimes the widow Smith's marshlands, no one in this year of 1983 can be sure of the exact spot. This was brought home to the Boro-Wide Association of Teachers back in 1930 when members tried to locate the site of the very first schoolhouse by searching available records. However, they did ascertain there was a Richard Shute and a William Haddon (sometimes Haiden) farming in the Eastchester sector in the 1680's.

Later on, in the 1700's, there were three more schools within the bounds of present-day Bronx. One was described as "the School near DeLancey's Bridge" and was possibly around West Farms Square, for the DeLancey mill was located at today's E. 180th St. and the Bronx River. The second schoolhouse was described as "the School near Widow Bartow's" and might have been in the Morris Park area where the Bartows lived.

The third schoolhouse was simply noted as "the School on Throgg's Neck" and with that kind of description it cannot be pinpointed at all. All three locations were well known at the time they were recorded, but today they are only a matter of conjecture.

SCENES FROM
THE OLD BRONX

The Bronx Old Timers Parade, Washington Avenue, May 30, 1932.
Washington Avenue had impressive mansions, a number of churches,
and quite a few theatres, social halls and restaurants. It was a favorite
route of most parades. (The Bronx Old Timers Collection, The Bronx
County Historical Society Research Library)

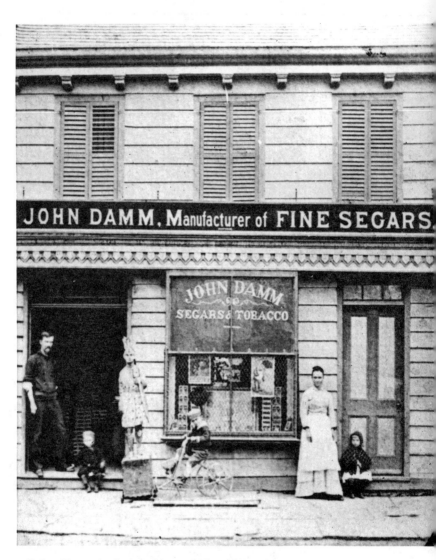

John Damm's Segar Store, West Side of Third Avenue at 166th Street, c. 1900. Morrisania had a number of small cigar factories employing a few "segar rollers" but also large establishments that employed forty or more men and women. Farmers from Connecticut brought the tobacco down Boston Road in large wagons. The wooden Indian was on wheels so that it could be taken in at night. (The Bronx Old Timers Collection, The Bronx County Historical Society Research Library)

Haffen Family, c. 1861. E. 162nd Street between Park & Morris Avenues. Caroline Haffen and Louis Haffen, Jr., are in the front seat. Louis Haffen became the first Borough President of The Bronx and the founder of The Bronx Old Timers. John E. Haffen in rear seat was co-owner of the Haffen Brewing Company. (The Robert R. Hall Collection, The Bronx County Historical Society Research Library)

Skating on Indian Pond in Crotona Park, c. 1900. Part of the Bathgate Farm was fed by springs, and in the 1860s, a brewer named Zeltner leased a pond to insure a supply of ice. The Parks Department of New York City acquired the farm, 1883–1888, and Zeltner's Pond became Indian Pond in Crotona Park. (The Bronx Old Timers Collection, The Bronx County Historical Society Research Library)

Bailey Avenue, 1912. A year of change for these residents, as a sewer line invaded this historic stretch of what had once been the Albany Post Road's junction with the road to Boston. This old settlement was known as Boston Hill to the people of Kingsbridge. Note the Broadway elevated subway train through the center. (The Bronx County Historical Society Research Library)

Diehl's Brewery on the east side of Westchester Avenue between Cauldwell and Trinity Avenues under the elevated train line. Originally a brewery in 1870s, the structure was later used as a Spanish live poultry market. Photographed on March 18, 1954. The structure was demolished in 1955. (The Bronx County Historical Society Research Library)

Leftover granite blocks used in sea wall at foot of Miles Avenue in 1919. Left to right, Claire Steneck, the author, John McNamara, at age 7, the author's mother, Betty McNamara, Marion and Jack McCaffrey, and John McNamara, Sr. author's father. (Courtesy of the author)

Looking north to Hunter Island Bridge, April 12, 1931. Low tide in the strait between Hunter Island on right and the mainland. This stretch was later dredged to become the Pelham Park lagoon. Large building in far background is New York Athletic Club. Small building on Hunter Island is "Mama Krauss" refreshment stand. One of the earliest photographs by John McNamara. (Courtesy of the author)

Pauline McNamara and Betty, wife and daughter of author in front of Baxter Mansion. Longstreet and Miles Avenues in January 1947. The Mansion was built in the 1880s, and later was a roadhouse. It burnt down in the 1950's (Courtesy of the author)

West side of Hunter Island where the wooden bridge touched the Island. John McNamara, author's son in foreground. c. 1952 (Courtesy of the author)

The Valentine-Varian House. Built in 1758 and listed on the National Register of Historic Places, this fieldstone farmhouse is now the Museum of Bronx History. Located on Bainbridge Avenue and East 208th Street. c. 1985. (The Bronx County Historical Society Research Library)

Edgar Allan Poe Cottage in 1985. Located in Poe Park at East Kingsbridge Road and the Grand Concourse. The final home for the noted author and his wife Virginia, it was here that he penned "Annabel Lee," "Ulalume" and "The Bells" during the years 1846–1849. Now operated as a literary landmark historic house museum by The Bronx County Historical Society. (The Bronx County Historical Society Research Library)

The Research Library building of The Bronx County Historical Society in 1986. Located at 3309 Bainbridge Avenue near 208th Street. It houses the largest collection of materials about The Bronx. (The Bronx County Historical Society Research Library)

Early Leaders of Historical Society, Nov. 11, 1960. The early leaders of The Bronx County Historical Society gather for the dedication of The Society's new tablet on Glover's Rock, the reputed site of the Revolutionary War Battle of Pell's Point in Pelham Bay Park. Left to right in the front row are Joseph Duffy, Theodore Schliessman, Fred E. J. Kracke, John McNamara and Bert Gumpert. In the back row are Ronald Schliessman, Theodore Kazimiroff and Vincent Hunt. (The Bronx County Historical Society Research Library)

Index

advertising 133
Aeronautic Society of New York 202, 203
African Church and Cemetery 166
Ahneman & Younkheere 149
Albany Post Road 236
Alexander Avenue 79, 226
Alexander Smith & Sons 107
Alf's Hardware Store 2
Allen's Drug Store 44
American Bank Note Company, The 26
American Monorail Company 193
Anvil Club 152
Archer family 84
Archer, John 122, 124, 129, 135
Armstrong, Harry 224
Arnold's Point 28
Arthur Avenue 111
artists 114, 116, 145
Asians 117
Associated Loyalists 9
Astor Avenue 10
Astor family 10
Astor, John Jacob 10
Avenues. See STREETS
aviation 202, 203

B. B. Theater 227
Bailey Avenue 126, 149, 236
Bailey, Nathaniel Platt 126
Bailor's Hotel 160
Baptist Church 15, 58
Bathgate, Alexander 62
bathhouses 5, 12
Baxter Mansion 238
Bear Swamp Road 201
Becker, C. Adelbert 110
Beller family 135

Belmont 111
Belmont Avenue 104
Belmont Street 87
Ben Riley's Arrowhead Inn 157
Benson Street 11
Bicentennial Veterans' Memorial Park 182
Biograph Studio 128
Birchall Avenue 205
Birchall, William 205
Bitter, Karl 145
Black Swamp 67
Blacks 11, 16, 50, 58, 65, 67, 79, 166, 221
Boller, Alfred Pancoast 94, 151
Bolte Brothers 227
Bolton Avenue 205
Bolton family 205
Bolton mills 205
Bolton, Robert, Jr. 232
Bonner Place 69
Bonner, Robert 69, 70
bootlegging 13
Borden's 172
Boston Hill Cemetery 236
Boston Road 95, 196
Boy Scouts 8
BRIDGES
    Broadway Bridge 94
    Brooklyn Bridge 3
    Central Bridge 97
    East 149th Street Bridge 94
    Henry Hudson Bridge 151
    High Bridge 64, 96
    Hudson Memorial Bridge 94, 151
    Hunter Island Bridge 237
    Macombs Dam Bridge 94
    Macomb's Bridge 97
    Madison Avenue Bridge 94

Spuyten Duyvil Bridge 138
Throgs Neck Bridge 183, 184
University Heights Bridge 94
wooden bridge 238
wooden footbridge 194
Broadway 138
Broadway Bridge 94
Brohmer Brothers 168
brokerage house 146
Bronck family 215
Bronck, Jonas 1, 14, 17
Bronx Botanical Garden 201
Bronx Community College 84
Bronx County Historical Society, The 20,
    121, 135, 182, 187, 239, 240, 241
Bronx County Jail 10
Bronx Home News 53, 56
Bronx Park 99, 102, 103, 115, 123
Bronx Press-Review xxi
Bronx River 27, 41, 133, 205, 207, 215
Bronx Star, The 193
Bronx Theatre 40
Bronx Zoo 112, 113, 114, 116, 153, 168
Bronx, The (the name) 215
Bronxdale Avenue 201, 205
Brook Avenue 3, 47
Brooklyn Bridge 3
Bruckner Boulevard 160, 180
Bungay Brook 52
BUSINESSES AND INDUSTRIES
  advertising 133
  Ahneman & Younkheere 149
  Alf's Hardware Store 2
  Alexander Smith & Sons 107
  Allen's Drug Store 44
  American Bank Note Company, The
    26
  American Monorail Company 193
  Biograph Studio 128
  Bolton mills 205
  bootlegging 13
  Borden's 172
  Brohmer Brothers 168
  brokerage house 146
  cigar factory 54, 234

counterfeiting 26
dairy farms 32
Damm's Segar Store, John 234
Diehl's Brewery 236
Dietrich's Restaurant 159
dry goods 146
Dutch West India Company 14
Edison Studios 127, 128
farming 176, 196, 197
foundry 3, 7
Freedomland 179, 197, 198
ironwork 3
Janes & Kirtland 3
Joe & Joe Restaurant 160
John Alf Hardware Store 2
John Damm's Segar Store 234
Kane's Park 173
Karl's Park 47
Kirchoff's Hall 15
Kyle's Park 71
Loeffler's Park 47
Lorillard Co. 133
Lorillard's snuffmill 201
Manhattan Sand Company 20
Mannello & Sons 57
Mott Iron Works 7
N. Johnston & Son 196
National Broadcasting Company 194
occupations 62, 221, 226
patents 7
pet sanitarium 49
Phil Dietrich's Restaurant & Tavern
  159
Piccirilli Studios 6
portrait engraving 26
poultry market 236
racetracks 69, 70, 97, 132, 199,
  200–202
railroads 58, 71, 120
restaurants 159, 160, 219
roadhouses 138, 209, 210, 211
sawmill 106
Sheffield Farms 172
Shorehaven 173
smuggling 195

Springhurst Dairy 32
sugar refining 231
Wray's Hall 101
Bussing Avenue 225
Bussing, Arent Harmanse 225
Butler Memorial Church 221
Burke Theater 227

Caesar Place 170
Camp Ranaqua 8
cartoons, films 127
Casanova mansion 29, 35
Casanova Street 35
Casanova Innocencio 22, 29, 35, 105
Casinos. See HOTELS
Castle Harbour Casino 167
Castle Hill Point 170
Castle Hill Avenue 168
Cedar of Lebanon 187
Cedar Park 68
Cemeteries 25, 27, 36, 39, 48, 108,
    115, 136, 162, 166, 195, 220,
    222, 223, 226, 236
Central Avenue 97
Central Bridge 97
Chateau Thierry Army Base Hospital
    119
Chevrolet, Louis 204
Chinese, 117
Chrysler, Walter 204
CHURCHES AND TEMPLES 169
  African Church and Cemetery 166
  Baptist Church 15, 58
  Butler Memorial Church 221
  Fordham Manor Reformed Church
      124
  Holy Cross Roman Catholic Church
      173
  Melrose Church 19
  Mott Haven Dutch Reformed
      Church 7, 16
  Our Lady of Solace Catholic Church
      175
  Reformed Protestant Dutch Church
      124

Saint Adalbert's Church 19
Saint Luke's Episcopal Church 221
St. Peter's Church 25
Saint Raymond's Church 165
Saint Thomas Aquinas Church 101
Temple Adath Israel 15
Temple Hand-in-Hand 15
Trinity Baptist Church 221
Cicero Avenue 170
cigar factory 54, 234
Cincinnatus Avenue 170
City Island 188, 194, 195
Civil War 70, 108
Claflin Ave. 146
Claflin, Horace B. 146
Claflin, Tennessee 146
Claflin, Victoria 146
Claremont Heights 67
Claremont Park 67, 69
Clason Point 161, 171
Clason Point Amusement Park 173
Clason Point Cemetery 171
Clason Point Military Academy 163
Clason, Isaac 163
Cohen, Jacob 47
College of Mount Saint Vincent 137, 154
COLLEGES
  Bronx Community College 84
  College of Mount Saint Vincent 137,
      154
  Fordham University 123, 136, 165
  Lehman College 97
  Saint John's College 136
Collins, James F. 214
Columbia War Hospital 119
Columbus Theatre 55
Comfort, Randall 3
COMMUNITIES (specifically named)
  Baychester *
  Belmont 111
  Boston Hill 236
  Bronxdale *

*See the section headings in the table of contents for names of these communities not otherwise specifically named in the text.

Bronxwood *
Castle Hill Point 170
City Island 188, 194, 195
Claremont Heights 67
Clason Point 161, 163, 171, 173
Concourse, The 7, 58, 82
Co-op City 196, 197
Country Club *
Crotona *
Dangerville 72
Dodgewood 158
Eastchester 190
Fieldston *
Fordham 150
Fordham Heights 83
Georgetown 58
Gun Hill *
Highbridge 66, 72
Highbridgeville 71, 75, 80, 226
Hub, The 2, 13, 39
Hunts Point 22, 23, 25–27, 30–33,
    35, 36, 39, 41, 105
Kingsbridge 4, 130, 131, 142, 147,
    149
Kingsbridge Heights *
Locust Point 183, 184
Longwood *
Melrose 11, 50, 51, 57, 58
Morrisania xxi, 8, 29, 48, 54, 58, 60,
    62, 79
Morris Heights 93
Mott Haven 5, 7, 16, 58, 59, 61, 65,
    79
Mount Hope 90
North New York *
Norwood *
Oak Point 21, 28
Old Morrisania 8
Parkchester 175
Park Versailles 162
Port Morris 18
Riverdale 157, 158
Silver Beach 180
Soundview *
Spuyten Duyvil 138

Throggs Neck *
Tremont 62, 90, 104, 109
Unionport 167, 169
Van Nest 203
Wakefield 229
West Farms 101, 102, 105, 107, 108
Westchester Square 164
Westchester Village 164
Western Reserve 90
Woodlawn *
Woodlawn Heights 226
Woodstock 50
Concourse, The 7, 58, 82
Conservatory, the 99
Copcutt, John 106
Cornell, Thomas 171
Corsa, Andrew 68
Cotter, James 118, 172, 175
counterfeiting 26
Courtlandt Avenue 11, 15, 19, 57
Croton Aqueduct 80, 87
Crotona Lake 52
Crotona Park 52, 60, 235
Cubans 22, 105

dairy farms 32
Damm's Segar Store, John 234
Dangerville 72
Dater Brothers 69
Daub, William 15
Debatable Lands 29
Decatur Avenue 127
DeLancey family 102, 103
DeLancey's Pine 103
DeLancey, Anne Charlotte 212
DeLong, George Washington 223
Deutsch, Stephen 167
Devil's Belt 185
Devil's Stepping Stones 185
Devoe Park 124
DiBrino, Nicholas 214, 227
Diehl's Brewery 236

*See the section headings in the table of
contents for names of these communities not
otherwise specifically named in the text.

Dietrich's Restaurant 159
Ditmars, Raymond 112, 113
Dodgewood 158
Drake Cemetery 36
Drake Park 23
Drake Street 23
Drake, Joseph Rodman 23, 36
dry goods 146
Duck Island 29
Duffy, Hugh 32
Duffy, Joseph 241
Dunninger, The Great 56
Dunsmore, John Ward 1
Dutch Broadway 57
Dutch names 88, 156
Dutch West India Company 14

East (street prefix). See STREETS
East 149th Street Bridge 94
Eagle Avenue 57
East River 27, 37, 93
Eastchester Bay 191
Eastern Boulevard 160, 180
Edgar Allan Poe Cottage 239
Edison Studios 127, 128
"El", Third Avenue 51
Elton Avenue 12, 19
End Place 8
English names 88

Faile estate 32
Faile, Edward 105
farming 176, 196, 197
Father Zeiser Place 150
Featherbed Lane 87
Ferncliff Place 10
Ferreira, Charles 189
ferryboats 33
Field, Robert M. 158
films, cartoons 127
Findlay, Andrew 50
Finns 78
fire departments 60, 63, 139, 192, 208
fishing 156
Fleetwood Avenue 70
Fleetwood Hotel 70

Fleetwood Race Track 69, 70
Fonthill mansion 154
Ford, William 26
Ford, Joseph 26
Fordham 150
Fordham Avenue 95
Fordham Heights 83
Fordham Manor 124, 129
Fordham Manor Reformed Church 124
Fordham University 123, 136, 165
Forest Houses 50
Forrest, Edwin 154
Fort Schuyler 188, 189
Fort Schuyler Road 181
forts 83–85, 142, 188, 189
foundry 3, 7
Fowler, Colonel 24
Frank, Solon 170
Franklin Avenue 43
Franz Sigel Park 10, 65
Freedomland 179, 197, 198
French, Daniel Chester 6
French names 88, 162, 219
Frey, Albert 121

gardens 75, 187, 201
General Slocum ship disaster 34
Georgetown 58
Gerard, Richard 224
Germans 11, 15, 44–47, 50, 54, 57, 61,
        79, 88, 167, 169
Giles Place 130, 142
Glover's Rock 241
Goldman, Albert 56
Grabe, Charles xxi
Graham, James 24
Grant Avenue 70
Grant, Ulysses S. 70
Gross, Martin xxi
Guerlain, Lewis 162
Gumpert, Bert 241
Gun Hill Road 217
gypsies 207

Haffen family 11, 235
Haffen Park 73

Haffen, Louis 73
Hammer's Hotel 51
Harlem River 71, 80, 93, 94, 96
Hart, Moss 54
Havemeyer Avenue 167, 231
Havemeyer, William 231
Havender, Joe 220
Hegney, Arthur V. 48
Hegney Place 48
Heintz, Louis 73
Hell Gate 34, 188
Henry Hudson Bridge 151
Henry Hudson Park 145
Hermitage, The 219
Hicinbothem, Walter 53
High Bridge 64, 96
Highbridge 66, 72
Highbridgeville 71, 75, 80
Highbridgeville Cemetery 226
High Island 194
Highway Department 120
Hispanics 11, 50, 88, 104, 105
Hoe, Colonel 30
Hoffmann, Adam 11
Hoffmann, Martin 167
Hoffmann's Casino 167
Holy Cross Roman Catholic Church 173
Homer Avenue 170
horse amulets 91
horse railways 95
hospitals 38, 83, 111, 119, 126
Hotel Clausen 89
HOTELS, INNS, CASINOS 51, 89
  Bailor's Hotel 160
  Ben Riley's Arrowhead Inn 157
  Castle Harbour Casino 167
  Fleetwood Hotel 70
  Hammer's Hotel 51
  Hoffmann's Casino 167
  Huber's Casino 167
  Hotel Clausen 89
  Kane's Casino 173
  North Side Hotel 89
  Pelham Heath Inn 209
  Riverdale Inn 138, 152

  Seebeck's Hotel 89
  Saint Mary's Park Hotel 89
  Trolley Inn, The 101
  Unionport Hotel 167
  Winona Hotel 89
  Woodmansten Inn 209, 210, 211
  See also roadhouses
Hub, the 2, 13, 39
Huber's Casino 167
Hudson Memorial Bridge 94, 151
Hudson River 93
Hungarian names 88
Hunt Cemetery 27
Hunt family 29
Hunt, Vincent 241
Hunter Island 238
Hunter Island Bridge 237
Hunts Point 22, 23, 25–27, 30–33, 35, 36, 39, 41, 105
Hunts Point Avenue 23
Hussar 18
Hutchinson, Anne 186
Hutchinson River 186

Indian Lake 52
Indian Pond 235
Indian Trail 180
Indian trails 86, 225
Indians 8, 11, 14, 27, 61, 67, 88, 102, 122, 140, 161, 171, 182, 183, 185, 186
industries. See BUSINESSES
inventions 30, 106, 107, 109, 212
Irish 14, 72, 75, 79, 87, 88, 91, 163, 226
ironwork 3
Italians 6, 11, 55, 77, 79, 88, 91, 111
inns. See HOTELS

Janes & Kirtland 3
Janes' Hill 3
Jerome Avenue 97, 218
Jerome Park Racetrack 97, 125, 132
Jerome, Leonard W. 97, 125, 132
Jesuits 136
Jews 15, 79, 88, 169
Joe & Joe Restaurant 160

jogging 78
John Alf Hardware Store 2
John Damm's Segar Store 234
John Peter Tetard Junior High School 4
Johnston, Nathan 196
Johnston, William 197
Joyce Kilmer Park 73
Jumbo's Corner 152

Kane's Casino 173
Kane's Park 173
Karl's Park 47
Kazimiroff, Theodore, Dr. 84–85, 88,
    215, 241
Kelly Street 52
Kerr, Joe xxi
Kidd's Brook 206
Kingsbridge 4, 130, 131, 142, 147, 149
Kingsbridge Road 83, 121
Kirchoff's Hall 15
Kracke, Fred E. J. 241
Kyle's Park 71

Laconia Theater 227
Lady Washington Engine Co. No. 1 60,
    63
Laguerre, Baudoin 219
landmarks 102, 103, 155, 186, 187
Lebish, Dr. 49
Leggett family 24, 25
Leggett, Gabriel 23
Leggett Mansion 22, 24
Leggett's Creek 29
Leggett's Lane 31
Leggett's Point 28
Lehman College 97
Lesh, Lawrence 203
Liberator, The 65
Liberty Bonds 56
Liberty Loan Drive 56
library 240
Lincoln, Abraham, assassination of 228
Lithuanians 79
Livingston, Philip 187
Loeffler's Park 47
loom, power 106, 107

Lopez, Matthias 105
Lorillard Co. 133
Lorillard estate 99, 133, 201
Lorillard snuffmill 201
Lowerre's Lane 167, 231
Lydig Estate 102
Lynch, Dominick 163

MacAdam, John L. 212
Maclay Avenue 228
Maclay, Isaac Walker 228
Macombs Dam Bridge 94
Macomb's Bridge 97
Macombs Dam Park 78
Madison Avenue Bridge 94
Major Deegan Expressway 17, 96
Manhattan Sand Company 20
Mannello & Sons 57
Mannello, Angelo 57
Manship, Paul 116
Marcher Avenue 75
Marcher estate 75
Matilda Avenue 224
McGlynn, Frank 128
McKeown, John 230
McLean Brook 220
McNamara family, the 237, 238
McNamara, John 241
Melrose 11, 50, 51, 57, 58
Melrose Avenue 19, 49
Melrose Church 19
Merrill Place 162
Miles Avenue 237
Mill Brook 14
Miller family 194
Miner, H. C. 40
Miner's 40
Minerva Place 132
Mohawk Athletic Club 78
monorail 193
Monterey Avenue 104
Monterey estate 104
Morgan, Appleton 121
Morrisania xxi, 8, 29, 30, 48, 54, 58,
    60, 62, 79
Morris, Ann Randolph 61

Morris Avenue 55, 69, 79
Morris, Ed 191
Morris family 10, 11, 29, 50, 68, 69,
    166, 200
Morris, Gouverneur 4, 11, 61
Morris Heights 93
Morris, John A. 201
Morris Manorlands xxi
Morris Mansion 81
Morris Park Racetrack 177, 199,
    200–204
Mosholu Parkway 73
Mott Avenue 58, 68, 73
Mott Haven 5, 7, 16, 58, 59, 61, 65, 79
Mott Haven Dutch Reformed Church
    7, 16
Mott Iron Works 7
Mott, Jordan L. 7, 16, 61
Mount Fordham 81
Mount Hope 90
Mount Morris Theatre 5
Mount Saint Vincent 137, 154
Museum of Bronx History 135, 239
Museum of the American Indian 171

N. Johnston & Son 196
National Broadcasting Company 194
Neighborhood Associations 101
New Found Passage 183
New York Botanical Garden 187
New York Catholic Protectory 174–176
New York Central Railroad 58
New York Harlem Railroad 120
NEWSPAPERS
    Bronx Home News 53, 56
    Bronx Press-Review xxi
    Bronx Star, The 193
    Liberator, The 65
    Parkchester Press, The xxi
    Westchester Patriot, The 105
nicknames, Bronx 90
Nieuw Haarlem 122
North Bronx xxii
North Brother Island 20, 21, 34, 37, 38
North Side Hotel 89

Oak Point 21, 28
O'Brien, Dynamite Johnny 195
occupations 62, 91, 221, 226
Old Morrisania 8
Olms, William 152
orphanages 169
Our Lady of Solace Catholic Church
    175

P. S. 3 – 58
P. S. 6 – 108
P. S. 31 – 65
P. S. 34 – 214
P. S. 36 – 169
P. S. 38 – 48
P. S. 58 – 109
Paderewski, Ignace Jan 19
Palmer Cove 191
parades 63, 82 119, 169, 208, 233
Parkchester Press, The xxi
Park Versailles Cemetery 162
PARKS
    Bicentennial Veterans' Memorial
        Park 182
    Bronx Park 99, 102, 103, 115, 123
    Cedar Park 68
    Claremont Park 67, 69
    Crotona Park 52, 60, 235
    Devoe Park 124
    Drake Park 23
    Franz Sigel Park 10, 65
    Haffen Park 73
    Henry Hudson Park 145
    Joyce Kilmer Park 73
    Macombs Dam Park 78
    Pelham Bay Park 237, 239, 241
    Poe Park 121, 239
    Pulaski Park 17
    Rose Hill Park 123
    Saint Mary's Park 3, 9
    Van Cortlandt Park 153, 218
    Weir Creek Park 182
Pastime Athletic Club 78
patents 7
Patti, Adelina 224

peace treaty 1, 14
Pearsall, Denton 210
Pelham Cemetery 195
Pelham Heath Inn 209
Pelham Bay Park 237, 239, 241
Pell, Thomas 194
Pell's Point 241
Penfield Street 229
Penfield, Frederick 229
pet sanitarium 49
Phil Dietrich's Restaurant & Tavern 159
Piccirilli, Attilio 6
Piccirilli Studios 6
picnic grounds 47
picnics 175
Pierce family 108
Ploughman's Bush 158
Pocahontas Line 3, 61
Poe, Edgar Allan 96, 121, 123, 124
Poe Park 121, 239
Poles 17, 19, 79, 88
Polish Hall 19
Pope John Paul II 55
Port Morris & Spuyten Duyvil Railroad 58, 61
Port Morris 18
portrait engraving 26
poultry market 236
printing press 30
Prohibition 13
Prospect Avenue 93
Public School. See P. S.
Puerto Ricans 11, 50, 105
Pugsley Creek 161
Pulaski, Count Casimir 17
Pulaski Park 17
puppet shows 55

Quinnahung 27

racetracks 69, 70, 97, 132, 199, 200–202
railroads 58, 71, 120
Rainey Memorial Gate 116
Ranaqua 86
Rasberry, William J. 108

Rattlesnake Brook 190
red-light district 87
Reformed Protestant Dutch Church 124
Refugee Corps 9
Reier, Sharon 94
reservoirs 97
restaurants 159, 160, 219
Revolutionary War 4, 9, 18, 24, 41, 66, 68, 83, 84, 87, 103, 124, 129, 130, 142, 183, 222, 241
Rice, Joel T. 202
Riggs, John A. 202
Riker, Abraham 37
Riker's Island 20, 37
Risse, Louis 73, 74
Riverdale 157, 158
Riverdale Inn 138, 152
RIVERS
    Bronx River 27, 41, 133, 205, 207, 215
    East River 27, 37, 93, 180
    Harlem River 71, 80, 93, 94, 96
    Hudson River 93, 180
    Hutchinson River 186
Riverside Hospital 38
roadhouses 138, 209, 210, 211
Rockefeller Foundation 116
Rocking Stone 102
Rose Hill Park 123
Ruppert, Colonel Jacob 20, 38
Russ, Horace P. 92
Russian names 88
Ryer Place 104
Ryer, Samuel 104

Sack, Bert 39
Saint Adalbert's Church 19
Saint Ann's Avenue 9, 51
Saint Barnabas Hospital 111
Saint John's College 136
Saint Lucia's Day 59
Saint Luke's Episcopal Church 221
Saint Mary's Park 3, 9
Saint Mary's Park Hotel 89
Saint Peter's Church 25
Saint Raymond's Church 165

Saint Thomas Aquinas Church 101
Samuel Street 104
Sanitation Department 91
sawmill 106
Scandinavians 59, 79, 88
Schliessman, Ronald 241
Schliessman, Theodore 241
SCHOOLS 232
   Clason Point Military Academy 163
   John Peter Tetard Junior High
     School 4
   New York Catholic Protectory
     174–176
   P. S. 3 – 58
   P. S. 6 – 108
   P. S. 31 – 65
   P. S. 34 – 214
   P. S. 36 – 169
   P. S. 38 – 48
   P. S. 58 – 109
   William Lloyd Garrison School 65
   See also COLLEGES
"Schultz, Dutch" 13
Schwab family 84
Scottish names 88
Sedgwick Avenue 83
Seebeck's Hotel 89
Segar Store, 234
Shakespeare Avenue 75
Sheffield Farms 172
Sheridan Avenue 70
Sherman Avenue 70
shipwreck 18
Shorehaven 173
Sigel, Franz 65, 68
Skinner, Halcyon 106, 107
Skinner, Joseph 106
Smith, Alexander 106
Smith, Hester 5
Smith, James 60
smuggling 195
Snuffmill Lane 201
Solon Place 170
South Bronx xxi, 59, 79
South Brother Island 20, 38

Southern Boulevard 115
Spencer Estate 191
Split Rock 186
Spofford Estate 32
Springhurst Dairy 32
Spuyten Duyvil 138, 139
Spuyten Duyvil, bridge at 138
Spuyten Duyvil Creek 140, 141
stagecoaches 134
Stahl, Jacob 54
statues 111, 145, 168, 223
steamboat racing 93
steamships 33, 143, 144
Steinman, David 151
street paving 92
streetcars 5
STREETS
   Albany Post Road 236
   Alexander Avenue 79, 226
   Arthur Avenue 111
   Astor Avenue 10
   Bailey Avenue 126, 149, 236
   Bear Swamp Road 201
   Belmont Avenue 104
   Belmont Street 87
   Benson Street 11
   Birchall Avenue 205
   Bolton Avenue 205
   Bonner Place 69
   Boston Road 95, 196
   Broadway 138
   Bronxdale Avenue 201, 205
   Brook Avenue 3, 47
   Bruckner Boulevard 160, 180
   Bussing Avenue 225
   Caesar Place 170
   Casanova Street 35
   Castle Hill Avenue 168
   Central Avenue 97
   Cicero Avenue 170
   Cincinnatus Avenue 170
   Claflin Avenue 146
   Concourse, The 7, 58, 82
   Courtlandt Avenue 11, 15, 19, 57
   Decatur Avenue 127

Drake Street 23
Eagle Avenue 57
Eastern Boulevard 160, 180
Elton Avenue 12, 19
End Place 8
Father Zeiser Place 150
Featherbed Lane 87
Ferncliff Place 10
Fleetwood Avenue 70
Fordham Avenue 95
Fort Schuyler Road 181
Franklin Avenue 43
Giles Place 130, 142
Grant Avenue 70
Gun Hill Road 217
Havemeyer Avenue 167, 231
Hegney Place 48
Homer Avenue 170
Hunts Point Avenue 23
Indian Trail 180
Jerome Avenue 97, 218
Kazimiroff Boulevard 88
Kelly Street 52
Kingsbridge Road 83, 121
Leggett's Lane 31
Lowerre's Lane 167, 231
Maclay Avenue 228
Major Deegan Expressway 17, 96
Marcher Avenue 75
Matilda Avenue 224
Melrose Avenue 19, 49
Merrill Place 162
Miles Avenue 237
Minerva Place 132
Monterey Avenue 104
Morris Avenue 55, 69, 79
Mosholu Parkway 73
Mott Avenue 58, 68, 73
Penfield Street 229
Ploughman's Bush 158
Prospect Avenue 93
Ryer Place 104
Saint Ann's Avenue 9, 51
Samuel Street 104
Sedgwick Avenue 83

Shakespeare Avenue 75
Sheridan Avenue 70
Sherman Avenue 70
Snuffmill Lane 201
Solon Place 170
Southern Boulevard 115
Theriot Avenue 162
Town Dock Road 196
Tremont Avenue 108, 172, 181, 212
Unionport Road 166
Villa Avenue 125
Villa Place 16
Virgil Place 170
Waldorf Place 10
Washington Avenue 63, 101, 233
Webster Avenue 100
West Farms Square 100
Westchester Avenue 236
Willis Avenue 6, 79
Zerega Avenue 168
130th Street 5
E. 134th Street 122
138th Street 5
E. 142nd Street 6
E. 145th Street 7, 16
E. 148th Street 56
E. 149th Street 7, 9, 11, 13, 53
E. 150th Street 57
E. 155th Street 79
E. 156th Street 12
E. 161st Street 51
168th Street 44
E. 169th Street 15
175th Street 64
E. 180th Street 108, 194
sugar refining 231
Swiss 79

Tallapoosa Club 50
Tangle Woods 206
Tarbox, Charles 101, 109
Tarbox, Hiram 109
Tarbox, William 101
telephones 101
Temple Adath Israel 15

Index

Temple Hand-in-Hand 15
THEATERS
  B. B. Theater 227
  Bronx Theatre 40
  Burke Theater 227
  Columbus Theatre 55
  Laconia Theater 227
  Miner's 40
  Mount Morris Theatre 5
  Victory Theatre 40
  Wakefield Theater 227
Theriot Avenue 162
Third Avenue "El" 51
Throgs Neck Bridge 183, 184
Tightrope walk 71
Titanic, sinking of 41
Town Dock Road 196
Tremont 62, 90, 104, 109
Tremont Avenue, 108, 172, 181, 212
Trinity Baptist Church 221
trolley 100
Trolley Inn, The 101
temples. See CHURCHES
Turn Verein Hall 15

U. S. Capitol Dome 3
U. S. Veterans Hospital 126
Underground Railroad 16
Unionport Hotel 167
Unionport Road 166
United Odd Fellows Home 169
University Heights Bridge 94

Valentine family 150
Valentine-Varian House 135, 239
Van Cortlandt Park 153, 218
Van Doren, Charles 16
Van Dyck, Hendrick 14
Van Horn, John 62
Van Nest 203
Van Schaick, D. L. 62
Van Zandt, Meyer 114
Vasa Hall 59
Veterans Hospital 83
Victory Gardens 169
Victory Theatre 40

Villa Avenue 125
Villa Place 16
Vineyard Beach 10
Virgil Place 170

Wakefield 229
Wakefield Theater 227
Waldorf Place 10
Watt, John 123
Washington Avenue 101, 163, 233
water supply 96
Webster Avenue 100
Weir Creek 182
Weir Creek Park 182
Welfare Island prison 37
Welsh names 88
West Farms 101, 102, 105, 107, 108
West Farms Civil War cemetery 39,
  108
West Farms Square 100
Westchester Avenue 236
Westchester Creek 164
Westchester Patriot, The 105
Western Reserve 90
Wickerscreek Trail, Ye 86
William Lloyd Garrison School 65
Williams, Percy 40
Willis Avenue 6, 79
Winona Hotel 89
Withers, William 228
wooden bridge 238
wooden footbridge 194
Woodlawn Cemetery 220, 222, 223
Woodlawn Heights 226
Woodmansten Inn 209, 210, 211
Woodstock 50
Wray's Hall 101
Wright's Island 183

Yankee Stadium 76
Yznaga, Fernando 105

Zeckendorf, William 198
Zeltner's Pond 235
Zerega Avenue 168

BOOKS FROM THE
BRONX COUNTY HISTORICAL SOCIETY

1. **The Bronx It Was Only Yesterday: 1935-1965.** (Ultan & Hermalyn)
   A glorious photo montage of The Bronx during this era
   of growth and stability..

2. **The Beautiful Bronx: 1920-1950.** (Ultan)
   A treasure chest of memories of the exciting years of The Bronx.....

3. **The Bronx in the Innocent Years: 1890-1925.** (Ultan & Hermalyn)
   Colorful first-person reminiscences and rare historical
   photographs provide a nostalgic glimpse into the past.....................

4. **History in Asphalt: The Origin of Bronx Street
   & Place Names.** (McNamara)   (Third Edition)
   Did you ever wonder how your street got its name? This fascinating
   560 page encyclopedia describes the history of Bronx names..........

5. **The Bronx in Print: An Annotated Catalogue of
   Books and Pamphlets About The Bronx.** (Kuhta & Rodriguez)
   A handy guide for researchers...

6. **Elected Public Officials of The Bronx Since 1898.** (Tosi & Hermalyn)
   A compilation of ten Bronx offices, the names of the officials,
   their party affiliations and years of service.This is the only
   work of its kind in New York City ....(Fourth Edition)

7. **History of Morris Park Racecourse.** (DiBrino)
   An illustrated history of the famous Bronx racecourse
   and the Morris Family ....

8. **Poems of Edgar Allan Poe at Fordham.** (Beirne)
   A collection of Poe's works while he lived in his Fordham Cottage ..

9. **Legacy of the Revolution.** (Ultan)
   A history of the landmark Valentine-Varian
   House, one of the City's oldest structures...

10. **The Bronx Triangle: A Portrait of Norwood.** (Mead)
    An illustrated history of this northern Bronx neighborhood...........

11. **Genealogy of The Bronx.** (Hermalyn & Tosi)
    An annotated guide to sources of information ....

12. **Theatres of The Bronx.** (Miller)
    Photographs of the famous movie theatres of The Bronx ....

13. **Latin Bicentennial.** (Serrano)
    This Spanish and English comic book discusses the Hispanic
    peoples of The Bronx ....

14. **McNamara's Old Bronx.** (McNamara)
    John McNamara's incomparable articles from his "Bronx in History"
    column in *The Bronx Press Review* spans the centuries with
    stories of the people of The Bronx..

15. **The Bronx in The Frontier Era: From The Beginning to 1696.** (Ultan)
    The first comprehensive volume in The Society's new series on
    The History of The Bronx ....

16. **West Farms Local History Curriculum Guide.** (Hopkins)
    Suggested objectives, lessons, activities, and resources
    for all grades ....

17. **Landmarks of The Bronx.** (Hermalyn & Kornfeld)
    Comprehensive list of designated and proposed landmarks of The Bronx;
    description of the landmark law and its process....**Revised Edition**

18. **The South Bronx and the Founding of America.** (Garrison)
    This activity book for teachers and students provides a concise
    historical account of the early settling of The Bronx.......................

19. **Morris High School and the Creation of the New York City
    Public High School System.** (Hermalyn)
    This is the story of the extraordinary educational reforms of the
    1890s which peaked with the opening of Morris High in 1897 ....

20. **Edgar Allan Poe at Fordham.** (McAuley)
    A teacher's guide and workbook on the life of this great writer.......

21. **The Signers of the Constitution of the United States.** (Quinn)
    Sprightly character sketches with original drawings of the Signers
    including The Bronx's own Gouverneur Morris...............................

22. **The Signers of the Declaration of Independence.** (Quinn)
    Interesting character sketches and original drawings of the Signers
    of the Declaration including The Bronx's Lewis Morris ....

23. **Presidents of the United States.** (Ultan)
    Absorbing character outlines of the men who have held the office;
    essays on the origins of the Presidency and the electoral college.....

24. **Chief Justices of The U.S. Supreme Court.** (Lankevich)
    The story of the men who have been the Chief Justices of the
    U.S. Supreme Court...

25. **The First House of Representatives and The Bill of Rights.** (Lankevich)
    The story behind the Bill of Rights and the men who established
    the first House of Representatives ....

26. **The First Senate of The United States.** (Streb)
    Explores the key figures in the upper house of the Congress in 1789 ......

27. **350th Anniversary of The Bronx Commemorative Issue.**
   This work celebrates The Bronx with essays on Jonas Bronck,
   transportation and The Bronx at the turn of the 20th century..............

28. **Bicentennial of the United States Constitution Commemorative Issue.**
   This special edition features articles on Gouverneur Morris, the
   Penman of the Constitution and a description of colonial money ....

29. **25 Year Index to The Bronx County Historical Society Journal.**
   This comprehensive index includes thousands of references to
   local events, individuals, institutions, schools and businesses.
   An invaluable research tool for New York history and genealogy..........

30. **Local History Classroom Resource Guide**
   Suggested activities, lessons and charts for all grades ....

GIFTS IN THE HISTORIC TRADITION

A.
THE BRONX AFGHAN
50" x 65" 100% cotton. Depicts scenes of Bronx institutions: The Zoo,
Wave Hill, Historic Houses, Botanical Garden and Yankee Stadium.
A wonderful gift.

B.
THE GRAND CONCOURSE PRINT
A top quality print of the 1892 proposed plan for the Concourse. It depicts the
entire west Bronx and upper Manhattan printed on 25" x 12" acid free stock.

C.
(a.) TILES OF THE VALENTINE-VARIAN HOUSE
(b.) AND THE EDGAR ALLAN POE COTTAGE
Each historic house is represented by a charming line drawing on a white ceramic
tile. They are decorative, useful and commemorate beloved Bronx landmarks.

D.
HISTORIC SCENES OF THE BRONX:
SET OF SIX OLD FASHIONED GLASSES
These unique glasses are each decorated with designs of historic sites.

When ordering books and gifts, please make your check payable to:
The Bronx County Historical Society
3309 Bainbridge Ave., The Bronx, NY 10467
Telephone: (718) 881-8900

EDGAR ALLAN POE COTTAGE

c. 1812

Poe Cottage is administered by The Bronx County Historical Society in agreement with the Department of Parks and Recreation of the City of New York

The Poe Cottage is open for guided tours:

Saturday	10:00 A.M.-4:00 P.M.
Sunday	1:00 P.M.-5:00 P.M.

Tours during week by appointment.

POE PARK

Grand Concourse & East Kingsbridge Road
The Bronx, New York
Telephone: (718) 881-8900

VALENTINE-VARIAN HOUSE
c. 1758

MUSEUM OF BRONX HISTORY

*The Valentine-Varian House is owned and administered by
The Bronx County Historical Society.*

Saturday 10:00 A.M.-4:00 P.M., Sunday 1:00 P.M.-5:00 P.M.
Open Monday to Friday 9:00 A.M.-5:00 P.M.
for Guided Tours by appointment

Bainbridge Avenue at East 208th Street
The Bronx, New York 10467
Telephone: (718) 881-8900

❖ ❖ ❖

Mr. William F. Beller purchased the Valentine-Varian House in 1905. His son, Mr. William C. Beller, donated the landmark structure to The Bronx County Historical Society in 1965. In recognition of this, the trustees in 1974 established The Society's most prestigious annual award, the William Beller Award of Excellence and Achievement.

THE BRONX COUNTY HISTORICAL SOCIETY

The Bronx County Historical Society was founded in 1955 for the purpose of promoting knowledge, interest and research in The Bronx. The Society administers The Museum of Bronx History, Edgar Allan Poe Cottage, a Research Library, and The Bronx County Archives; publishes books, journals and newsletters; conducts school programs, historical tours, lectures, courses, archaeological digs and commemorations; designs exhibitions, sponsors various expeditions, and produces the *Out Of The Past* radio show and cable television programming. The Society is active in furthering the arts, in preserving the natural resources of The Bronx, and in creating a sense of pride in the Bronx community.

Members of The Bronx County Historical Society receive:

A subscription to
The Bronx County Historical Society Journal
published semi-annually

The Bronx Historian Newsletter

Free admission to
MUSEUM OF BRONX HISTORY
Bainbridge Avenue at East 208th Street
The Bronx, New York

EDGAR ALLAN POE COTTAGE
Kingsbridge Road and Grand Concourse
The Bronx, New York

Invitation to
The Society's Annual High School
Valedictorians Awards Program,
Historical Tours, Lectures, Exhibitions
and other Educational Projects

To join, please write or telephone:
THE BRONX COUNTY HISTORICAL SOCIETY
3309 Bainbridge Avenue, The Bronx, New York 10467
Telephone: (718) 881-8900